GENDER AND EXPERTISE

GENDER AND EXPERTISE

Edited by
Maureen McNeil

'. . . an association in which the free development of each is the condition of the free development of all'

Free Association Books / London / 1987

Gender and Expertise
Radical Science Series, no. 19

Published in June 1987 by
Free Association Books
26 Freegrove Road
London N7 9RQ

British Library Cataloguing in Publication Data

Gender and expertise.—(Radical science
series, ISSN 0305–0963, no. 19)
1. Sex role
I. McNeil, Maureen II. Series
305.3 GN479.65

ISBN 0–946960–26–7 Pbk

Cover by Carlos Sapochnik

Typeset by Input Typesetting Ltd, London SW19 8DR

Printed in Great Britain by Short Run Press Ltd, Exeter

CONTENTS

INTRODUCTION

Maureen McNeil

The emergence of a sexual politics concerned with expertise is a fairly recent phenomenon. Charting the dimensions of such a politics has not been straightforward. Some of the most recent attempts to canvas this territory – particularly in relationship to women and technology – have been rather eclectic.

Our collection, *Gender and Expertise*, maps out some common pointers on this relatively new terrain. This is not to say that there would be total agreement amongst the contributors on these issues, or that every article tackles each point. Taken together, however, these essays do demonstrate the need for a feminist politics around expertise which: (1) emphasizes the need for transformative strategies; (2) is not idealist – that is, does not make changes in ideas and images our only goal; (3) is not defined by recourse to 'nature'; and (4) is constructed around gender relationships rather than women or masculinity as fixed categories.

Transformative Strategies

Ruth Schwartz Cowan has succinctly formulated a fundamental observation relevant to this book: 'We have trained our women to opt out of the technological order as much as we have trained our men to opt into it' (Cowan, p. 6). The lesson which might be drawn from the present collection is that an 'opting into' the 'technological order', or into any sphere of expertise, must involve a political awareness of what we are opting into and a strategy for transforming it.

Confronted with WISE (Women into Science and Engineering Year in Britain), women and computing groups, or women into management courses, some of us have become wary of jumping onto the women's training bandwagon. Undoubtedly there have been some excellent feminist initiatives in education and training, which make it seem churlish to express scepticism about *any* new opportunity for women to gain expertise. Nevertheless, feminist political strategies around expertise far too often begin and end with the principle that women must get more of it. At worst, this results in a technicist approach to expertise: the expectation that we can extract the knowledge without ourselves entering into the power relations. This also often involves individual adaptation – often at considerable costs – by the women involved.

Feminists have begun to develop more transformative ways of entering into previously male worlds: women-only classes, group projects, discussions about sexual politics to accompany teaching of the physical skills of self-defence. This collection reflects these innovations and underlines the need for a transformative strategy within every feminist initiative in the area. That includes challenging the terms of 'opting in' and being clear about what men have 'opted out of' (e.g. child care, housework, etc.) along the way.

Against Idealism

Too much of the discussion about gender and science and technology has been conducted in terms of the relationships amongst scientific ideas, masculinity and femininity. This begs many questions about the historical and cultural specificity of masculinity and femininity. In addition, such formulations ignore the fact that scientific ideas emerge from a complex of material relations which include – but, as many feminists have indicated, are not restricted to – the economic relations of capitalism. Some feminists have pushed for a much broader sense of 'materialist', which includes control of labour power (both paid and unpaid), production and reproduction, forms of physical control and violence.

While these insights have transformed other political realms, they have often been neglected in the analysis of expertise. This neglect can result in forms of politics which are idealistic, presuming that all necessary changes will follow from a change in the nature of scientific ideas. The resulting strategy is also individualistic and elitist. This can best be illustrated by the work of two influential analysts of science and gender, Brian Easlea and Evelyn Fox Keller.

Both these writers have been admirably involved in pioneering the study of the history of science from the perspective of gender. Nevertheless, there are political limitations in their frameworks. In Easlea's case, his impressive sweep of the history of science constructs a chronicle of the imagery and ideas of science and their applications (see Easlea, 1980; Easlea, 1981; Easlea, 1983; Jordanova's review in this collection). He neglects the institutional dimensions of science, including its economic roles. This neglect yields a political strategy which pleads for individual scientists to be gentler, more loving, creatures, who will thereby produce non-violent (feminine) scientific ideas.

Evelyn Fox Keller begins from a different tack, but arrives at a similar implication: 'Modern science is constituted around a set of exclusionary oppositions in which that which is named feminine is excluded – be it feeling, subjectivity, or nature' (Fox Keller, 1985, pp. 9–10). Her detailed work in the history of science investigates 'gendered discourses' within evolutionary biology. She has also written a biography of Barbara McClintock – one of the most intriguing success stories amongst women is science (see Grobicki's review in this collection).

While Keller's work is a welcome intervention within biology, there are limitations in a political programme which relies primarily on the institutionalization of feminine discourse as the key to transforming scientific expertise. In effect, the foundations of expertise would remain untouched. Such prescriptions rely on individualistic initiatives by women or by sympathetic (feminine-thinking?) men in importing more feminine ideas and ideals into science. Moreover, professionals are implicitly designated as the agents of change: science can be changed only by the scientific elite. Its power structures are left intact. Indeed, in other idealistic approaches, such as that offered by Fritoj Capra, no political change is even called for. He presumes that feminism, positive Eastern philosophies and high-level physics will inevitably come together in a desirable unity towards conservation, non-aggression, and holism (see Capra).

In the face of such proposals, we might do worse than return to the early *Radical Science* formulations about 'science as social relations'. These can remain mere rhetorical phrases; they have not, in the context of *Radical Science*, provided sufficient stimulus to investigate the specific power relations around gender. However, they do indicate that we must examine the social, political, and economic context from which experts' ideas emerge – not just the ideas themselves.

No Recourse to Nature

When confronted with male expertise, some feminists have called for a return to nature, which they see as an alternative to the male-dominated cultural realm. The contributors to this collection would take issue with such a move. They argue that it is impossible to separate out a pristine 'nature' from 'culture' and that, as women, we are inescapably part of the cultural realm, even in our rebellions. 'Nature' is a cultural category, as Lukács, Douglas, and Williams have emphasized over and over again (see Lukács, Douglas, 1960, 1970; Williams). Some feminists have developed this general argument to illustrate the inadequacy of a sexual politics which relies on the nature/culture dichotomy (see Brown and Jordanova). From a zany and controversial post-modernist position, Donna Haraway insists that there can be no 'organic or natural standpoint' from which feminism or any other politics can be constructed (Haraway, p. 75).

Yet many women see the trump card of 'nature' as one of the few available to them. This means that its use bespeaks the limitations of our power: that we do not expect to be heeded on other grounds – for example, by saying 'we don't want this' or 'this doesn't meet our needs'. However, it is just for this reason that, as feminists, we must distance ourselves from the appealing discourse of nature. Bolstering an argument by maintaining that 'it is natural' insulates us against political struggle and abrogates our claims to power. In effect, it prevents us from consciously espousing our political priorities and setting out to achieve them.

Ruth Hubbard stresses this point in her discussion of feminism and child-rearing: 'The question we as feminists need to ask is not which is more "natural" but to what extent the different constructs empower women or, alternatively, decrease our power to structure child-rearing around our own needs and those of the people with whom we live our daily lives' (Hubbard, p. 332). The reliance on the discourse of nature is by definition a reliance on the status quo in so far as it does not encourage women to acknowledge and develop our own political powers.

There are further difficulties with the discourse of nature. How can disparate definitions of the 'natural' be adjudicated? Feminists may describe surrogacy as unnatural, while others label lesbian motherhood as unnatural. 'Nature' is a notoriously arbitrary and unreliable reference point in this respect: it gives us nowhere to stand.

Expertise as a Gender Relationship

In exploring different kinds of expertise, the various contributors to this collection are examining gender *relationships*. In this sense, expertise is not just a women's problem. For this problem is fully present – and, indeed, is fully reproduced – even in all-male settings. Cynthia Cockburn's study of the male-dominated print industry exemplified this, since it was in fact a study of gender relations (see Cockburn). This point has been taken even further by the questioning of presumptions about the unity underpinning the categories of 'women' or 'female'. So, for example, Donna Haraway argues: 'There is nothing about being "female" that naturally binds women. There is not even such a state as "being" female, itself a highly complex category constructed in contested sexual scientific discourses and other social practices' (Haraway, p. 72).

Some of the authors of this book might not carry the questioning of categories quite so far. They might also have reservations about the political implications of Haraway's approach. Nevertheless, whether examining the position of men or women around expertise, they would agree that gender relationships should be the focus. This is crucial for avoiding a politics of expertise which pictures women as needing to catch up with men or as passive victims. In addition, the stress on relationships provides a way out of debates – such as that between Barry Richards and Brian Easlea (see Richards; Easlea, 1985) – about whether or not the problems of expertise stem from the existence of 'masculine evil'.

Our Approach

In the light of recent feminist politics concerned with expertise, this collection raises some novel questions about strategies for change. Immersed in various ways in political struggles around women and expertise – as schoolteachers, university lecturers, journalists, adult education organizers, authors, technology network organizers, and scientific researchers – we have reflected on the direction of our politics. In some cases, the result has been a mapping of the terrain with reflections on our bearings: for example, in Mary Kennedy's survey of the gender politics of expertise within adult education in Britain, or in my own account of the emergence of a feminist politics in the area of knowledge production. In other cases, the authors have highlighted crucial issues or problems that have often been ignored or insufficiently explored by feminists. Thus, Pam Linn challenges the preoccupations with hardware in alternative projects; she seeks to unsettle assumptions about what constitutes technology. While praising Cynthia Cockburn's *Machinery of Dominance* as a valuable, concrete examination of gender relations around technology in paid employment, I express my reservations about attributing too much power to technology, and about underestimating the ideological dimensions of claims about technical power. Pam Linn, Judith Williamson and I are also concerned that feminists are sometimes too presumptuous about the uniformity of women's experience and the politics which results from such presumptions. The specificity of the needs of women in Western industrialized countries must be acknowledged and integrated into our politics. This is a lesson that both Judith Williamson and Pam Smith wish to draw from their readings of, respectively, *Sex and Destiny* and *The Wonderful World of Mrs Seacole*.

The resources available to feminists in challenging male expertise provide the focus for some of the following articles. While praising Brian Easlea's accessible opening up of debates on gender and science, Ludi Jordanova suggests that he uses a rather dehistoricized conception of feminity and that he fails to explore the sexual politics at stake in different views of creativity. Donna Haraway similarly welcomes Janet Sayers' book *Biological Poli-*

tics, whilst warning feminists against the dangers of reconstructing male expertise – of merely creating new heroes and new ideological taxonomies. Smith reminds us that we can learn much that is directly relevant to political practice today from those (like Mary Seacole) who tussled with male expertise in earlier periods. Looking at a more contemporary figure at the forefront of scientific research, Ania Grobicki finds the Nobel Prize-winning Barbara McClintock a much more innovative figure than Evelyn Fox Keller's biography acknowledges. It is the absence of a gender dimension in Fox Keller's account which makes it a limited rendering of women's struggles within professional scientific work.

Sonia Liff and Alison Ravetz probe the complexities of women's work and technology. In both cases, they use recent and exemplary studies of women's work (in Ravetz's case unpaid housework) to explore the parameters of feminists' understandings of the technological dimensions of women's work. Their reflections are stimulated by writings from Australia, America, and Canada suggesting that British feminists have much to learn from our sisters elsewhere, but also that we need to assess the peculiarities of British technology, both in the home and in sites of paid labour.

The Process

It might seem strange to describe the work of bringing together this collection as a 'labour of love'. But given the labour, angst and frustration involved in love, perhaps this is an appropriate way to label my experience with this book. Spelling out some to these difficulties is not merely self-indulgent or cathartic, though I feel fairly justified in seeking a little of both. Rather, this description might serve to illustrate some of the political difficulties in comprehending and transforming gender dynamics around expertise, whilst providing a way into the collection.

The Radical Science Collective would agree that this volume was more difficult to produce than any of its predecessors. This difficulty was not surprising, partly for reasons internal to the history of the Radical Science project. Although there have been articles in earlier collections which tackled gender, the main focus has been on science in capitalism, with a primary focus on class relations. This was despite the fact that some of the most characteristic formulations associated with Radical Science – for example 'science is social relations' – could, sometimes did and indeed *should* have included attention to gender inequalities.

Furthermore, the Collective itself was not the most propitious context from which to embark on such a project. Oh, the spirit was willing, but. . . . We were a mixed Collective (in gender terms) and the three women members who were around when the project was launched had originally become involved because of our commitments to Marxism. In different ways we three would describe ourselves as feminists, but Radical Science was not the main site of our feminist politics. Moreover, as in virtually every mixed left grouping, sexism reared its ugly head within the Collective and was sometimes 'the enemy within'.

The women within the Collective, again not atypically, were overstretched with other commitments. Thus, although it did not work out this way in the end, I was initially faced with the rather daunting prospect of trying single-handedly to assemble a volume on gender within a mixed Collective. (This is perhaps the appropriate moment to thank one of the men in the Collective, Les Levidow, for his patience and commitment in doing the behind-the-scenes work on this project.)

Finally, we realized fairly early on that our collective tool bag for analysing science and expertise as gender relations was pretty lightweight. (A preliminary brainstorming session was experienced by me at least as somewhat feeble.) This is not surprising, given, as Hilary Rose describes it, 'during the 1970s . . . those who sought to analyse and critique capitalist science's existing forms and systems of knowledge often produced critiques that are theoretically sex blind' (Rose, p. 73).

With preceding Radical Science collections we were able to draw on both internal and external resources (in the form of submitted articles, internally generated analyses, and approachable contacts); these were not so readily to hand in this case. Our attempts to forge some Radical Science perspectives on gender and expertise seemed plagued with pitfalls: we were often let down by would-be contributors, or ourselves simply not able to come up with the goods. In most cases, these problems related directly to the sexual division of labour which is the central concern of this collection: we were dealing with women who were overworked and underpaid (and totally unpaid by us), who had been intimidated by forms of male expertise, who were doing more than their fair share of caring and/or domestic labour, who were daunted by what they considered to be the masculinist mode of Radical Science or who were just exhausted. In short, the production process has been difficult, though not without its own rewards.

Finally, we must note that this is a unique product for the Radical Science Collective. This is the only issue of Radical Science written exclusively by women. This represents a definite decision on our part, arrived at along the way. However, we are not thereby advocating that only women have anything relevant to say on these matters, or any separatist politics. Instead, it represents a gesture towards rectifying the imbalance in preceding issues and the hope that women's voices will be heard more often on these issues. Nevertheless, all the articles were discussed by the mixed Collective; thus, the final product was also shaped by the collective process, making it unusual for such a collection on gender politics. Coming from that unusual background, this collection offers fresh perspectives on one of the most exciting dimensions of recent feminism.

References

Books are published in London unless otherwise noted.

P. Brown and L. J. Jordanova, 'Oppressive Dichotomies: the Nature/Culture Debate', in Cambridge Women's Studies Group, ed., *Women in Society: Interdisciplinary Essays,* Virago, 1981, pp. 224–41.

F. Capra, *The Turning Point,* Flamingo, 1982.

C. Cockburn, *Brothers: Male Dominance and Technological Change,* Pluto, 1983.

M. Douglas, *Purity and Danger: an Analysis of Concepts of Pollution and Taboo,* Harmondsworth, Penguin, 1970.

M. Douglas, ed., *Rules and Meanings: The Anthropology of Everyday Knowledge,* Harmondsworth, Penguin, 1973.

B. Easlea, 'Exploding Masculinity', *Science for People* 59 (Autumn 1985), 17–20.

B. Easlea, *Fathering the Unthinkable: Masculinity, Scientists and the Nuclear Arms Race,* Pluto, 1983.

B. Easlea, *Science and Sexual Oppression: Patriachy's Confrontation with Woman and Nature,* Weidenfeld & Nicolson, 1981.

B. Easlea, *Witch-Hunting, Magic and the New Philosophy,* Brighton, Harvester, 1980.

E. Fox Keller, *A Feeling for the Organism: The Life and Work of Barbara McClintock,* New York, W. H. Freeman, 1983.

E. Fox Keller, 'How Gender Matters, or Why It's So Hard for Us to Count Past Two', Speech to the British Association for the Advancement of Science Annual Conference, August, 1985.

D. Haraway, 'A Manifesto for Cyborgs: Science, Technology, and Socialist Feminism in the 1980s', *Socialist Review* 80 (1985), 65–107.

R. Hubbard, 'Personal Courage is Not Enough: Some Hazards of Childbearing in the 1980s', in R. Aditti, R. Duelli Klein and S. Minden, eds, *Test-Tube Women: What Future for Motherhood?* Pandora, 1984, pp. 331–5.

G. Lukács, *History and Class Consciousness: Studies in Marxist Dialectics* (1923), Merlin, 1971.

B. Richards, 'The Bomb: Men or the State' (review of B. Easlea, *Fathering the Unthinkable* and R. Aronson, *The Dialectics of Disaster*), *Science for People* 57 (Spring 1985), 12–15.

R. Schwartz Cowan, 'From Virginia Dare to Virginia Slims: Women and Technology in American Life', *Technology and Culture* 20 (Jan. 1979).

R. Williams, 'Ideas of Nature' in R. Williams, ed., *Problems in Materialism and Culture: Selected Essays*, Verso, 1980, pp. 67–85.

B. Young, 'Science *is* Social Relations', *Radical Science Journal* 5 (1977), 65–129.

Women's Nature and Rationality

BEING REASONABLE FEMINISTS

Maureen McNeil

The recent phase of the women's movement has distinguished itself from its predecessors in its fundamental challenging of many presumptions about knowledge and expertise. From at least the eighteenth century to the 1970s, women anxious to improve their lot and that of their sisters often began by probing why women were 'deficient' in knowledge and/or less rational than men. The new women's movement – which emerged in America, Britain, Australia and much of Europe in the 1960s and 70s – has begun to break with the traditional framework for conceptualizing female oppression. This essay analyses the new forms of sexual politics around knowledge production which have characterized this period of feminism.

The novelty and significance of these new forms of politics can be assessed only with reference to what preceded them. For this reason, I begin by highlighting some features of earlier feminist approaches to issues of rationality and gender. I have chosen to do this by considering three major figures – Mary Wollstonecraft, Virginia Woolf and Simone de Beauvoir. My intention is to contrast earlier feminists, who saw women as unfairly deprived of rationality, with contemporary ones, who identify male rationality as the problem.

From there, I move on to 'Body Politics' and the recent women's health movement, which I regard as the first popular movement to construct a gender analysis and politics in an area of scientific knowledge. I consider this to be the first of two major feminist movements – the second being the women's peace movement – which mobilized around issues of male expertise.

In the wake of the women's health movement, since the late 1970s in Britain and America, there have followed various explorations of the gender politics of expertise. I sketch some of its numerous threads, including the patriarchal character of scientific knowledge,[1] a gender dynamic in the history of science, women and nature, and a feminist epistemology.

This brings me to the second mass political movement focused on gender and expertise: the women's peace movement. Situating the movement historically, I analyse how it incorporated a politics of expertise, posing new questions about gender and rationality. As suggested above, I see this movement as a turning point in the history of feminist debates about rationality. I argue that it has constituted a watershed, transforming feminist agendas about science, epistemology and rationality.

The last part of the article reviews some of the most interesting assessments of how we might tackle the knowledge–gender dilemmas of a nuclear age. In different ways, this is the concern of Christa Wolf, Rosalie Bertell, and Hilary Rose. Thus, I examine their strategies for tackling contemporary dilemmas in this field. By way of conclusion, I offer my own suggestions about where to go from here.

My main focus is on developments within British feminism. However, international connections have been extremely important to the recent phase of the movement, so I have cast my net beyond these shores for reasons of principle when it seemed appropriate. This has meant looking at imported texts which have been influential and, in some instances, drawing comparisons and contrasts.

My purpose in writing this article is to get some sense of the changing face of feminist politics around issues of rationality, epistemology, expertise, and science and technology. As a feminist, I have found this one of the most exciting and yet most confusing features of the movement. I mount arguments on two levels. First, I make critical comments about specific developments and debates within the movement in this domain. Feminism has made me wary of pronouncements from the critic – from on high. I hope that it will be clear that this is not what is on offer here. Rather, I hope that my comments will be taken as musings on common problems, on shared political projects. I suppose my interest might be described as pushing for, and trying to pull myself towards, some forms of feminist 'good sense', in Gramsci's sense (see *Prison Notebooks*).

On a more general level, I am stressing the importance of the interrelationships between popular movements and debates about the gender politics of knowledge. Just as the nineteenth-century working-class movements in Britain sought 'really useful knowledge' for class emancipation (see Johnson), today's women's movement requires its counterpart. Perhaps more controversially, I am suggesting that the feminist politics of expertise is currently facing a cul-de-sac. This results from the reduction of this politics to a series of options for or against female intuition, an abstract rationality, or a feminist science. Such foreclosures carry us away from acknowledging the depth of the problem that we face in the struggle for 'really useful' feminist knowledge.

EARLIER FEMINISTS AND RATIONALITY

Mary Wollstonecraft

What was perhaps the first feminist manifesto published in Britain – Mary Wollstonecraft's *A Vindication of the Rights of Woman* (1792) – condemned women's 'deplorable state' that resulted from 'their innocence, as ignorance is courteously termed', from the fact that 'truth is hidden from them' (p. 131). Wollstonecraft (1759–97) herself was a true daughter of the Enlightenment and active in the intellectual circles most concerned with the spread of its principles in Britain. As she saw it, women's position would improve only when women became as rational as men; it was their ignorance which thwarted them constantly: 'I may be allowed to infer that reason is absolutely necessary to enable a woman to perform any duty properly, and I must again repeat, that sensibility is not reason' (p. 156). Masculinity was linked to rationality for Wollstonecraft, so that women would have to become more 'masculine' – more like men – in order to improve their lot.

Of course, the complexities of Wollstonecraft's own controversial life (Wollstonecraft, 1796; Tomalin; Walters) and her fictional explorations of the position of women – in *Mary* (1788) and *The Wrongs of Woman* (1798) – belied such a narrow strategy for female emancipation. But that is another story.

Behind the many campaigns to improve women's access to education in various phases of feminism there have been assumptions fairly similar to Wollstonecraft's: women were insufficiently rational or deficient in knowledge, and their attempts to 'catch up' with men needed to be facilitated. Virtually every feminist resurgence from the eighteenth century to the present day was accompanied by struggles around access to education. (For some recent feminist versions of these campaigns see Byrne; Deem; Spender and Sarah.)

This feminist tradition emphasized female deficiencies around rationality and set out to rectify them: masculine knowledge was to be acquired. It never examined or questioned the nature or desirability of that knowledge, nor did it investigate – other than dismissively – the kinds of knowledge that women already had.

Virginia Woolf

Virgina Woolf (1882–1941) was an extremely important figure in this debate. She asked profound questions about the gendered character of education and knowledge. Woolf deepened the argument about women and rationality by probing the gendered nature of educational institutions and the formal and informal male power networks around these; by reflecting on the material conditions which made intellectual work possible; and by probing the way in which gender relations became embodied in formalized knowledge itself.

When Woolf looked at education and the professions, she saw bastions of male power. Unlike her predecessors, her main focus was not on *access* for women to these institutions; rather it was on the forms of power they structured and reproduced:

> Your world, then, the world of the professional, of public life, seen from this angle undoubtedly looks queer . . . It is from this world that the private house (somewhere, roughly speaking, in the West End) has derived its creeds, its laws, its clothes and carpets, its beef and mutton. (1977, p. 22)

Here, and in her concern for the conditions of intellectual production, Woolf developed a kind of materialist analysis.

This brings me to Woolf's second innovative contribution to debates about women and rationality. Woolf's familiar preoccupation with 'a room of one's own' was indicative of her interest in sketching the constraints on women as intellectual creators. It was these determinations which shaped, channelled and confined the forms of women's public intellectual production. For Woolf, writing in Britain during the first half of the twentieth century, fiction was materially designated as *the* primary female mode:

> Thus, when I came to write, there were few material obstacles in my way. Writing was a reputable and harmless occupation. The family peace was not broken by the scratching of a pen. No demand was made upon the family purse. (1979, p. 57), The cheapness of writing paper, is, of course, the reason why women have succeeded as writers before they have succeeded in the other professions. (p. 58), Fiction was, as fiction still is, the easiest thing for a woman to write . . . A novel is the least concentrated form of art. A novel can be taken up or put down more easily than a play or a poem. George Eliot left her work to nurse her father. Charlotte Brontë put down her pen to pick the eyes out of the potatoes. (p. 46)

The last quotation in particular vividly relates outstanding achievement by women novelists to domestic labour. For Woolf, it was no coincidence that women's main cultural achievement took the form of novels; the cultural form was a product of the material realities of women's domestic lives.

But Woolf also went a step further in investigating gender relations and intellectual production. She felt that, just as novels were a determined cultural form, so were other intellectual forms also shaped by the gender relations from which they emerged. Her brazen pronouncement in *Three Guineas* (1938) – that 'Science, it would seem, is not sexless; she is a man, a father and infected too' – eloquently signals this. In this book Woolf probed the relationship between male dominance and the disturbing ideas and value systems of fascist militarism. Male control of the institutions of education had provided the breeding ground for these horrifying intellectual products, which hovered threateningly over the world in the 1930s. Woolf was certain that this connection would have to be understood in order to prevent the spread of the militarist spectre.

There were, of course, real limitations in Woolf's original questioning. Her perspective and insights were primarily about the relative disadvantages of middle-class women as compared with men of their class. Thus, the institutions she focused on were middle-class institutions: the professions and higher education. Likewise, in unpacking the material conditions of intellectual production, she looked at the division of labour between middle-class men and women. Indeed, a striking lacuna for someone so concerned with the division of labour was her failure even to comment about servants and maids, whose labour was so taken for granted as to be rendered invisible. Moreover, it is the domestic rather than the larger economy which primarily concerns her – again presuming the perspective of women who did not need to bring money into the home. Note in the earlier quote that the issue for Woolf is with women as *consumers* and their limited call on family resources.

There is also the further difficulty that Woolf's profound questions reached a limited audience. She wrote for and interacted with the intellectual elite of Britain. The organs in which she pursued these issues were the journals and periodicals patronized by these people, as well as her two nonfiction texts – *A Room of One's Own* (1929) and *Three Guineas* (1938) – which circulated to a very limited audience.

But there were further restrictions in the take-up of Woolf's concerns. While Woolf's novels gained intellectual acclaim, her nonfiction books were relatively neglected. Woolf's appeals for closer examinations of the gendered nature of intellectual work were largely ignored. They were often attributed to the quirkiness of an overly intellectual or 'mad' woman or, more charitably, as the notes on difficulties in the production of her infinitely superior literary 'masterpieces'.

Simone de Beauvoir

Nine years after Virginia Woolf died, Simone de Beauvoir (1908–86) published *The Second Sex* (1949). This 'book on women' (p. 13) was to become a sort of bible of the post-World War 2 women's movement in the West. Addressing the *problem* of femininity, it seeks an explanation for this problem in the inferior status of women as 'the Other'. De Beauvoir's diagnosis was that the female was closer to her animality, closer to nature than the male. This enslavement prevented women from transcending their immediate situation and thereby entering into the world of cultural creativity. Women were, for the most part, 'shut up in immanence' (p. 726).

For Simone de Beauvoir, as for Mary Wollstonecraft, women were insufficiently rational and transcendent of their immediate environment. However, unlike Wollstonecraft, she saw more reason for hope around her: 'The "modern" woman accepts masculine values: she prides herself on thinking, taking action, working, creating on the same terms as men; instead of seeking to disparage them, she declares herself their equal' (p. 727). Equality meant acting 'on the same terms as men' and – what is crucial for us – '*thinking* . . . on the same terms as men'. De Beauvoir's aspirations for women were that they too would become progressively more transcendent. 'When she is productive, active, she regains her transcendence; in her projects she concretely affirms her status as subject . . .' (p. 689).

Within de Beauvoir's analysis there is a strong bond between rationality and masculine accomplishment represented in technology:

> . . . it is the male principle that has triumphed. Spirit has prevailed over Life, transcendence over immanence, technique over magic, and reason over superstition. The devaluation of woman represents a necessary stage in the history of humanity, for it is not upon her positive value but upon man's weakness that her prestige is founded. In woman are incarnated the disturbing mysteries of nature, and man escapes her hold when he frees himself from nature. It is the advance from stone to bronze that enables him through his labour to gain mastery of the soil and to master himself . . . This world of tools could be embraced within clear concepts: rational thought, logic, and mathematics could now appear. The whole concept of the universe is overthrown. The religion of woman was bound to the reign of agriculture, the reign of irreducible duration, of contingency, of chance, of

> waiting, of mystery; the reign of *Homo faber* is the reign of time manageable as space, of necessary consequences, of the project, of action, of reason. (pp. 106–7)

It is not surprising to find that many of the extrapolations from de Beauvoir's framework identified technological innovation as a paradigmatic example of male transcendence (for example, Ortner, p. 75). Nor is it surprising that questions about the desirability of technological domination of the natural world have generated critiques of this aspect of de Beauvoir's views (Easlea, 1981, pp. 35–40).

From the vantage point of 1980s feminism, the weaknesses of de Beauvoir's analysis seemhto stem partly from her almost exclusive focus on women. While femininity is to be destroyed (de Beauvoir, p. 728), masculinity is seen as unproblematic. Nevertheless, occasionally she was more ambiguous about both the possibility and the wisdom of a total conversion to masculine forms of thought and creativity.

In writing about the new 'free woman' who is 'just being born' (p. 723), she was reflecting about the more independent women of the period. She is unsure about the results of the modern woman moving into the worlds of creativity that men have hitherto exclusively occupied:

> It is not certain that her 'ideational worlds' will be different from those of men, since it will be through attaining the same situation as theirs that she will find emancipation; to say in what degree she will remain different, in what degree these differences will retain their importance – this would be to hazard bold predictions indeed. (p. 724)

Even allowing for her uncertainty here, her baseline remains that the key to female emancipation lies in the conversion to male modes.

Stepping further back from de Beauvoir's views, it is striking how idealistic her approach to intellectual creativity is. This is not to say that she is unaware of the real, lived differences between the positions of men and women as cultural creators. Her accounts of the dilemmas of intellectual women are vivid, concrete and intimate. She comments on such details as women's invisible labour on their appearance and dress and other forms of female labour: 'Obedient to the feminine tradition, she will wax her floors, and she will do her own cooking instead of going to eat at a restaurant as a man would in her place. She wants to live at once like a man and like a woman, and in that way, she multiplies her tasks and adds to her fatigue' (p. 694). Perhaps significantly, de Beauvoir does not include child (and other forms of family) care with housework in her sketch of women's double burden of labour.

Women find it difficult to move beyond the world of these specific forms of female labour, whose demands leave little time, space or energy for the transcendence that de Beauvoir associated with male creativity. The problem is that once again she does not devote enough attention to the male equivalent (though she makes passing references to various forms of female servicing of men). If she had done so, she might have recognized that male cultural production does *not* transcend its conditions of production – it takes forms that flow directly from it. For example, abstraction is possible only for those who can afford to detach themselves from their immediate environment. Furthermore, can we presume that a move away from the concrete and immediate situation necessarily constitutes the most desirable option? Is all cultural creativity based on transcendence? The very polarization between transcendence and immanence blinds her to the ways in which male cultural production is intimately related to its conditions of production.

There is a further problem with her notion of transcendence. It cuts off any questions about the nature of intellectual achievement or cultural production. By its very definition, such products no longer bear the mark of their origins. Thus de Beauvoir separates her acute insights about the sexual division of labour, and its concrete experienced form for female intellectuals, from her far more idealistic investigation of cultural creativity. The two are simply never brought together.

There was a world of difference between her personal situation and that of Virginia Woolf in terms of financial independence. Woolf's 'room of her own' was negotiated within the affluent, patriarchal domestic economy of upper-middle-class Britain, where she depended on male benevolence. De Beauvoir sees financial independence as a *sine qua non* for all women; the nature of her own room was literally determined by her own earning power – as a teacher, then writer.

But we must be much more mindful than she was of the conditions of intellectual production, and hers in particular. *The Second Sex*, like all de Beauvoir's writing, was generated in the bohemian world of Left Bank post-World War 2 Paris. De Beauvoir and Sartre were at the centre of an artistic circle which was alternative, marginal, though nevertheless increasingly influential. Cafés and hotels were their haunts, eliminating some pressures of domestic labour. Whilst deeply immersed in the politics of their period, their lifesyles testified that there could and should be individuals who labelled themselves as 'intellectuals' and sustained themselves an adequate – if often precarious – living through intellectual production. This, again, presupposed that there were those who set themselves apart – who transcended their immediate environment in cultural production – and those who did not. This presumed a certain mental/manual division of labour. Cultural production was not a part of everyday life; for de Beauvoir, it was an exclusive function realized by a few – the intellectual avant-garde – albeit often in rather insecure circumstances.

The Second Sex was rediscovered by the second wave of twentieth-century British feminism. There was a gap of almost twenty years between the appearance of its first English edition (1953, Cape) and its second, paperback form (Penguin, 1972). In Britain, as in much of the West, de Beauvoir's book came to be regarded as a key text for the new women's movement.

In turning to this new movement, I am aware of the difficulties around what happened to feminist ideas in Britain from the First World War until the late 1960s. However, such a leap is necessary in this analysis because there was no literature or movement in the intervening period which addressed itself to the questions of intellectual production which so preoccupied Woolf and de Beauvoir. As I shall suggest, the new feminists were drawn into these questions much more through practical political campaigns than through intellectual dilemmas or the difficulties of would-be intellectuals.

BODY POLITICS

Birth control and abortion were key concerns fairly early on in this period of feminism. Free contraception and abortion on demand was one of the initial Four Demands of the first national women's conference in Britain, held in Oxford in February–March 1970 (Wandor, p. 2). The formulation of this demand recognized the centrality of the control of female sexuality and fertility in the oppression of women. Most important for my vantage point, it was virtually impossible to tackle these issues without investigating the nature and power of medical expertise.

The late 1960s and 1970s witnessed the emergence of various forms of politics centred on women's bodies. The anthologies of the movement document the importance of this channel of feminist activities. The first collection of feminist papers was itself called *The Body Politic* (Wandor), while a section of the second anthology was devoted to 'Body Politics' (Allen *et al.*, pp. 8–58). Each of the subsequent collections records the continuing significance of campaigns around reproduction and health issues (Rowe, chs 8 and 9; Kanter *et al.*, ch. 7).

Here we have the documentation of a very practical movement around women's health issues. Indeed, the 1970s and 1980s saw the flourishing of many women's health groups and much experimentation around 'alternative' forms of health care and self-help (e.g. Brent Women's Centre; Leeson and Gray, pp. 190–200). This practical orientation was commented upon in the introduction to the section on 'Our Bodies' in the feminist anthology for the 1981–3 period: 'Although not much has been written about the politics of women's health recently, much practical work has been done. Women have fought the cuts in a crumbling health service, encouraged self-help activities, and there has been increasing interest in alternative forms of healing' (Kanter *et al.*, p. 203).

Much of this published material is an experiential literature: first-hand accounts of women's experience of medical treatment or neglect of various kinds. As such, it recorded a different kind of knowledge about medical phenomena from that provided by medical science itself. Women's dissatisfactions with the treatment they received, mainly at the hands of male doctors, led them to question the nature of and status attributed to medical expertise. The revealing title of one article on this topic which appeared in 1974 was 'Medical Mystifications' (Comer). It claimed that it would be a 'mistake to assume that medical science is any more free from traditional assumptions about female inferiority than any other so-called "science" ' (p. 45). By challenging medical expertise on grounds that it did not meet the needs of women and, often, contributed to the maintenance of female oppression, this approach encouraged the development of 'self-help' strategies. Behind these lie the belief that women could develop new kinds of knowledge and skills which drew on their own experience and needs.

Our Bodies, Ourselves

The textbook or, more accurately, the handbook for this new body politics was *Our Bodies Ourselves*, produced by the Boston Women's Health Collective. Very much the product of the women's health movement, its collective authorship and various transformations are indicative of this origin. Its first incarnation was as the papers for women's health courses. These were duplicated for wider circulation and then assembled into a cheap edition published by the New England Free Press. The commercial edition first appeared in the USA in 1971, and in Britain in 1978 in revised form. The royalities from the American edition were used to help finance further health education. This history itself documents the alternative educational channels and communication networks around the women's health movement in America in the 1970s.

Our Bodies Ourselves became an alternative manual with wide popular appeal. Most copies are, I suspect, like mine – extremely well-thumbed. Like many of my friends and, no doubt, countless women around the world, I have used its index for numerous mini-consultations. In this sense, it has been used as a medical reference text. But it is rather different from any standard text of this sort. First, and perhaps foremost, it was not written by doctors or medical experts. The authors make no claims to special expertise; they present themselves simply as 'women'. Moreover, its operating definition of knowledge challenges the parameters of medical textbooks. The first chapter after the introduction begins with the heading: 'Our Feelings' (p. 17). The approach is subjective – an unusual tack for a chapter on the '*Anatomy* and *Physiology* of Sexuality and Reproduction'. In setting out from women's feelings about their bodies, the authors implicitly challenge the men who 'through the ages have considered themselves experts on us [women]' (p. 11). The use of 'we' binds the individual experiences of women together assertively, in a political stance against the isolation and divisions which structure female oppression. But there is a less positive side to the use of the umbrella 'we'. With few exceptions, the differences and disagreements – amongst the authors, and amongst women more generally – are obscured. This is particularly worrying because the book was written by white, middle-class American women between the ages of twenty-nine and forty-five – a rather homogeneous group from a very specific context.

There were certain identifications within the text which were characteristic of the new body politics. The title asserted and seemed to welcome the fact that, as women, we are defined by our bodies; we *are* our bodies. Moreover, in so far as most of the book was devoted to sexuality and reproduction, it implies that this is what being a woman is about. I can remember scanning the index of *Our Bodies Ourselves* in a futile search for an entry on 'haemorrhoids'. This was a most disconcerting experience: Was I suffering from a 'man's' ailment and what did this mean? Why did my body not respect sexual divisions? I was left wondering why this problem did not constitute a woman's problem. The new body politics, focusing on female aspects of the body, seemed to contradict its avowed intention of challenging traditional divisions.

The Women's Health Movement

The women's health movement of this period in Britain and America was perhaps the first popular movement to construct a gender analysis and politics around a body of scientific knowledge. The issue was not restricted to female access to such knowledge – to campaigns (as in the earlier feminist movement) to permit women to undertake medical education. Instead, the campaigns hovered around Woolf's perception that scientific knowledge was gender-laden – at least within the medicine that shaped women's lives.

The movement also unleashed a number of hares, one of which pursued the historical trail of the construction of male expertise. How had medicine come to be such a repository of patriarchal values? Despite its weaknesses (see Jordanova), the research of Barbara Ehrenreich and Deirdre English was extremely influential; indeed, almost paradigmatic in this field. In two popular pamphlets – *Witches, Midwives and Nurses: A History of Women Healers* (1973) and *Complaints and Disorders: The Sexual Politics of Sickness*, both first published in 1973 – they traced what they saw as the growth and consolidation of male expertise against the interests of women. Accompanying this was a 'recovered' history of female health knowledge and its marginalization. Here was a message about the gender politics of knowledge addressed to a far wider and more diverse audience than Virginia Woolf reached. Interestingly, Ehrenreich's and English's work was the product of two worlds. As teachers in an American institution of higher education (the State University of New York), they had benefited from the post-World War 2 expansion of such education in the West; they were products of increased female access to higher education. So, they were professional 'knowledge producers', earning an income through intellectual production. But they were also part of 'a women's health movement – composed of women health workers, community activists, and dissatisfied health care consumers' which was operating by 1972 in the Northeastern United States as 'a distinct feminist force' (Ehrenreich and English, 1979, p. vii).

Despite their employment by a university, their research was clearly beyond the academic pale and orientated towards a popular readership. Referring to *Witches, Midwives and Nurses: A History of Women Healers* (1973), they described how its publication came about:

> We filled the text with illustrations, paid to have it printed, and for over a year mailed it to people who wrote for copies, working from a kitchen-table office. To our surprise, demand for this pamphlet quickly

> outgrew our capacity to distribute it. Fortunately The Feminist Press, in Old Westbury, New York, offered to take over publication and distribution . . . The response to the two booklets (which were never advertised) was both overwhelming and unexpectedly diverse. (pp. vii–viii)

They sketch the range of their readers: 'dissident grass-roots health organizations', 'elite nursing schools', 'university women's studies programme:' and 'women hospital workers' who apparently passed it from hand to hand (p. viii).

Embedded in this account are elements in the emergence of a new feminist politics about knowledge production: the securing of new institutions designed to disseminate forms of knowledge which were not male-dominated, such as feminist publishing and women's studies courses. In addition, it also suggests that there was a broad and deep concern about the sexual politics of expertise.

Ehrenreich's and English's original pamphlets were not isolated examples of the growing disenchantment with male medical knowledge. Caroll Smith-Rosenberg's more conventionally academic examination of female hysteria in nineteenth-century America revolved around similar issues (C. Smith-Rosenberg; also C. Smith-Rosenberg and C. Rosenberg); she demonstrated that medical men played a pivotal part in defining potential roles for women during this period. In addition, when Ehrenreich and English presented their original research in book form (Ehrenreich and English, 1979), they extended their analysis to scientific theories of child-rearing and domestic science.

The writings of Juliet Mitchell, in particular, register the influence during the early stages of the recent women's movement in Britain, of another political movement centred on the critique of expertise – the anti-psychiatry movement (see Mitchell, 1971; Mitchell, 1974, esp. pp. 227–92). The latter, to some extent, attempted to validate the experience and knowledge of psychiatric patients. It was sceptical about the knowledge and treatment on offer from experts in this field. As such, it complemented similar strategies within the women's movement in relationship to the medical profession in particular. Although some would claim that anti-psychiatry quickly generated its own set of 'alternative' experts (virtually all male, of course), this connection was influential in the beginnings of the women's health movement in Britain.

A Turning Point

So, by the 1970s, we had come a long way from Mary Wollstonecraft's presumption that women were insufficently rational and needed to have more access to male knowledge to realize their emancipation. Many feminists had powerful and concrete critiques of at least one form of male knowledge – scientific medicine. There were several noteworthy features of what was perhaps the first popular movement orientated around the gender politics of knowledge. First, it challenged the systemic knowledge produced by experts in a profession which largely excluded women. In this respect, when Ehrenreich and English did extend their analysis, their chosen target was knowledge produced by similar sorts of male-dominated professions. Indeed, in terms of conceptual frameworks for criticizing knowledge production, professionalization became the main focus – the identified 'cause' of gender inequalities in this area.

Another significant feature of the women's health movement was that it saw problems only in those forms of knowledge production which had an obvious ideological function in the construction of female roles. It was only here that a gender politics was seen to be in operation. None the less, the movement did encourage a popular scepticism amongst women. This encouraged forms of resistance which easily spilled over from the doctor–patient relationship to other power relations involving expertise.

The women's health movement, and the investigations in the history of expertise that it fostered in the 1970s shared a critique of systemic medical knowledge. But there were different ways of accounting for its deficiency. For the most part, such critiques were based on the belief that medical knowledge (and the other forms of expertise women directly encountered) was insufficently rational – distorted by irrational male prejudices against women (see Jordanova, p. 126). This is clearly exposed in the concluding chapter of *For Her Own Good*:

> Claiming the purity of science, they [the experts] had persisted in the commercialism inherent in a commoditized system of healing. Claiming the objectivity of science, they had advanced the doctrines of sexual romanticism. They turned out not to be scientists – for all their talk of data, laboratory findings, clinical trials – but apologists for the status quo. Confronted with something resembling the essence of real scientific thought – the critical and rationalist spirit of the new feminism – they could only bluster defensively or mumble in embarrassment. (p. 285)

Effectively, for Ehrenreich and English as for many others, the women's movement had put a wedge between existing scientific medical knowledge and rationality. Systemic, established knowledge was not necessarily rational.

Returning to my starting point – Mary Wollstonecraft's ideas – it is crucial to recall that Wollstonecraft's world was one of unified and unitary truth and knowledge. Access to education was vital to women because access to the knowledge it would provide would help them to function as more rational beings – to be more like men. By the 1970s, feminism was declaring that it was the male 'experts' who were irrational.

The evidence for their irrationality could be found where Mary Wollstonecraft would have been shocked to find it – in scientific (mainly medical) knowledge. This certainly undermined any straightforward strategy of regarding education as the primary tool for female liberation. Perhaps most important of all, it was no longer just intellectuals or writers who were asking questions about the sexual politics of knowledge.

With the floodgates now open, the streams flowed in many directions. If medical knowledge – as one form of scientific knowledge – was patriarchal, then what about the rest of science, in which men were similarly dominant? And what about other forms of systemic knowledge? Was the whole intellectual realm gender-biased? The scientists who formulated the facts and theories challenged by the women's health movement *claimed* to be invoking rationality. Nevertheless, Ehrenreich and English wrote of an opposing 'critical and rationalist spirit' within the new feminism. Was there more than one kind of rationality? Was there a 'male' and a 'female' rationality? Or was 'rationality' itself a tainted concept denoting a blinkered and limited approach to understanding the human situation?

It would not be an exaggeration to claim that since the 1970s there has been some feminist exploration of virtually every one of these questions. Moreover, and perhaps more importantly, there have been different feminist answers offered to each one. I do not think it is just my jaded perspective as someone reflecting on recent developments in this area which brings me to observe that the pace of this debate has been dizzying.

NEW EXPLORATIONS OF EXPERTISE

In order to tease out the features of recent explorations in the gender politics of knowledge production, I will consider how the various questions mentioned earlier have been pursued. These issues include scientific knowledge as patriarchal, women and nature, and feminist epistemology. Here I will sketch the continuation of feminist debates about knowledge and rationality to the present day.

Scientific Knowledge as Patriarchal

I recently came across my reading lists for an MSc. course on Women and Science which I taught between 1978 and 1980 at the Liberal Studies in Science Department, University of Manchester. The course was divided up into units of the 'Women and . . .' variety, except for the first unit on 'women as scientists'. So, from there we looked at 'women' and science education, medicine, technology, biology. Three things strike me about those courses now.

First, 'women and science' issues were defined around either access to scientific education and/or careers, or medical or biological appropriations of the female body, or the failure to use scientific knowledge to meet the needs of female labour via technology. The only section of the course which revolved around an evaluation of the politics of scientific knowledge as such was the unit on medicine and biology. And here, as suggested above, it was far too easy to attribute the gendered nature of the knowledge to the topic. The problem seemed to be that, in tackling certain topics relating particularly to female biology, male scientists found it impossible to keep wearing their intellectual lab coats (trousers?) – their objectivity. Their generally maintained objectivity gave way; they exposed themselves as *men*, rather than scientists. I can remember being extremely pleased when the Ehrenreich and English book appeared because it was one of the few texts which centralized questions about scientific knowledge itself rather than merely the use or abuse of such knowledge. But, as noted previously, there were limitations in the framework of this text. I continued to find it difficult to get students to consider scientific knowledge as political, in any sense. My own framework for doing this around gender politics was clearly limited at this time; I probably found it easier to debate some of the capitalist features of scientific knowledge, rather than its patriarchal ones. Nevertheless, it was hard to develop *any* political perspective on scientific knowledge.

My second reflection is that the course seemed to embody the assumption that biology and medical science were the only sciences in which gender relations were significant. I remember feeling uneasy about this at the time, particularly when we delved into issues of science education. Most of the literature on women and science education concentrated on the issue of access (see, for example, Kelly, 1981). Now I was adamant that this just wasn't good enough: it begged questions about the *nature* of the education and the *nature* of the science on offer; there were clearly real forms of resistance (perhaps political) going on in the classroom. Such resistances amongst working-class males could be diagnosed as politically significant. Although I felt certain about this in the microcosm of the classroom, I could not quite work it out on a larger scale. Women's absence from the world of science was not just a problem of exclusion, requiring campaigns for access. There were real feminine resistances to scientific knowledge – which suggested that it was not just biology and medical science which embodied sexual politics.

My final point about my course is a bit more nebulous. It identified a sexual politics around science only in sites where women were: biological knowledge of female anatomy, women working inadequate washing machines, women banging on the door of higher education for science courses, women scientists. This now appears a real blinkering; from feminists working on a range of other issues, we have learned that gender relations are virtually always with us – in our heads (both men's and women's) and in the structures of our institutions, environments, etc. Cynthia Cockburn's research on all-male chapels of the British print industry graphically illustrated the presence of gender relations in single-sex environments (Cockburn).

Although I have dwelt on my own experience teaching about women and science in higher education, similar patterns emerged elsewhere. The Brighton Women and Science Group's *Alice Through the Microscope* (1980) was devoted almost totally to examinations of biological and medical sciences and technologies as they related to women. Except for an article on science education, only Ruth Wallsgrove's contribution – 'The Masculine Face of Science' – breaks out of this mould. The others' spotlight is very much on women's bodies, their sexuality and reproduction.

The preceding account sets the stage for describing what I take to be fairly dramatic developments since then in the analysis of the sexual politics of scientific knowledge. To illustrate concretely the transformation in thinking about gender and science, I would say that if I had set my course only one year after I stopped teaching it, we would have been examining the ways in which *all* scientific knowledge can be seen as patriarchal. New research in the history of science, and a growing awareness of the cultural identification of women with nature, were largely responsible for this dramatic transformation.

Who would have predicted that the first systematic work on the gender politics of modern science would come from the study of the Scientific Revolution? On second thought, this is not so surprising, given that this Revolution was considered to have established the foundations for modern science – for a 'scientific method' which has dominated the Western world ever since. Carolyn Merchant and Brian Easlea published their detailed investigations of the sexual politics within the Scientific Revolution almost simultaneously. In 1980 *The Death of Nature* and *Witch Hunting, Magic, and the New Philosophy* traced the attacks on traditional forms of female knowledge and its practitioners (witches) as integral to 'the New Philosophy'. These two books also examine how this heralded a more aggressive and ruthless exploitation of the natural world. Easlea's sequel, *Science and Sexual Oppression: Patriarchy's Confrontation with Woman and Nature* (1981), argued that the Scientific Revolution had established a constitutional link between male sexual insecurity and science, that the link was based on domination of women and nature, and that it has pervaded the history of science since then.

Much could be said about Merchant's and Easlea's work (and some important differences between them). What is crucial for my present concerns is that it provided the historical underpinning for the claim that all science was patriarchal – a claim which had increasing credibility in America and Europe. But it was worth noting that Easlea at least evaded any straightforward designation of science as such as problematic. He is interested in 'the reasons why modern science has not been *applied* in a way that enriches... the lives of all people' (Easlea, 1981, p. ix). He comments on how class interests 'distorted scientific enquiry' and on how scientific Marxism 'adopted a distorted view of science' (p. 198); it is 'scientific *practice*' which 'has been overwhelmingly irrational'. Somewhere – though it remains unclear, since he ranges over five centuries of the history of science and finds it distorted – there is implicitly a set of pure, rational, undistorted scientific ideas.

I am often surprised that the hesitancies in Easlea's analysis have not been given more attention. Perhaps this is because the generalized version of his argument that science is patriarchal had considerable popular purchase, particularly among feminists. But it is also important that it was no longer exclusively in the interface between *women* and science that a sexual politics could be identified. If Merchant and Easlea were right, then *all* of science was patriarchal, from biology to physics. The question of the relationship between women and rationality was slightly fudged by Easlea, though in a way which was very indicative of subsequent developments. On the one hand, he suggested that it was the scientific *practice* and application which were so irrational, not scientific knowledge itself. He seemed to want to defend something like a scientific rationality. However, his hopes for change led in a rather different direction – to mysticism, a more communal and less aggressive form of interaction with the natural world.

Women and Nature

Easlea and Merchant were very much influenced by the ecology movement in America and Europe. They highlighted the correspondence between the way men treated women in particular historical periods and the way they used nature. This facet of their work coincided with a growth in awareness of the links between women and nature. I use that word 'link' deliberately, because the use of female metaphors for nature and natural metaphors for women have long existed in Western culture. What was distinctive about the late 1970s onwards was a growing self-consciousness about these metaphors, an investigation of them as indicative of female oppression and of ruthless exploitation of natural resources and, in some quarters, a celebration of the bonds between women and nature. Undoubtedly, it was the conjunction of feminism and the ecology movement which encouraged these developments.

Susan Griffin's book *Woman and Nature: The Roaring Inside Her* (1978),[2] documented poetically the extensive use of the bond between woman and nature in Western thought. Hers was a literary celebration of the bond which, somewhat ironically, had been seen as a cornerstone of female enslavement. Whereas Simone de Beauvoir had regarded female immersion in the natural realm as precisely a confinement with dire consequences, Griffin and others took it as the starting point – the foundation for a new feminist politics. For some it would be expressed in involvement in the anti-nuclear protests; for others it would take the form of a full-blown nature mysticism. Whatever form it took, it fostered considerable scepticism about science.

Towards a Feminist Epistemology

From Easlea and Merchant's accounts, and increasingly in many feminist circles, Western science became labelled as patriarchal. But this was to be the thin end of the wedge, as gradually more and more forms of systematized knowledge and expertise were diagnosed as patriarchal. Perhaps the fullest statement of this burgeoning and extensive critique came in Mary Daly's *Gyn/Ecology: The Metaethics of Radical Feminism* (published in the USA in 1978, in Britain in 1980). For me that book was brilliant, witty, and intensely irritating. Daly spins – the metaphor she would choose – a new metaphysics. She labels it a new 'metaethics' because it is deliberately pro-feminist – value-laden, thus challenging notions of objectivity. She counterposes it to what she sees as the patriarchal values of dominant Western thought. Her tools are a perceptive dissection of language to suggest its sexual politics, together with a new feminist vocabulary (see Index of new words, pp. 469–71); historical instances of the oppression of and violence against women; a rich repertoire of excerpts from women writers; irreverent attacks on established bastions (institutions and individuals) of Western knowledge and expertise; a sense of 'theological' mission (not surprising, given that Daly is herself a professor of theology). Incidentally, I find it an irritating text precisely because you are so easily caught in its webs, in its pronouncements about patriarchal knowledge. There is virtually no space to disagree or ask in *what way* patriarchal values are embodied in particular forms of expertise or ideas. Here is a typical formulation:

> It is impossible to miss symptoms of this male fertility syndrome in the multiple technological 'creations' (artificial wombs) of the Fathers – such as homes, hospitals, corporate offices, airplanes, spaceships – which they inhabit and control (p. 61).

Here was a new bible of feminism, very different from de Beauvoir's, which endorsed and extended the earlier feminists' observation of male dominance in the intellectual realm. However, unlike de Beauvoir, who beckoned women to enter that male domain, Daly calls on her sisters to reject it and to construct their own alternative. She also influenced those who documented, in less flamboyant ways, male control of the tools and products of intellectual production (e.g. Dale Spender's work). Most systematized knowledge was labelled as patriarchal; indeed, by 1980 language itself had been labelled 'man-made' (Spender, 1980).

In a real sense, Daly and some other feminists were revolting not only against male expertise, but its very epistemological foundations. Evidence for this can be found in countless evocations in Daly's text: 'Sisterhood and female friendship burn down the walls of male-defined categories and definitions. However, hagiocratic separatism/separation is not essentially about walls at all. Rather, it is expanding room of our own' (p. 380). With an allusion to Virginia's Woolf's *A Room of One's Own*, Daly's is a shrill cry against the Enlightenment values which she sees represented in Western patriarchal thought. It would be a fair guess to describe these values, as they are not explicitly sketched, as revolving around a series of dichotomies: the subjectivity/objectivity distinction; fact vs value; public vs private; division and dissection vs wholeness; man vs woman; man vs nature; intuition vs scientific knowledge.

I have given Daly considerable attention as one of the 'most outrageous' (to quote a cover blurb from *Gyn/Ecology*) and controversial expositors of a new feminist epistemology. Although you would find little indication of it if you consulted the curricula of British universities (an issue to which I shall return later), feminists were storming the barriers of epistemology. What had been embryonic insights for Virginia Woolf have been elaborated and extended in confident, collective and popular forms.

Nevertheless, unveiling the patriarchal nature of knowledge in the Western world involved feminists in a number of contradictions and quagmires. Was all knowledge patriarchal? Eventually, a sort of common sense emerged which posited that formal, systematized, publicly validated knowledge production – often associated with professionalization, and generally linked to Western science since the Scientific Revolution – was the target of feminist attack. But was it possible for women to step outside this patriarchal epistemological order? How might they do so? Daly opted for linguistic innovation and often striking wordplay. With French feminists such as Monique Wittig and Luce Irigary (see Wittig; Marks and de Courtivron), she effectively opted for a feminist avant-gardism, with all the problems associated with such cultural forms.

Thus, their appeal was somewhat elitist. Daly's quotation above, for example, presumes familiarity with Virginia Woolf.

Furthermore, they were placing a premium on expressiveness, rather than on communication. This could (and in some cases did) result in a rather authoritarian style. In Daly's work I find the assertiveness of the author overbearing. The very power of its unveiling of patriarchal knowledge leaves little opportunity to question any of her judgements. Other solutions were more flat-footed. Indeed, very often the problems were side-stepped. Quite radical arguments, such as Dale Spender's proposal that language was 'man-made', were made in surprisingly conventional ways. I am not arguing that Spender should have presented her argument differently but, rather, suggesting that feminists have been selective and more or less self-conscious about what parts of the patriarchal epistemological order should be abandoned.

In addition, the blanket label 'patriarchal' has sometimes obscured the need for detailed consideration of the social relations of knowledge production. The formulators of patriarchal science and expertise, both in the past and in the present, have been not just any men, but almost always white, middle-class men. This suggests a pattern of the politics of knowledge production which is very complex indeed – placing not only women but, in some instances, certain men at a disadvantage. The brandishing of the label patriarchal has encouraged the skating over of crucial differences between, for example, medical knowledge in nineteenth-century Britain and its counterpart in 1980s Britain, or Western scientific medicine compared to its counterparts in Africa and other parts of the world. In other words, there are grave dangers of ahistorical and imperialist generalizations. But – perhaps more immediately important to us as feminists – it has made it difficult for us to decide concretely about what constitutes 'really useful knowledge'.

In America, questions of epistemology were pursued by feminist philosophers, many of whom were working in academia. The Society for Women in Philosophy was one group which provided support for this development (see Jagger, acknowledgements). The growth of professional feminist philosophy yielded major works. These included – in addition to Daly's work – collections edited by Sandra Harding and Merrill B. Hintikka (1983), by

Carol C. Gould (1984), and Alison M. Jagger's *Feminist Politics and Human Nature* (1983).

This did not happen in Britain, where academia took little notice of feminist epistemological challenges. In fact, the only substantial attempt to tackle the philosophical dimensions of feminism was equivocal about the women's movement as a whole. Janet Radcliffe Richards' title – *The Sceptical Feminist: A Feminist Enquiry* (1980) – in this sense, speaks for itself. It reduces feminism to a limited campaign in pursuit of an abstract notion of social justice. Many of the most interesting and important feminist insights about sexuality and gender roles are neglected. I and many other feminists agreed with Radcliffe Richards that there was a need for some rigorous thinking about the arguments and implications of feminism. Nevertheless, she seems to stand outside the movement and pronounce a series of philosophical judgements on it. Far from considering the challenges which feminism has offered to traditional philosophy, she reprimands the movement for not taking on the latter: 'there is undoubtedly evidence that feminism has some tendency to get stuck in the quagmire of unreason from time to time, or at least get dangerously close to its brink' (p. 33). In mounting her arguments, she often seems to be constructing straw feminists – the largely unidentifiable 'liberators', as she calls them. As Jean Grimshaw points out, Radcliffe Richards' version of sexual politics is 'decontextualized and dehistoricized' (Grimshaw, 1982, p. 6). This is the old Enlightenment perspective of Mary Wollstonecraft applied to contemporary feminism. Richards finds *feminists* insufficiently rational. But if we have learned anything over the last two centuries, we have learned that a return to abstract, dehistoricized and monolithic notions of reason are no longer possible or desirable.[3]

Feminism came under more direct attack in the name of traditional philosophy in Carol McMillan's *Women, Reason and Nature* (1982). Using a Winchian framework, McMillan characterizes feminism as a revolt against 'nature and not patriarchal institutions' (p. 108). Like Radcliffe Richards, her version of contemporary feminism is limited; represented in the book only by the writings of Shulamith Firestone and Kate Millett. For McMillan, biology is destiny:

> I have dwelt at some length on the biological realities of birth, of the relation of the mother to her infant and of the helpless dependence of the human infant, in order to show that the difference in the child-rearing roles of men and women are fundamentally and significantly biological. (p. 95)

McMillan's is an impassioned defence of the belief in value-free knowledge and epistemology (see esp. p. 74) in the face of feminist challenges in the hope that this will return women to their traditional, 'natural' roles. (For critical reviews of McMillan see Grimshaw, 1983; Hardie.)

It is interesting that in Britain the main reactions to the new philosophical dimensions of feminism were equivocal or outright antagonistic towards the movement. The sole exception to this pattern was the special issue of *Radical Philosophy* (no. 34) on 'Women, Gender and Philosophy'. There is some interesting material in this, including some reviews, discussions of the Greenham Common protest, and articles about the treatment of women in the work of specific philosophers. But there is not much sense of the way feminism was storming traditional epistemological barriers. Somewhat ironically, that comes across more strongly in the writings of those critics of feminism who considered that it was threatening traditional philosophical frameworks.

Against this background of considerable rhetorical flourish about patriarchal knowledge in general and some defensive rejoinders from the philosophical community in Britain, there have been some more concrete and exciting ventures. Liz Stanley's and Sue Wise's *Breaking Out: Feminist Consciousness and Feminist Research* (1983) is one such exploration. Using some specific examples, they try to work out what it would mean to integrate a feminist perspective into the methods of social research. Part of the appeal of their project for me is that they concentrate their energy not on identifying and condemning ubiquitous patriarchal forms but on the more positive, if difficult, task of seeing what feminism has to offer. There are still traces of the idealism (see Fee, 1983) which, as I have hinted above, has plagued feminist forays on to the terrain of epistemology. The book has, for example, no discussion of funding priorities for social research – a strange omission for those interested in the social construction of knowledge in 1980s Britain. This aside, Stanley and Wise demonstrate the potential of the epistemological challenges of recent feminism when they are made concrete in social research at least. However, by the time their book appeared, debates about the gender politics of knowledge were being given a much more public airing in relationship to the women's peace movement.

THE WOMEN'S PEACE MOVEMENT

The women's peace movement which emerged in Britain in the 1980s has been the object of much attention and controversy both within and outside the women's movement. The encircling of the Greenham Common Air Base on 12 December 1982 captured international interest and publicly pronounced that the campaign against nuclear weapons was, in some way, a women's issue. Since then there has been much deliberation about what that means.[4]

This was not the first instance of an active women's peace movement in Britain. Various women's groups campaigned for peace from the period before World War 1 until World War 2 (see Wiltsher). Two of the most notable episodes in this history were the Women's Peace Crusade during World War 1, which has been sketched by Jill Liddington (Liddington), and the important contribution of women's groups to the Peace Ballot of 19334 (Branson and Heinemann, pp. 302–7). The interwar period witnessed the flourishing of international women's initiatives for peace; a number of British women, including Vera Brittain and Winifred Holtby, devoted much time and energy to these efforts.

Women had played leading roles in challenging the expertise which justified and sustained nuclear weapons, even before the emergence of a specifically women's campaign. Alva Myrdal's *Game of Disarmament* (1977), Helen Caldicott's *Nuclear Madness* (1978) and Mary Kaldor's *The Baroque Arsenal* (1981) have become international reference texts for the nuclear disarmament movement. In their different ways, each challenged the experts by constructing its own arsenal of 'facts' about the nuclear issue.

There were probably critical perspectives on expertise around these earlier phases of the women's peace movement in Britain. Virginia Woolf's *Three Guineas* (discussed above) can be cited as evidence of this. It would seem almost inevitable that any women's peace campaign takes at least part of its inspiration from a critique of male-dominated political/military elites. Nevertheless, the current women's peace movement, in contrast with any which preceded it, has produced a much more explicit critique of expertise. In addition, because of its specifically technological focus as a nuclear disarmament movement, it has opened and extended the politics of expertise, to include a challenge not only to political/military elites but, in some cases, to scientific/technological elites as well. This is not to say that every woman who has been active in (or who identifies with) the movement would describe herself as involved in the politics of expertise. Nevertheless, the various manifestations of protest – from slogans like 'take the toys away from the boys', to detailed arguments about nuclear deterrents – have revolved around the politics of knowledge.

The new women's peace movement has not been orientated around the experts' facts as such. In different ways, Myrdal, Caldicott and Kaldor used their own expertise in opposing the nuclear weapons establishment. The Greenham encirclement signalled the appearance of a mass movement, which permitted many women – who were not legitimated by their scientific credentials or research – to speak out against nuclear weapons. In addition, they were protesting *as* women, making gender the explicit pivot of the movement, though often in unspecified ways.

The women's peace movement which emerged in Britain in the early 1980s did not have universal support within the women's movement. While some black and working-class women have become involved, most of them would give priority to different campaigns against the state, or define peace more broadly in terms of wider social conflict (see Brown). Such women challenge the way the peace movement defines violence and equates it with masculinity. In addition, radical feminists have been unhappy with the way specific women's issues (e.g. fighting for women's rights) seem to get pushed to the background in favour of the 'greater' general cause of world peace (see Wallsgrove; Feminism and Non-

Women dance at dawn on a Cruise missile site in USAF Greenham Common, 1 January 1983. Photo: Raissa Page.

Violence Group). Some women have also felt that this protest reinforces traditional gender roles, in particular, consolidating motherhood as a lynchpin of female identity. Of course, the movement has never been restricted to mothers, but it has relied heavily on appeals to women *as* mothers or to their motherliness. (The collection of articles edited by Dorothy Thompson is illustrative in this respect, in so far as the experience of motherhood or an interest in mothering are constant reference points for the various contributors.) What I am saying is that the movement would not have so much appeal to women who do not regard motherhood or mothering as an essential part of womanhood. In highlighting the differential composition and appeal of the women's peace movement, my intention is not to discredit the movement but to guard against glib presumptions that this cause is naturally or universally a feminist one. Easlea has claimed that 'the single most important issue facing humankind today is surely the nuclear arms race' (Easlea, 1983, p. 3). For many different reasons, particularly the immediacy and enormity of many other political struggles, no such consensus exists among women.

Gender and the Politics of Expertise

The women's peace movement, for many of its participants, has been first and foremost a protest against the control and power of experts. They identify and attack the hallmark of expertise – experts' language or, as it is more critically described, jargon. Thus, in her introduction to a collection of articles from the movement, Dorothy Thompson refers to 'the weapons jargon by which so many "experts" try to obscure the basic moral and political questions' (Thompson, p. 2). Her implication is that there is a deliberate conspiracy of expertise. Not all women active in the movement might view the nuclear weapons establishment in quite this light. Nevertheless, most would assent to Thompson's subsequent assertion that 'the questions we are considering [relating to nuclear armaments] are too important to be left to self-selected "experts" ' (Thompson, p. 2). This view was not unique to the women's movement. In this respect it shared the concern of the broader anti-nuclear campaign to draw attention to the contradictions between the power wielded by nuclear technocrats and principles of democracy,

The women's movement, however, was distinguished from other parts of the nuclear disarmament movement in its concern for male dominance within the nuclear arms elite. Connie Mansueto spelled out the fundamental observation that engaged many women: 'It is no coincidence that the overwhelming majority of these individuals are white educated men because the governments, military forces, scientific and business establishments involved in the nuclear arms race were created and are now maintained by white, educated men' (Mansueto, p. 118). That is, expertise does not transcend vested interests. This argument became a significant lever for the movement. However, it should be noted in passing that the movement's focus was almost entirely on the fact that arms race experts were men, rather than on the fact that they were mainly white and middle-class. This again may be a factor in the movement's greater strength amongst white middle-class women.

Ordinary citizens, both male and female, have asserted their right to speak on the nuclear issue: 'I am no expert in anything, not history, not psychology, not medicine nor peace studies, neither (least of all) strategic planning. I am simply a child of the nuclear age' (Carter, p. 13). This sort of introduction is typical, implying that lack of expertise in these fields should not silence the speaker. But the women's peace movement has characteristically linked these claims to an examination of what constitutes expertise on the issue of nuclear arms and of how this relates to the division of labour. Stark questions have been posed: Are knowledges either of formal international politics or of nuclear technology the only sorts of knowledge relevant to decision-making regarding nuclear arms? What kind of expertise qualifies one to make the awesome decisions associated with nuclear weapons? Counter-posing traditional qualificatory criteria with the skills acquired by many women in their daily domestic lives, women peace campaigners have argued their case: 'It is particularly relevant in this connection that women should speak. For by virtue of their role in human reproduction, their statements are given the authority of experiences that men do not have' (Soper, p. 170). Here is a profound critique of the impoverishment of established criteria of relevant knowledge. Two contrasting images, in diverse variations, have been invoked to illustrate these arguments: a mother caring for a child (in some versions, a sick or dying child), versus the emotionally detached daily life of the international politician or nuclear technocrat. So, for example, there is Rosalie Bertell's ecological argument about women's qualifications: 'Traditionally charged with birthing and assisting the dying, women have been generally more attuned than men to the signs of sickness and death in the earth's biosphere' (Bertell, p. 307).

Taking the opposite tack, but once again through the spectrum of the sexual division of labour, Christa Wolf uses Greek mythology to explore the limitations of contemporary political expertise:

> In Priam's day, when kings ruled smaller realms (and enjoyed the additional protection of being considered divine), perhaps they were not screened off from normal everyday life as totally as today's poli-

> ticans, who arrive at their decisions not on the grounds of personal observation and sensory experiences but in obedience to reports, charts, statistics, secret intelligence, films, consultations with men as isolated as themselves, political calculation, and the demands of staying in power. Men who do not know people, who deliver them to destruction; who by inclination or training can endure the icy atmosphere at the tip of the pyramid. Solitary power affords them the protection they have not received, and could not receive, from everyday life, where they would rub shoulders and skins with normal people. (Wolf, pp. 256–7)

The call to re-examine what counts as expertise, and the sexual division of labour which sustains accepted definitions of it, has been one of the most important contributions the movement has made to contemporary politics. The negative evaluations of the knowledge and skills of relatively powerless women offered by Wollstonecraft and De Beauvoir have been replaced by critical assessments of the capabilities of relatively powerful men. Nevertheless, Wollstonecraft's and de Beauvoir's critiques were pivots for change in the sexual division of labour. In contrast, some of the more recent positive re-evaluations of women's traditional skills seem almost to celebrate and entrench that division.

GENDER AND RATIONALITY IN THE NUCLEAR AGE

Just as warriors of this and preceding ages (including Reagan) claim to have God on their side, the exponents of nuclear armament claim to have rationality on theirs. This has provoked some members of the women's peace movement to declare that this cloak of rationality is like the emperor's new clothes: 'It took nuclear weapons to make me realize the full extent of the paltriness, the impoverished understanding and the sheer irrationality of most of those who govern me' (Soper, p. 171). When the currency of rationality is so devalued, it is not surprising that women wish to distance themselves from it, Angela Carter explains this phenomenon as follows: 'And, over the years, I've grown rather tired of rational, objective arguments against nuclear weapons. To approach rampant unreason with the tools of rational discourse is something of a waste of time' (Carter, p. 147). Soper puts it slightly differently:

> I will argue through the irrationality of deterrence and current nuclear policy with anyone who cares to take me on: I will do so in detail, coldly and even clinically. But in a final moment of feminine intuition, I might well want to add that much of the 'rationality' of those who offer their 'realistic' scenarios is utterly and completely out of touch with the reality of what nuclear weapons can do – and thus in turn with a significant part of the reason for not wanting to have them. (Soper, p. 178)

Obviously, the recent women's peace movement seems far removed from de Beauvoir's framework, which celebrates the bond between rationality and masculine accomplishment as the key to cultural creativity. But de Beauvoir's analysis did draw on a widely accepted presumption. The threat of the massive destruction of nuclear war is a disturbing component to fit into this framework. Thus it is no exaggeration to say that for many the threat of nuclear war constitutes a crisis in Western values and epistemology. This is the sort of crisis which Christa Wolf identifies:

> The realization that the physical existence of us all depends on shifts in the delusional thinking of very small groups – that is, on chance – to be sure unhinges the classical aesthetic once and for all, slips it from its mountings, which, in the final analysis, are fastened to the laws of reason. (Wolf, p. 226)

For many of the women in the peace movement there is a gender dimension to this crisis. If the campaign against nuclear armaments involves a clash with male reason, it is not surprising to find members invoking female intuition or instinct. The term 'feminine intuition' is smuggled into Kate Soper's preceding statement, but it has appeared in more full-blown invocations: 'We must back our instincts, and do all we can to take peace – the only sane option for the world – into practical politics, beginning with the absolute renunciation of nuclear weapons' (Assiter, p. 206). Whatever our response to such calls, we must acknowledge that they constitute popular oppositional stands. I for one would far prefer to put my faith in the intuitions of Greenham women rather than in the rationality of Defence Ministers. In invoking feminine intuition or instinct as an oppositional tool, women are offering a positive evaluation of women's contribution to the world order (in contrast to de Beauvoir) and are displaying a healthy scepticism about what is done in the name of rationality.

Nevertheless, fighting the nuclear (or any) issue on the terrain of intuition or instinct is very limited. Terms like intuition and instinct denote a special, natural knowledge which women as women are presumed to have acquired. Linked to these notions is a return to the polarization of women with nature and men with culture. This has been a strong, though not uncriticized, strand within the women's peace movement, most notably symbolized by the web as the icon of the movement. But women's spinning, like all forms of women's work and thought, are cultural processes, in contrast to the activities of spiders. In this respect – and although we might dislike the analogy – women's spinning and thinking are more like the labour (performed presumably by men) involved in the construction of the perimeter fences at military establishments than they are like the spider's spinning.

This bold confrontation between feminine intuition and male knowledge emerging from the women's peace movement represents a watershed in feminist explorations of the politics of knowledge. The problem with which I began – the deficiency of reason amongst females as posited by Mary Wollstonecraft – has been completely turned on its head. Male rationality is now posited as the problem. Here also is a synthesis of many of the strands of recent feminist investigations of gender dynamics already outlined: the linking of women and nature is celebrated; there is a revolt against the values of the Enlightenment and the Scientific Revolution and their contemporary legacies. As the second popular political movement revolving around the gender politics of expertise, the women's peace movement has had much in common with its predecessor, the women's health movement: autonomous women's groups as the main organizational unit; a reliance on informal networks, and efforts to break with hierarchical modes of organization; the investigation of women's experiences as sources of alternative kinds of knowledge. But the focus has shifted from the bodies of women to the body politic.

The women's peace movement has been central to the unfolding of the complex issues involved in the gender politics of expertise on a popular basis. But the invocation of feminine instinct or intuition prematurely forecloses the political explorations and debates within feminism. My views on this would seem to be shared by many other feminists. At least this is what I detect in some of the most interesting writings which have appeared in the wake of the women's peace movement. I have chosen to look at what Christa Wolf, Rosalie Bertell and Hilary Rose make of the dilemmas the women's peace movement have posed, because they are all concerned to find a way forward from the watershed I described earlier.

Christa Wolf

I consider Christa Wolf's *Cassandra* the most complex exploration of where feminism is, and should be, in tackling the political dimensions of epistemology in the nuclear age. Wolf is an East German writer – whose novels are popular amongst British feminists (as published by Virago, e.g. *A Model Childhood* and *The Quest for Christa T.*). *Cassandra* is written from within the women's peace movement. Its core is a re-examination of the myth of Cassandra in order to help unravel the related options of twentieth-century women who aspire to Cassandra's knowledge and concomitant power. It is by no means an easy text, working as it does through allusions, and it is sometimes confusing (and, I would say, confused). I suppose I see these confusions as symptomatic of a wider uncertainty within feminism about where we go from here on questions of knowledge production, science, etc.

For those of us who cannot accept the simplifications involved in the 'female intuition versus male rationality' dichotomy, it feels as if we are in a kind of suspended animation. In countless concrete instances we must deal with such difficult questions as: In what ways are particular forms of knowledge patriarchal? What forms of social relations might transform knowledge production? Is gender the only social variable that matters? (And these are only a few of the many questions we might pursue.) Wolf's mythological framework seems to make it possible to sketch some of these issues, while holding them in an appropriate suspended animation. Perhaps her tentativeness and confusions are preferable to foreclosure.

Yet Wolf offers far more than muddles. She concretely and forcefully draws out insights from the women's peace movement. So, for example, the campaign against nuclear weapons has made her aware of the dangers of scientism and its recent manifestations.

> Delusion is mathematicized of course. (Just as, paradoxically, mathematics – if you begin to *believe* in it as an independent structure whose laws should be transferred to other structures, there to prove or even generate one of the most life-preventive myths of our time: 'scientificness' – just as mathematics, with its indisputable exactitude, peculiarly lends itself to incorporation into a delusion, and to fortifying the delusion so that it is unassailable.) Twice in the past week, the US computer has sounded the alarm: Soviet rockets are flying toward the United States. In such a case, we are told, the President has twenty-five minutes to make a decision. The computer (we hear) has now been switched off. The delusion: to make security dependent on a machine, rather than on an analysis of the historical situation possible only to human beings with an understanding of history that includes understanding of the historical situation of the other side. (Wolf, p. 228)

Likewise, she scrutinizes faith in progress from the vantage point of the sexual division of labour:

> Recently I was discussing the problems of modern science with a company of younger scientists, and we also talked about the history of woman in the West. One of the young men – evidently determined to come clean at last – declared: 'People should stop complaining about the lot of woman in the past. The fact that she was subordinated to the man, took care of him, served him – that was the precondition for the man's ability to concentrate on science or on art, and to achieve peak results in both fields. Progress was and is possible in no other way, and all the rest is just sentimental twaddle.' A murmur arose in the room. I agreed with the man. The kind of progress in art and science to which we have grown accustomed – extraordinary peak achievements – *is* possible only in this way. It is possible only through depersonalization. I suggested that a kind of Hippocratic oath should be introduced into the mathematical sciences which would forbid any

> scientist to collaborate in research that served military ends; and the debaters declared that this was unrealistic. If scientists here did not break the oaths (they retorted), they would in any case be broken somewhere else; there could be no taboos on research. 'For me,' I said, 'the price is now too high for the kind of research that science as an institution has been producing for some time.' Later I heard that some of the participants had detected in me a trend of hostility toward science. A ridiculous misunderstanding! I thought in the first moment. Then I paused. Could I be 'amicably' disposed toward a science which has moved so far from the thirst for knowledge it derives from, and with which I still secretly identify it? (p. 284)

This passage intrigues me because, in revealing her own thought in progress, Wolf is also unpacking some of the wider confusions amongst feminists about science and knowledge in the nuclear age. The excerpt is composed of a series of juxtaposed reflections about these issues. Their juxtaposition establishes that they are interrelated, but it is never quite clear how. For this reason, the paragraph is choppy. It begins with the reflection on the relationship between progress and the sexual division of labour. This observation of 'the young scientist' links the transcendence associated with male cultural creativity with the sexual division of labour. Wolf's endorsement of this analysis provides a tentative, although not altogether satisfactory, transition to her own thoughts about how science could be demilitarized. Her musings represent a gesture towards democratic control of the kind many of those looking for the first time at the scientific face of nuclear arms might entertain. Informed of likely resistances to even such a limited measure from within the scientific community, Wolf is brought to recognize that contemporary science seems resistant to democratic control. For her, and many opponents of nuclear arms, this is a shocking revelation. Her proposal brands her as 'hostile to science'. Once again, like many other anti-nuclear arms protesters, she is forced to confront the disparity between her own idealistic view of science – based on 'the thirst for knowledge' – and its current form.

Somewhat clumsily, Wolf has represented a typical way in which many women peace campaigners have come upon the plethora of questions relating to knowledge and science embedded in the nuclear issues. While she successfully evokes the questions, she is not offering any answers. In fact, she definitively rejects the view that there is one easy answer:

> I feel a genuine horror at that critique of rationalism which itself ends in reckless irrationalism. . . . But it does not make it any easier to achieve maturity if a masculinity mania is replaced by a femininity mania and if women throw over the achievements of rational thought simply because men produced them, in order to substitute an idealization of prerational stages in human history. (p. 260)

Of course, this formulation has its own problems, depending as it does on the dubious notion of stages in 'rational development'. I would find it difficult to imagine any historical period as simply 'prerational'.

The rebellion against patriarchal rationality, an important thread in the women's peace movement, comes under critical scrutiny here. Taken together, the various quotations I have drawn from *Cassandra* indicate Wolf's dilemma. Although she has not worked out the detail, she has sketched some of the ways in which gender relations underpin the expertise operational in the world of nuclear weapons. For her, this raises enormous epistemological questions. Nevertheless, she is shocked to be labelled as hostile to science and draws the line at throwing over 'the achievements of rational thought simply because men produced them'. So, despite her fascinating explorations, Wolf is pulled back to abstract formulations in terms of male rationality versus female intuition. Once on this terrain, concrete political investigations of really useful knowledge get left behind. The point is not whether 'the achievements of rational thought' should be abandoned because they are the product of male thinking. Rather, in specific political situations we must investigate how male interests become embodied in particular forms of knowledge. Indeed, 'the achievements of rational thought' can mean just about anything. This phrase has a pretentious ring and makes me suspicious, as it discourages investigation of the social and political usefulness of particular kinds of knowledge on the ground of a spurious pedigree. (Could concentration camps be described as 'achievements of rational thought'?) On the whole, I found Wolf's opening up of questions about the interrelationship between gender and knowledge exciting, and her recoil from quick or easy resolutions refreshing. But the choice between male rationality and female intuition haunts *Cassandra*, as it has haunted too many contemporary feminist debates, thereby obscuring the way forward.

Rosalie Bertell

As its name suggests, the object of the women's peace movement was the termination of the nuclear arms race. In Britain, the immediate goal was to stop the deployment of nuclear weapons on British soil. But some women felt strongly that the nuclear threat was not confined to its military potential; they were also drawn into opposition to nuclear power. Rosalie Bertell's *No Immediate Danger: Prognosis for a Radioactive Earth* (1985) addressed itself to this broader issue. Thus, strictly speaking, it is not written from within the women's peace movement. Nevertheless, it very much comes out of the debates which emerged from that movement, attempting to extend its framework to construct a feminist perspective on nuclear energy.

Bertell herself is a Catholic nun and a nuclear expert with a Ph.D in mathematics and a prestigious career as a research scientist. She marshals this expertise efficiently against the pro-nuclear power experts. She demonstrates 'the problem' (nuclear radiation and its biological effects: Part I of the book), 'the practices' (the technological applications – military and civil: Part II), and the 'cover-ups' about these (Part III). Her text amasses the scientific facts about radioactivity which other scientists have hitherto failed to compile, ignored or covered up. This is perhaps the most technical text to come out of women's anti-nuclear protests. Its use of established expertise in the nuclear field is not dissimilar to Myrdal's, Caldicott's, and Kaldor's. In fact, she is much more embedded in nuclear expertise in so far as she is a research scientist rather than a researcher on science policy (Kaldor), an economist (Myrdal) or a doctor (Caldicott). However, unlike theirs, her analysis of nuclear development centralizes gender and is explictly feminist.

My interest in Bertell here is in her particular path through the quagmires, sketched above, that have faced feminists in the wake of the peace movement. She picks up one of those themes – the reliance on feminine instinct – in her proposals for reconstructing the world order: 'Women, who have not become so unnaturally separated from their instincts, need at this moment in history to assume special roles of idea input, facilitating consensus decision-making and seeing to the equitable implementation of plans and sustainability of the society's work' (Bertell, p. 374). Of course, in her formulation not all feminine instinct is reliable, and it is not clear or obvious how we determine which women are in touch with their instincts. This aside, counterposed to the positive evaluation of feminine instinct is the scientificity of the text itself. The whole structure of scientific expertise remains unexamined, and Bertell rejects the view that such expertise is implicated in the nuclear proliferation that she so deplores: 'It is not the scientific understanding of the global system in all its basic chemical and physical properties which is disordered; it is rather the policy, planning and operational judgements which have gone awry' (p. 382). She explains that 'The slow erosion of health and genetic integrity is judged "acceptable" to policy-makers who rely on "experts" who rely on funding from military strategists or big business' (p. 382). Apparently, she proposes to attach 'pure' science to a policy infrastructure which would be more in touch with human needs and in which feminine instincts would be an influential component.

No Immediate Danger effectively poses the question: How socially expert are the experts? Thus far, I have no objection to Bertell's strategy. The book is addressed to a broad readership and the discourse of scientific fact is a powerful tool, particularly when wielded against those who claim exclusive rights to it. However, I do find her unusual amalgam of feminine instinct and a pristine science unpromising as a solution to the problems of the nuclear age. It begs many of the questions about feminine instinct touched on earlier, but it also ignores so much that feminists and others have learned about the way in which scientific knowledge itself embodies gender, racial and class inequalities. Specific and concrete challenges to experts on their own terms, valuable though they may be, cannot substitute for the more full-blown feminist critiques of expertise required in the 1980s.

Hilary Rose

Hilary Rose's investigation of a feminist epistemology for the natural sciences is framed by references to the women's peace movement. In one article (Rose, 1983) she begins starkly: 'This paper starts from the position that the attitudes dominant within science and technology must be transformed, for their telos is nuclear annihilation' (p. 73), and ends with a reference to 'the baby socks, webs of wool, photos and flowers threaded into the wire fences by thousands of women peace activists ringing Greenham Common' (p. 90). This piece is more specialized than either Wolf's or Bertell's writings, being published in *Signs* (a journal read mainly by feminists in academia). Moreover, it is addressed primarily to those engaged in the critique of the natural sciences or interested in their reconstruction along feminist principles. She criticizes the lack of a feminist perspective in radical critiques of science. The integration of such a perspective requires, she argues, the inclusion of reproduction within materialist critiques of the division of labour in science and of the gender dimensions of abstraction within ideological critiques of science. These are mirrored in her prescription for a feminist reconstruction of the natural sciences. She feels they should make space for and acknowledge the importance of 'caring labour' (p. 83) and operate with an epistemology which 'will bring together subjective and objective ways of knowing the world' (p. 87).

Rose has been working and reworking her central themes over the past few years (see Rose, 1982; Rose, 1986). She is clearly much more willing than Wolf or Bertell to tackle science head on. The purpose is to work towards 'a different, alternative science' (1983, p. 74) – towards the reformation of science. The key words of recent feminism are integral to her project: reproduction, the sexual division of labour, 'caring labour', 'subjective shared experience of oppression' (1986, p. 87).

However, there are clear points where Rose's interpretation of science as socially and politically constructed stops short. She does not seem to acknowledge the fact that the term 'nature' is a powerful and changing cultural category. Thus she writes of living 'in harmony with nature' (1983, p. 73) and 'defending nature' (1986, p. 57) as feminist goals. Would this include not fighting diseases (since they are natural)? This somewhat facetious question merely illustrates the dangers of using the term 'nature' uncritically.

Rose hovers around the slippery slope of biologism in her project for a feminist epistemology. It is difficult to know exactly what it might mean for us 'to admit biology' (1983, p. 84). This could involve embracing accepted definitions of sex differences. In any case she implies that biology, unlike other sciences, stands above the social and political order. Her elevation of biology makes her wary of (what she sees as) an exaggerated social constructivist analysis. These attitudes are consolidated in her call for 'biosocial knowledge' (1986, p. 73). Precisely what this would be, and how it could be squared with feminist critiques of biology, is not at all obvious.

These specificities aside, there are further difficulties about Rose's programme. While much of it is politically promising at the rhetorical level, it is difficult to know what it would mean concretely. According to her prognosis, a feminist epistemology 'transcends dichotomies, insists on the scientific validity of the subjective, on the need to unite cognitive and affective domains; it emphasizes holism, harmony, and complexity rather than reductionism, domination and linearity' (p. 72). To stop at just one of the issues that is glossed over in this formulation, what would it mean to embrace the 'scientific validity of the subjective'? Does this mean that every expression of feeling, every intuition, becomes a scientific fact? Furthermore, how might 'caring labour and the knowledge that stems from it' (1983, p. 90) be integrated into the operations of science?

Referring to recent feminist debates about gender and rationality, Rose's work tends to channel such concerns into the goal of a feminist science, as a reform of science as it currently exists. That is, she seems to be addressing mainly professionals, to whom she appeals to incorporate the missing element – 'the heart'. Her proposal to include subjectivity within science begs crucial questions about the fundamental character of scientific institutions in contemporary society, where 'science' is defined precisely by its pretensions to exclude subjectivity. Is not her new science a contradiction in terms? Rose evades the question of why we should want to salvage something called 'science', much less what social forces could create her 'new science'.

Thus Wolf, Bertell and Rose all address the dilemmas which emerged for feminists in the wake of the women's peace movement. In Wolf's case she is bristling against, yet confined to, the choice between male rationality and female intuition. She fears being labelled as 'hostile to science', as if this would constitute being irrational – Wollstonecraft's irrational woman in a new guise. In contrast, Bertell sees nothing wrong with scientific practices as such; for her, science policy-making institutions must be reformed by harnessing them to feminine intuition. Rose proposes to reform science practice itself by creating space within it for 'caring labour' and subjectivity, the redeeming qualities of feminist practice and theory. For all three writers, some core of science remains sacred.

Being Reasonable Feminists

The recent phase of feminism has elaborated a new sexual politics of expertise. In a sense, this essay has been concerned with the progress of feminism within that politics. No longer do feminists consider women the problem, deficient in rationality. Moreover, the democratization of this politics, most notably through the women's health movement and the women's peace movement, has been one of its most remarkable features. The domain of the isolated intellectual has been opened out – not only to make space for more women, but to invite new questions about the sexual division of labour and what counts as expertise. As I have also suggested, the scope of this politics has also been extended, most notably through a shift from a feminist politics of the body to feminist strategies for the body politic.

However, within feminism as elsewhere, presumptions about progress are misleading. Wollstonecraft's femininist aspirations for male rationality and de Beauvoir's aspirations for male transcendence were unsatisfactory because they masked social and power relations under the guise of transhistorical categories. Likewise, today's feminists have tended to get bogged down in similar ossifications when they feel forced to choose between rationality or feminine intuition or some integration of the two. Such models start from a given dichotomy between a grand Rationality as defined by science and an intuition rooted in female Nature. Neither Rationality nor Nature is seen as the historically specific social products that they in fact are.

The skills that we need to develop for overcoming female oppression can come only from transformed social practices which involve redefinitions of rationality and intuition. We do not wish to be reasonable in the sense of limiting ourselves by the conservative principles of rationality and nature as this society defines them. Instead, we want our reasonableness to constitute broader visions of what is humanly possible and desirable. In short, if we are to be reasonable feminists, we need to redefine what society means by reason.

Notes

1. I have chosen to use the term 'patriarchal' throughout this article, despite the difficulties of the term. (See Barrett, pp. 10–19; Rowbotham; Alexander and Taylor; Beechey for discussions of these problems.) I have taken this option for two reasons: 1) I prefer this to terms with more biologistic connotations, such as 'masculinist'; 2) it is the term most frequently used in relation to issues of gender and knowledge. In using this term I do not wish to imply that it refers to a transhistorical social order.
2. See Judith Williamson's review of this book in this collection. For an uncritical exploration of the link between women and nature, see Ortner. For a more critical examination of this link, see MacCormack; Brown and Jordanova.
3. No doubt some of the appeal of the work of Michel Foucault for some feminists was that it challenged notions of monolithic and eternal regimes of knowledge. Tracing these appropriations is beyond the scope of this article. For a minimal introduction to this set of perspectives, see Foucault.
4. For accounts of the women's peace movement from within, see Thompson, Caldecott and Leland. For debates about the relationship of this movement to feminism more generally, see Feminism and Non-Violence Group, Finch *et al.*; from Hackney Greenham Groups, Soper and Assiter, and Wallsgrove.

References

S. Alexander and Barbara Taylor, 'In Defence of "Patriarchy" ', in R. Samuel, ed., *People's History and Socialist Theory*, Routledge & Kegan Paul, 1981, pp. 370–3.

S. Allen, L. Sanders, J. Wallis, eds, *Conditions of Illusion: Papers from the Women's Movement*, Leeds, Feminist Books, 1974.

A. Assiter, 'Womanpower and Nuclear Politics: Women and the Peace Movement', in D. Thompson, ed., *Over Our Dead Bodies: Women Against the Bomb*, Virago, 1983, pp. 199–206.

M. Barrett, *Women's Oppression Today: Problems in Marxist Feminist Analysis*, Verso, 1980.

S. de Beauvoir, *The Second Sex*, trans. and ed H. M. Parshley, Harmondsworth Penguin, 1973 (first published as *Le Deuxieme Sexe*, 1949).

V. Beechey, 'On Patriarchy', *Feminist Review* 3 (1979).

R. Bertell, *No Immediate Danger: Prognosis for a Radioactive Earth*, The Women's Press, 1985.

Boston Women's Health Collective, *Our Bodies Ourselves: A Health Book By and For Women* (British Edition), eds A. Phillips and J. Rakusen, Harmondsworth, Penguin, 1978.

N. Branson and M. Heinemann, *Britain in the Nineteen Thirties*, Weidenfeld & Nicolson, 1971.

Brent Women's Centre, 'How to Run a Health Course', *Spare Rib* 94, reprinted in M. Rowe, ed., *Spare Rib Reader*, Harmondsworth, Penguin, 1982, pp. 416–20.

Brighton Women and Science Group, *Alice Through the Microscope: The Power of Science over Women's Lives*, Virago, 1980.

P. Brown and L. J. Jordanova, 'Oppressive Dichotomies: the Nature/Culture Debate', in Cambridge Women's Studies Group, ed., *Women in Society: Interdisciplinary Essays*, Virago, 1981, pp. 224–41.

W. Brown, *Black Women and the Peace Movement*, Bristol, Falling Wall, 1984.

E. Byrne, *Women and Education*, Tavistock, 1978.

L. Caldecott and S. Leland, *Reclaim the Earth: Women Speak Out for Life and Earth*, The Women's Press, 1983.

H. Caldicott, *Nuclear Madness*, New York, Bantam, 1978.

A. Carter, 'Anger in a Black Landscape', in Thompson, pp. 146–56.

C. Cockburn, *Brothers: Male Dominance and Technological Change*, Pluto, 1983.

L. Comer, 'Medical Mystifications', in Allen *et al.*, pp. 45–50.

M. Daly, *Gyn/Ecology: The Metaethics of Radical Feminism*, The Women's Press, 1979 (first published in the USA in 1978).

R. Deem, *Schooling for Women's Work*, Routledge & Kegan Paul, 1980.

B. Easlea, *Fathering the Unthinkable: Masculinity, Scientists and the Nuclear Arms Race*, Pluto, 1983.

B. Easlea, *Science and Sexual Oppression: Patriarchy's Confrontation with Woman and Nature*, Weidenfeld & Nicolson, 1981.

B. Easlea, *Witch-Hunting, Magic and the New Philosophy*, Brighton, Harvester, 1980.
B. Ehrenreich and D. English, *Complaints and Disorders: The Sexual Politics of Sickness*, Writers & Readers, 1976 (first published in the USA in 1973).
B. Ehrenreich and D. English, *For Her Own Good: 150 Years of the Experts' Advice to Women*, Pluto, 1979.
B. Ehrenreich and D. English *Witches, Midwives and Nurses: A History of Women Healers*, Writers and Readers, 1976 (first published in the USA in 1973).
E. Fee, 'Critiques of Modern Science: The Relationship of Feminism to Other Radical Epistemologies' in R. Bleier, ed., *Feminist Approaches to Science*, Oxford, Pergamon, 1986, pp. 42–56.
E. Fee, 'Women's Nature and Scientific Objectivity' in M. Lowe and R. Hubbard, eds, *Woman's Nature: Rationalizations of Inequality*, Oxford, Pergamon, 1983.
Feminism and Non-Violence Group, *Breaching the Peace: Feminism and Non-Violence*, Onlywomen Press, 1979.
S. Finch *et. al.* from Hackney Greenham Groups, 'Socialist-Feminists and Greenham', *Feminist Review* 23 (Summer, 1986), 93–100.
M. Foucault, *Power/Knowledge*, ed. C. Gordon, Brighton, Harvester, 1980.
C. Gould, ed., *Beyond Domination: New Perspectives in Women and Philosophy*, Totowa, NJ, 1984.
A. Gramsci, *Selections from the Prison Notebooks of Antonio Gramsci*, ed. and trans. Q. Hoare and G. Nowell Smith, Lawrence & Wishart, 1971.
S. Griffin, *Woman and Nature: The Roaring Inside Her*, The Women's Press, 1984 (first published in the USA in 1978).
J. Grimshaw, 'Feminism: History and Morality', *Radical Philosophy* 30 (Spring 1982), 1–6.
J. Grimshaw, Review of C. McMillan, *Women, Reason and Nature, Radical Philosophy* 34 (Summer 1983), 33–5.
A. Hardie, Review of C. McMillan, *Women, Reason and Nature, Radical Philosophy* 34 (Summer 1983), 36.
S. Harding and M.B. Hintikka, eds, *Discovering Reality: Feminist Perspectives on Epistemology, Metaphysics, Methodology and Philosophy of Science*, D. Reidel, 1983.
A.M. Jagger, *Feminist Politics and Human Nature*, Brighton, Harvester, 1983.
R. Johnson, ' "Really Useful Knowledge": Radical Education and Working-Class Culture', in J. Clarke, C. Critcher and R. Johnson, eds, *Working-Class Culture: Studies in History and Theory*, Hutchinson, 1979, pp. 75–102.
L. Jones, ed., *Keeping the Peace: A Women's Peace Handbook*, The Women's Press, 1983.
L. Jordanova, 'Conceptualizing Power over Women' (review of B. Ehrenreich and D. English, *For Her Own Good: 150 Years of the Experts' Advice to Women*), *RSJ* 12 (1982), 124–8.
M. Kaldor, *The Baroque Arsenal*, André Deutsch, 1981.
H. Kanter, S. Lefanu, S. Shah, C. Spedding, eds, *Sweeping Statements: Writings from the Women's Liberation Movement 1981–83*, The Women's Press, 1984.

A. Kelly, *The Missing Half: Girls and Science Education*, Manchester, Manchester University Press, 1981.

J. Leeson and J. Gray, *Women and Medicine*, Tavistock, 1978.

J. Liddington, 'The Women's Peace Crusade: The History of a Forgotten Campaign', in Thompson, pp. 180–98.

C. MacCormack, 'Nature, Culture and Gender: a Critique' in C. MacCormack and M. Strathern, eds, *Nature, Culture and Gender*, Cambridge, Cambridge University Press, 1980, pp. 1–24.

E. Marks and I. de Courtivron, eds, *New French Feminism: An Anthology*, Brighton, Harvester, 1981.

C. Mansueto, 'Take the Toys from the Boys: Competition and the Nuclear Arms Race' in Thompson, pp. 108–19.

C. McMillan, *Women, Reason and Nature*, Oxford, Blackwell, 1982.

C. Merchant, *The Death of Nature: Women, Ecology, and the Scientific Revolution*, San Francisco, Harper & Row, 1980.

J. Mitchell, *Psychoanalysis and Feminism*, Hardmonsworth, Penguin, 1974.

J. Mitchell, *Woman's Estate*, Harmondsworth, Penguin, 1971.

A. Myrdal, *The Game of Disarmanent*, Manchester, Manchester University Press, 1977.

S.B. Ortner, 'Is Female to Male as Nature is to Culture?' in M. Zimbalist Rosaldo and L. Lamphere, eds, *Women, Culture and Society*, Stanford, Stanford Press, 1974, pp. 64–87.

J. Radcliffe Richards, *The Sceptical Feminist: A Philosophical Enquiry*, Harmondsworth, Penguin, 1980.

Radical Philosophy Collective, eds, 'Special Issue: Women, Gender and Philosophy', *Radical Philosophy* 34 (Summer 1983).

H. Rose, 'Beyond Masculinist Realities: A Feminist Epistemology for the Sciences in R. Bleier, ed., *Feminist Approaches to Science*, Oxford, Pergammon, 1986 pp. 57–76.

H. Rose, 'Hand, Brain and Heart: A Feminist Epistemology for the Natura Sciences' *Signs: Journal of Women in Culture and Society*, *9*, 1 (Autumn 1983) 73–90.

H. Rose, 'Making Science Feminist' in E. Whitelegg *et al.*, eds, *The Changin Experience of Women*, Oxford, Martin Robertson, 1982, pp. 352–72.

M. Rowe, ed., *Spare Rib Reader*, Hardmonsworth, Penguin, 1982.

B. Ruehl, 'The Balance of Terror: Deterrence and Peace-Keeping', in Thompso pp. 32–48.

C. Smith-Rosenberg, 'The Hysterical Woman: Sex Roles and Role Conflict Nineteenth-Century America', *Social Research* 39 (1972), 652–78.

C. Smith-Rosenberg, C. Rosenberg, 'The Female Animal: Medical and Biologic Views of Woman and Her Role in Nineteenth-Century America', *Journal American History* 60 (1973), 332–56.

K. Soper, 'Contemplating a Nuclear Future: Nuclear War, Politics and the In vidual', in Thompson, pp. 169–79.

K. Soper and A. Assiter, 'Greenham Common: An Exchange', *Radical Philosophy* 34 (Summer 1983), 21–4.

D. Spender, *Man-Made Language*, Routledge & Kegan Paul, 1980.

D. Spender and E. Sarah, eds, *Learning to Lose: Sexism and Education*, The Women's Press, 1980.

L. Stanley and S. Wise, *Breaking Out: Feminist Consciousness and Feminist Research*, Routledge & Kegan Paul, 1983.

D. Thompson, ed., *Over Our Ded Bodies: Women Against the Bomb*, Virago, 1983.

C. Tomalin, *The Life and Death of Mary Wollstonecraft*, New York, Mentor, 1976.

R. Wallsgrove, 'Greenham Common – So Why Am I Still Ambivalent?', *Trouble and Strife* 1 (Winter 1983), 4–6.

M. Wandor, ed., *The Body Politic: Women's Liberation in Britain*, Stage 1, 1978 (first published in 1972).

M. Walters, 'The Rights and Wrongs of Women: Mary Wollstonecraft, Harriet, Martineau and Simone de Beauvoir' in J. Mitchell and A. Oakley, eds, *The Rights and Wrongs of Women*, Harmondsworth, 1976, pp. 304–78.

J. Williamson, 'Gone With the Wind' (review of S. Griffin, *Women and Nature*), *Gender and Expertise/Radical Science* 19, Free Association Books, 1987.

A. Wiltsher, *Most Dangerous Women: Feminist Peace Campaigners of the Great War*, Pandora, 1985.

M. Wittig, *Les Guerilleres*, trans. D. LeVay, The Women's Press, 1979 (first published in 1969).

C. Wolf, *Cassandra: A Novel and Four Essays*, trans. J. Van Heurck, Virago, 1984 (first published in German in 1983).

C. Wolf, *A Model Childhood*, trans. U. Molinaro and H. Rappolt, Virago, 1983 (first published in German in 1976).

C. Wolf, *The Quest for Christa T.*, Virago, 1982 (first published in German in 1968).

M. Wollstonecraft, *Letters Written During a Short Residence in Sweden, Norway and Denmark*, 1796.

M. Wollstonecraft, *Mary (1788) and The Wrongs of Woman (1798)*, ed. J. Kingsley and G. Kelly, Oxford, Oxford University Press, 1980.

M. Wollstonecraft, *A Vindication of the Rights of Woman (1792)*, ed. and intro. M. Kramnick, Harmondsworth, Penguin, 1975.

V. Woolf, *A Room of One's Own* (1928), Collins, 1985.

V. Woolf, *Three Guineas* (1938), Harmondsworth, Penguin, 1977.

V. Woolf, *Virginia Woolf: Women and Writing*, ed. and intro. M. Barrett, The Women's Press, 1979.

CONTESTED BODIES

Donna Haraway

Essay review of Janet Sayers, *Biological Politics: Feminist and Anti-Feminist Perspectives*, Tavistock, 1982, £4.95 pb/£10.95 hb.

> Finally, I hope I have demonstrated . . . that the answers to the woman question are not to be found solely in biology as many radical feminists and conservative anti-feminists have claimed. Nor can they be found in the flat denial by liberal feminists that biological factors like menstruation affect women's lives, nor in the claim of some socialist feminists that biology influences women only via its social construction within patriarchy. The account of women's destiny provided by classical Marxism, though it is . . . incomplete, is nevertheless one of the few theories underlying contemporary feminism that begins to do justice to the fact that biology does have a direct influence on women's lives, and to the fact that, despite their shared biology, women of different classes nevertheless have different, and sometimes conflicting, interests even in regard to their shared biology. Moreover the recent resurgence of feminism has resulted in a number of extremely useful elaborations of the ways in which the Marxist theory of social class can and should inform feminist theory and practice. (Sayers, pp. 200–1)

This quotation demonstrates for me both the strengths and problems in Sayers' recent interesting exploration of nineteenth- and twentieth-century, white, largely English-speaking, feminist and anti-feminist arguments about the facts and meanings of women's sexualized bodies. Sayers cares about women's material, historical bodies; and she is not impressed by claims that these bodies are sufficient ground for a trans-historical unity of women. I want to affirm this strong thread in *Biological Politics*. On the other hand, Sayers is resolutely taxonomical: feminists come in neat brands and ideological packages, like radical, socialist, liberal, or Marxist. Despite the book's dedication to historical materialism and good discussions of nineteenth-century contexts, too little attention is paid to the specific historical moments from which recent feminist texts, forms of political action, and slogans emerge – moments which might disperse a neat taxonomy into a complex field of ideological negotiations and crossed boundaries. The same impulse that assembles feminists in tidy boxes seems to drive two other tendencies in *Biological Politics*: a kind of literal insistence on the letter of a document outside history deprives the book of any sense of humour, a great aid to dissecting women's sexualized bodies, and results in the unintended irony of the re-establishment of the sacred texts of the fathers. Feminist authors fare badly in Sayers' account; the authors who are trustworthy guides to the politics of women's bodies, at least methodologically, turn out to be Marx, Engels, Freud, and Darwin.

Feminists who do well have been obedient in principle to these fathers. The patronymic list – which makes me slightly hysterical in my nineteenth-century uterine brain and stresses my twentieth-century neuroendocrine system – alerts me to re-examine the historical constitution of sexual politics in *Biological Politics*. The clue of my nervous disorder with Sayers' frequently well-argued and politically sympathetic book lies in a quirk of rhetorical style. The word *biology* is a stand-in for the body itself. 'Biology' is repeatedly claimed to do or not to do this or that; biology here is a thing, itself without history, not a socially constructed discourse with highly mediated connections to what I will call our bodies. For Sayers, biology is a social text, not a body. But her apparent firm materialism seems finally rooted in a curious idealism that mistakes the discourse for the body.

Sayers would correctly accuse me of the opposite and equal idealism, perversely reading the social and historical contests (one modern form of which is biology) for what will count as our bodies, and never resting in the earth of reliably physically developing, birthing, menstruating, female bodies – who offer themselves to the differentiations of interpretation and social appropriation, as nature to culture. In good Marxist, Freudian, Darwinian (and Aristotelian) fashion, Sayers' analytical strategy depends upon the dualism numbingly involved in struggles for hierarchical reversals: nature/culture, materialism/idealism, resource/appropriation. Dialectics has been no final solution, only a mechanism for driving another form of the dichotomy. I think this logical, political issue underlies Sayers' drive to taxonomize, to ascertain which arguments are materialist and which idealist, to discipline the process of feminist and biological politics with the whip of the univocal name which claims to mark the real thing. No wonder the fathers come out on top in this explanatory incest. These rules legitimate their law, and the daughters are put in their place.

Let us proceed appreciatively and critically by exploring the plot of Sayers' discussion, which is organized into two sections. Throughout both, Sayers emphasizes two main points: (1) biology must be taken seriously for its direct effects upon women's lives, effects that none the less differ as a function of class and race; and (2) biology does not exert its effects in a fixed or mechanistic way, but through the mediation of social and personal interpretation. Sayers refuses to let her text degenerate into another diatribe against biological determinism or into an appeal to biological essentialism; she wants to find a third way, rooted in classical Marxism. She also documents the considerable diversity among feminists in their relation to arguments about biology and social construction; when the taxonomic impulse recedes, Sayers has a good ear for feminist cacophony on the touchy issues of sexual politics.

Anti-Feminist Biology

Part I, considerably less problematic for me than the second section, examines biological arguments against feminism, comparing and contrasting nineteenth- and twentieth-century debates. In 'Sexual Equality as Reproductive Hazard', she compares the nineteenth-century debate about the effects of extensive education for women on their reproductive efficiency with current disputes about occupational hazards and appropriate jobs for reproducing women. She persuasively shows the selective application of biological arguments in both periods; it seems to be only higher education and good jobs with money and security that interfere with women's biological well-being. 'Social Darwinism and the Woman Question' (chapter 3) examines nineteenth-century evolutionary doctrines, showing feminists embracing social Darwinism with enthusiasm and noting that Darwin was a better biologist than Spencer (or Jane Addams), whose doctrines on the evolution of social efficiency were ubiquitous in social theory of the second half of the nineteenth century. Sayers concludes with the correct moral: evolution does not give a valid account of the development of human society, but is valid as biology; and women's advance comes only through political struggle, the real cause of changing opinions about the deterministic influences of biology.

Sayers tells her histories well, but tends to simplify the history of science to make the final moral clearer. No historical relativist, Sayers judges her historical actors by her late twentieth-century judgement of correct biological opinion. In an unacknowledged way that links her to the subject of her own book, she lets her claims about good biology buttress her moral, political positions. Is this fidelity to Spencer in method, if not in content? Since I think biology is inherently about political contests, in the form of embodied symbolic systems structuring and expressing basic personal and social meanings – and that this state of affairs is not only not equal to bad science, but is how a science develops – this question bothers me less than it might Sayers. For example, the sciences of monkeys and apes are major discourses in biology and anthropology. The bodies of primates are constructed in complex story-telling practices about the origins of individuality, family, and society. These constructions are simultaneously fact and fiction, and to lose either pole of that tension would gut the political scientific practice of primatology. Perhaps stronger examples could be chosen from the history of illness, from chlorosis in the nineteenth century to stress in the late twentieth. The line between relativism careless of the resistant realities of living bodies and careful historical specificity is a delicate one, but it is very important to the development of Marxist accounts of biology and medicine.

The issue of biology *as* political argument is critical to chapters 4 and 5, both treating aspects of current sociobiology debates. 'Sociobiology on the Relations between the Sexes' argues that three offensive claims of modern sociobiologists (Robert Trivers of 'parental investment' fame stands in for this troop – or hive) about biological grounds for human social-sexual relations are false. Thus, women's subordination through their role in child care, the sexual double standard, and the battle between the sexes are not rooted in biology but in social structure and its derivative cultural assumptions. Sayers argues that Trivers' parental investment explanations derive from the capitalist market-place, that Darwin was a better biologist than Trivers, and that cultural assumptions regularly account for the flawed structure of sociobiological argument. This account has become dogma on the left and among feminists. Offensive biology has to be bad biology, caused by bad politics. As critics, the left (including the feminist left, and I am not immune from this criticism) readily adopts a double standard of argument and evidence. It is easy to show the cultural foundation of the enemy's biological argument – because it is there, I would argue. It is also easy to obscure the cultural foundation of one's own argument by appealing to available evidence and counter-explanatory strategy – also because they are there, since real biologists have constructed these alternatives.

I am not arguing that all explanations are equally good 'biology,' but I am arguing that the struggle for what will count as explanation is much messier than Sayers shows in her book. (Sayers tends to misrepresent arguments like this one. For example, in her footnote 2 in chapter 4, she claims that Robert Young sees capitalist science as 'nothing but ideology'. The argument I have read in the same sources by Young has consistently been that ideology is a misleading term, and the problem for us is multiple mediations of social relations, culminating in a notion of science as a labour process.) If in the end we cannot appeal to the 'correct biology' (a term unnervingly reminiscent of the label 'politically correct', which has got a very bad reputation among feminists) to displace an unacceptable account of nature, then the political struggle for our bodies permanently remains very complex. Without succumbing to politically and intellectually lazy relativism or cynicism, a very real question for me, and I think for us, becomes then: how do we respect and engage in the construction/discovery of our biological politics and political biology? We have become accustomed to an analogous question in political economy, where Marxist scientism has (I hope) become an unnecessary ploy in the rational and experiential political struggle for determining a standpoint to know and change the social world. Nancy Hartsock's fine Marxist-feminist book *Money, Sex, and Power*, is a good example; we need similar left feminist epistemological scrutiny in natural sciences.[1]

Chapter 5, 'Physical Strength, Aggression, and Male Dominance', argues that various claims that male dominance is biologically based are patently false and rooted in social argument. Sayers develops two counter-positions, the first that since male dominance is not universal among people, it cannot be biological, and the second that since other primates learn behaviours like dominance, so do people. Therefore, change is possible. The entire structure of this argument depends on the fiction that social causation is required if change is to be possible. Fiction does not mean false; it means here 'required by the story'. The predictability of Sayers' arguments is disturbing. In this chapter, she uses dated material on primate social organization and behaviour, selects what she wants, and moves on. That is exactly what she is accusing the bad guys of doing, but she calls her narrative better science. I find her argument regularly oversimplifies accounts by biologists, on her side or not, and tends not to examine much primate biology after the mid-1970s. When she uses Eleanor Leacock to prove that 'male dominance' ('male supremacy'?, 'patriarchy'?, each term is loaded with different practical and theoretical weight) is not universal, she jumps over an entire contentious and very much unresolved political and anthropological debate. Sayers quotes Leacock as if that were an examination of standards of argument in this very touchy matter. It is not accidental that Leacock is the most faithful modern feminist interpreter of Engels.

Chapter 6 is a persuasive demonstration that social factors have determined the rise and fall of arguments about sex differences in the brain since the nineteenth-century. Recent debates are no exception, but there is the nasty quirk today of women biologists advancing some of the most anti-feminist accounts. Sayers notes the relevance of current claims about brain asymmetry and sex differences to women's struggles for professional opportunity in the sciences. But also fromwithin scientific disciplines, women and men are putting forward cogent objections to misogynist accounts. Sayers' main point is that the future of these objections depends less on advances in brain science than on success in struggles for sexual social equality, particularly within the scientific professions. What is certain is that the brain is an important contested political terrain.

Psychoanalysis and Biology

Part II, Feminist Theory and Biology, a four-chapter examination of varieties of feminism in relation to female biology, contains the most interesting and the most controversial aspects of Sayers' project to demonstrate the superiority, on grounds of attention both to bodily and to social-experiential aspects of life, of classical Marxism as a foundation for feminism. I should admit a prejudice at the start. Sayers' concerns are overwhelmingly about versions of psychoanalysis, among which she finds classical Freudianism superior to Lacanian or object-relations frameworks, on the same grounds on which classical Marxism is to be preferred. I find all the psychoanalytic accounts bizarre. Nothing makes me into an unreformed positivist faster than the ease with which claims are made about infantile experience and stages of psychodynamic development and their relevance to what it means to be human, e.g. to have language. These claims make Sayers' sociobiologists look positively dedicated to high standards of evidence. The status of psychoanalytic debate in feminist theory overdirects our attention to predetermined aspects of female bodies and experience, making it difficult to remember that female bodies and experience, hunger and metabolism, or mortality and disease patterns, might be more important feminist issues than those more readily sexualized into debates about oedipal versus pre-oedipal development. Women's roles in agriculture should be getting at least as much attention as early mother–child relations in modern feminist theory, but they will not and cannot from presently valued theoretical preoccupations.

What accounts for the extraordinary immersion in psychoanalytic debates among current feminist theorists? The psychoanalytic accounts have to be ultimately about sex, in the precise ways that women have been constituted as the sex (or the difference – same thing) since the nineteenth century in life and human sciences. The debates then turn on whether the phallus or the clitoris (completely absent, by the way, in Sayers' book, despite her insistence on the developmental importance of the real penis) matters more, or whether the symbolic or real penis is the object of concern, or whether innate or social constructionist accounts get closer to explaining the nature of mother–child relations, etc. Without a sexualized body, women simply do not exist for any of the major prestigious theoretical traditions. That is part of the 'woman question', to say the least, and I agree that understanding how psychoanalytic theory works is important. But I think that psychoanalysis and biology share the dubious distinctions of being the leading discourses in the construction of woman, and that the task for feminist theory is at least as much to learn how to construct/discover female bodies and experience outside the boundaries imposed by these discourses, as to endlessly elaborate them ourselves.

Sayers' psychoanalytic preoccupation predictably degenerates into fine discussions about which accounts are materialist (classical Freudian) or idealist (Lacan and feminist Lacanians) or too social constructionist (object relations and associated socialist feminism) or properly balanced between body and history (again, classical Freudian). That debates about psychoanalysis are at the centre of contemporary feminist theory is both true and outrageous. These debates are no small part of the taxonomic exuberance of the second half of Sayers' book. The nuances of one's allegiance to psychoanalytic options allow endless elaboration of categories in the name of contributing to theory. The intersection of psychoanalytic possibilities and versions of Marxism raises the stakes by orders of magnitude and increases the taxonomic riches markedly. We do have to contest for psychoanalytic stories, as we must for biological ones, but we need at least some sense of irony in this state of affairs. Instead, we get claims about the true story and correct theory; i.e., biological politics, feminist and anti-feminist perspectives.

But Sayers' discussions of various theorists are regularly interesting, and her positions deserve a hearing. In 'The Social

Construction of Female Biology', after dismissing structuralism (and Sherry Ortner's version of the relation of woman and nature) as too idealist, Sayers turns to the problem of menstruation. The problem is that women bleed regularly, often enough with a fair amount of pain, and any account that looks only to symbolic meanings, either positive or negative, will miss important dimensions of issues crucial to menstruating women – like the need for proper facilities at work. Further, women of different social classes have different interests in relation to shared biology, so an effort to ground a unity of women on the basis of positive meanings of the body will fail. From this perspective, Sayers rejects versions of radical feminism which 'fall into the masculine trap of enclosing ourselves in our differences' (from de Beauvoir, p. 118).

She ridicules the Baltimore Bleed-In from this perspective, completely missing, in my opinion, the wonderful sense of humour and theatre behind that action, and choosing to interpret it in a literalist fashion. The Bleed-In occurred in the period of late 1960s and early 1970s street theatre and people's exuberant and public re-symbolization of politics. A common menstrual play in that context was a potent and serious joke, but not a new ontology calling for heavy Marxist-feminist chastisement. Radical feminism gets a bad press for its marvellous generation of metaphor at a particular and very brief moment of recent feminist history. Those who pour their venous blood on the Pentagon do not get such a hard metaphysical time.[2] But the merit of Sayers' chapter is her concern for serious different relations to the body for women of different classes. Those differences will charge different metaphors in constructing feminist politics, and it remains too easy to mistake one's favourite symbolic actions for the route to universal sisterhood.

In 'Freud and Feminism' Sayers lays out in detail her reasons for preferring Freud to most of his feminist interpreters, at least methodologically. She objects to 'biological essentialism' in Jones, Horney, and Irigaray – quite a combination, and one that depends on a literalist reading of Irigaray, a dangerous tack. Sayers notes evidence against essentialist accounts, but glides easily over the same problem in classical Freudian approaches. Socialist-feminist accounts – e.g. those of Juliet Mitchell or Rosalind Coward – fail on the ground of providing no theory which could ground hope for social change through concrete struggle. Prey to Lacanian interpretations, these theorists sin through idealism, underestimating both social action and physical bodies. For Sayers, Freud alone gives balanced space to both environment and body.

In 'Biology and Mothering' Sayers argues that the biological processes of childbirth matter, and so the 'object-relations' socialist-feminists err by stressing too much the social relation of mother and child and too little the processes of physical existence. Sayers is careful to align herself with Deutsch; the effects of the body are not mechanistic, but are mediated by interpretation. Sayers uses Alice Rossi and Adrienne Rich to illustrate the opposite error to that of the socialist-feminists. Rossi and Rich are both accused of stressing innate factors in mothering and end up as biological essentialists, whatever their differences. The compulsion to sort out the theorists along lines of essentialism versus constructionism leads to bizarre reductions of complex positions, like those of Rich, into caricatures of what she says about 'thinking with the body'.

In her final chapter, 'Biology and the Theories of Contemporary Feminism', Sayers summarizes her positions by proposing an elaborated summary of the allegiances of liberal, radical, and socialist-feminists compared to classical Marxist feminists. Engels provides the reference text, particularly as interpreted by Eleanor Leacock. Engels plus Freud provide the resources to understand the different interests of middle-class and working-class women and to avoid false theoretical notions like a unitary class of women. Conflicts of women across class (in the Marxist sense) foreclose the utopian hope of sex-class unity (in the radical feminist sense). Economic conditions, not men, are feminist enemies, so radical feminists are wrong. I am caricaturing here too, but I want to stress the disservice to the messy and rich world of feminist discourse that results from labelling as a strategy for exhibiting a predetermined correct method. I lose the nuances of Sayers' discussion in her insistence on labels. But this review would be a caricature of its own criticism if it did not stress Sayers' own final word and the priorities it makes plain:

> The goals and priorities of the women's movement should not be determined on the basis of abstract theory, whether it is the theory of liberalism, radicalism, cultural feminism, or structuralism. [Marxism is conspicuously not on this list . . . Why not?] These aims should instead be determined by examining the concrete ways in which the majority of women are oppressed within their sexual and familial relations and at work. . . . The struggle is by no means over. . . . (p. 201)

Beyond Taxonomy

In conclusion, Sayers' book should also be read as an entry into the growing feminist debate on women's relation to scientific expertise, both as knowledge and as technology. Accounts of the history of science and medicine are simultaneously prescriptive of political positions on current struggles. For example, Barbara Ehrenreich and Deirdre English's *For Her Own Good* was an early story about the history of scientific-medical expertise that was immersed in the politics of self-help and female control of reproductive health care. Carolyn Merchant's *Death of Nature* was a story whose main action was in the sixteenth and seventeenth centuries, but whose meanings were commitments to particular technologies and organicist attitudes to 'nature' in the twentieth century. The early days of the second wave of feminism developed a powerful symbol from the speculum of gynaecological practice. It could be a hand tool for the empowerment of women, despite its sordid history as part of the male takeover of women's bodies. (Note the part-for-whole relation: feminists here reduced women's bodies to the area revealed by the tools of gynaecology.)

The speculum as a symbol will not do for the historical moment we are now in, where ultrasound scanners and gene probes are the relevant reproductive technologies, and women's bodies are as much constructed by video-display terminals as by other forms of bodily copying. My own 'Cyborg Manifesto' is an anti-organicist account of recent biological and technological history that tries to persuade left feminists that ironic, active feminist constructions of the body and of identity from the resources of mythic machine-organism hybrids (cyborgs) allow more sensitive analysis of the differences among women and of political possibility than more traditional socialist-feminist myths. Pleasure in machine embodiment is not a feminist sin. The riches of feminist science fiction are a major imaginative source for political rethinking about these issues.

Sayers' book is helpful in its resolute insistence on the specific social relations that alter the meanings of a shared biology. There can be no one feminist position on an abstract 'expertise', but a multiplicity of allied, carefully chosen strategies on the meanings of specific social relations of technology and science. Technologies are frozen social relations; Marx would have said 'dead labour'. Bodies too are like time slices through the fabric of social lives; bodies tell a contested political history. Technical expertise about these matters can be a form of responsible political struggle. It is as true for the feminist left as for the owners of multinational capital: our politics construct our tools.

Notes

1. Hartsock develops a theory of feminist standpoint from the starting positions suggested by Lukács, Marx, and Gramsci. The basic point is that some social positions allow, but do not determine, a more adequate view of the totality of social relations than others. In addition to providing carefully argued criteria for what can count as a standpoint and stressing that an epistemological position is potentially available only from the experiential ground of women's immersion in care for daily life, Hartsock provides a rich exploration of the relations of eros and power in feminist accounts of community.
2. A nice touch on this is the pouring of menstrual blood by a fine group of feminist witches on the Lawrence-Livermore nuclear weapons design labs in California in the summer of 1984. The blood had been collected in the kitchen freezer of a Collective, in store for just such an occasion. Pollution can still make effective politics.

References

Barbara Ehrenreich and Deirdre English, *For Her Own Good: 150 Years of the Experts' Advice to Women*, NY, Anchor Doubleday, 1978.

Donna Haraway, 'Cyborg Manifesto', *Socialist Review* 80 (1985), 65–108.

Nancy Hartsock, *Money, Sex and Power*, Longman, 1982, reissued by Northeastern Univ. Press, 1984.

Carolyn Merchant, *Death of Nature: Women, Ecology and the Scientific Revolution,* San Francisco, Harper & Row, 1980.

GONE WITH THE WIND

Judith Williamson

Review of Susan Griffin, *Woman and Nature – The Roaring Inside Her*, Women's Press, 1984, £4.95

Susan Griffin's book about woman and nature was first published in America in 1978. The issue of 'woman's place' in the discourses, the patterns of speech and thought, of our society is an extremely important one both for feminists and for all those on the left who wish to benefit from feminism. It was noticeably absent from a book on women's liberation written by the leader of the Socialist Workers Party (Tony Cliff, *Class Struggle and Women's Liberation*, Bookmarks, 1984). I criticized his book on publication for belittling recent feminist attempts to theorize the position of women in our culture. Such a book claims to speak *for* oppressed groups, rather than listening to them; the white, male left has never been all that good at letting 'other' people speak.

However, on receiving the 1984 British reprint of Griffin's book *Woman and Nature – The Roaring Inside Her*, I could immediately see why certain feminist ideas are so open to ridicule. 'Come back Tony Cliff, all is forgiven!' – was my first reaction to this book. But my second, and more serious reaction, was one of frustration at being caught between the two extremes of an argument – two positions, each of which seems bent on acting out its caricature in the eyes of the other.

We have the whole of the 'Left' apparently unable to recognize the politics of the very *act* of speech from those who traditionally have been silent, unwilling to listen as those who have been the bearers become the wielders of symbolic meanings. And then, in *Woman and Nature – The Roaring Inside Her*, we do indeed have speech from the silent – but not just from women: we have speech from the *very* silent – rocks, stones and trees.

I do not intend to make fun of this book (easy though that

would be, as with all works that lack their own humour): it is a serious philosophical project, an investigation of the ways Western culture has viewed nature through the spyglass of science, and of the ways women have been either worshipped or reviled as part of that 'nature'. An enormous amount of fascinating historical and scientific research goes into it: in fact, the book sits on material which I wish Griffin would actually deliver instead of merely referring to in a sort of generalized 'male' scientific discourse. But then the book is, in a way, more about discourse itself than just science and male domination, and this is both its greatest interest, and its weakness.

It is structured – and this is the best idea in it – as two opposing voices, the 'scientific', pseudo-objective voice of patriarchy, and the 'great chorus of woman and nature' [*sic*] which enters into struggle with the patriarchal voice and finally drowns it out. 'We', apparently, speak with the wind, we say things like 'we are the mothers', 'we are the volcano', etc. 'We know this earth is made from our bodies . . . and we are nature . . . the red-winged blackbird flies in us, in our inner sight . . . We fly . . .', etc. Apart from the fact that I find this sort of thing impossible to stomach, just as *writing* (it always reads like a parody of itself), there are three major problems involved in the whole enterprise.

First, you cannot just say 'we' for all women. Subjective speech is fine, but don't steal my subjective speech from me; personally I do *not* speak with the volcanoes or feel like the mother of the earth. And, as Tony Cliff would be the first to point out, there is that bothersome issue of *class* and the *difference* in peoples' experience. Since feminism has 'claimed' subjectivity, some feminists seem to go overboard and claim *all* subjectivity. We are not one with the earth, we are not even one with each *other*.

Second, there is an inherent philosophical problem in that the underlying drive of the book is for a pre-linguistic state, a desire to get back to an unfallen Eden of 'no names': nature stands for this state, while men are supposed to have named everything. 'Behind naming, beneath words is something else . . . all this knowledge is in the souls of everything, behind naming, before speaking, beneath words.' Of course it is true, language is the primary and most powerful of the tools by which we organize the undifferentiated world. Yet we can never know either the world, or ourselves, *without* language; and indeed part of the positive project of the book is precisely to *give* language to those that don't have it. Cows speak, we hear the voices of the wind and water, of nature itself – and yet nature's great mystery, it is said, is 'her' lack of language. (However, when nature does speak, I wish she wouldn't use so many clichés.)

Finally there is the basic confusion about women and nature which has a much wider application than in this book alone – it is the same issue which manifests itself in some aspects of Greenham Common women or in parts of the ecology movement. Griffin's own position on it is confused and seems to shift from the first premise of the book. In the preface she observes that 'men consider women to be more material than themselves, or more a part of nature.' Very true, women traditionally have been identified with nature, dumb as cows, murky as mud, unpredictable as hurricanes, etc. This is an ideology. Now, the same society based on the profit motive, which mechanizes childbirth, demands work to be done for free by women in the home, oppresses women in hundreds of ways, is indeed the one which pours chemical waste into rivers, runs factory farms, and manufactures the atom bomb. This is a fact. The fact is perpetuated in part by the aforementioned ideology. But that does not mean that women have to *identify* with nature (thereby confirming that ideology) just in order to oppose the ravages on both ourselves and the globe. We do not have to *be* the earth in order to save it.

Woman and Nature could have been a fascinating exposé of the naturalizing language of our oppression. But *we* need not speak pidgin to please the colonizers. You can count me out of this particular chorus.

INTIMATE IMPERIALISM

Judith Williamson

Review of Germaine Greer, *Sex and Destiny*, Secker & Warburg, 1984, £9.95 hb.

The 1980s have been a time for many reappraisals of the early 1970s women's movement, both by feminists and by those in the media who have long been waiting on the sidelines of this marathon for a leading figure to trip and fall. A few years back a Sunday colour supplement delighted in featuring an array of once 'hardline' feminists who had all, apparently, discovered that there was after all much to be said for men and babies and 'settling down'. In an atmosphere where many feminists are, in fact, anxious to reclaim more 'feminine' roles, and where the press are just itching to say 'told you so', it is hardly surprising that Germaine Greer's latest book *Sex and Destiny* has been hailed as a great turn-around by the original high priestess of sexual liberation – a fact which appears to delight some, while being seen by others as evidence of a sell-out. Common to almost all these reactions is first, the idea of Greer as somehow symbolic of the Pill-taking 1960s, and second, the belief that *Sex and Destiny* primarily advocates the 'withdrawal method' to replace the Pill for women today.

Only a culture as individualist as ours would appoint one person as the representative of a generation; only a culture as emotionally desensitized as ours would assume that contraception must be the key issue in any discussion of sexual relations; and only a culture as ethnocentric as ours would assume that a description of what *other* cultures do must really be a prescription for ourselves – since we are only interested in what *we* do. For the most basic misreading of Greer's book is that it is in any way a set of directions for Western feminists. I mention the emphasis on the 'withdrawal method' simply because it is the one aspect of the book that everyone who hasn't read it seems to have heard about. But Greer is not concerned with exhorting sisters in Britain and the US to practise withdrawal (or abstinence) as the latest feminist contraceptive fad: she is pointing out that for centuries people in other cultures have used these methods of controlling their fertility within sexual relationships, and that *their* established patterns are being destroyed by the importation of *ours*.

For what *Sex and Destiny* is really about is imperialism. Greer may not use that word explicitly, but what she so lucidly traces and documents in the realm of human reproduction is just that: at the economic level, as chemical companies reap millions from contraceptive sales; at the political level, as Western nations worry at the thought of rapidly multiplying foreigners – many of them black, to boot – and at the ideological level, as in imposing fertility controls on others we convince ourselves that we are liberating them, certain that everyone would, really, choose to be more like us if they could. But as Greer asks at the beginning of the book: 'What is our civilization that we should so blithely propagate its discontents?'

In answer to this, the picture of our 'civilization' that gradually builds up is one of enormous sterility – both literal and metaphorical. As she charts its concerted attempt to limit the population of the rest of the world, Greer points to the deficiencies of our own culture through comparison with those it destroys – where children are *not* regarded as a nuisance, where childbirth is *not* seen as an illness, where women do *not* struggle to bring up children in isolation, where the old are *not* treated as a useless burden. The politics of reproduction are not just about sex, but about the value of life, and its continuance: and despite all our machinery and medicines, we appear to have less regard for life than those societies where both its beginning and its ending are attended with respect and affection.

The throwaway quality of our own society is particularly hard on women: in most other parts of the world, you do not have to 'stay young and beautiful/if you want to be loved.' Greer outlines the importance of women's roles within cultures based on the extended family, which she terms Family – an importance which increases, rather than decreases, with age. In such cultures women are guaranteed not only respect but practical support, both in the rearing of children and in old age, from relatives, the community, and society at large. By contrast, Greer remarks that

> outside English supermarkets rows of parked baby-carriages can be seen, because the merchants who take billions of pounds from mothers' purses cannot be bothered to design a facility to accommodate them. Instead they have the gall to announce that perambulators and strollers are not permitted inside the store. Feminists are often accused of downgrading motherhood. The accusation is ridiculous: motherhood hit rock-bottom long before the new feminist wave broke. The wave itself was caused by the groundswell.

In this light, the notion that we may really be reading *our* discontents into other civilizations becomes particularly vivid: feminists, however well-meaning, have no special exemption from the generally missionary attitude of the colonizing culture, and we can all too easily find ourselves zealously exporting 'solutions' to problems which are in fact our own. Yet none of this is to suggest that Western women should artificially imitate women from the cultures with which our own compares so unfavourably. As Greer says,

> The point of the contrast is simply to caution the people of the highly industrialized countries which wield such massive economic and cultural sway over the developing world against assuming that one of the things they must rescue the rest of the world from is parenting. That motherhood is virtually meaningless in our society is no ground for supposing that the fact that women are still defined by their mothering function in other societies is simply an index of their oppression. We have at least to consider the possibility that a successful matriarch might well pity Western feminists for having been duped into futile competition with men in exchange for the companionship and love of children and other women.

This reminder of other forms of companionship might make us question the Western hierarchy of relationships in which the sexual bond between a man and a woman is given precedence over all others. This precedence has come to seem entirely natural to us, though it is not a part of those more 'primitive' cultures which we often obscurely associate with Nature. In those cultures, collectivity is the key to social order: only in our own, 'civilized' society does the law of the jungle rule, as commodities and sex are dangled before nuclear couples as the prizes of competitive capitalism. Sex itself has become an essential component of the consumer society and appears as its supreme form of human activity. Yet our definition of sex is as limited and hierarchized as our notions of relationships. We believe that heterosexual intercourse must be available on demand at all times, like any other commodity, while at the same time requiring more commodities precisely to counteract its probable effects. In her chapter entitled 'Polymorphous Perversity' Greer points out that where mechanical or chemical contraceptives have not been available, couples have always been perfectly able to prevent conception by elaborating forms of sex that do not involve ejaculation inside the vagina on the part of the man – something to which our own society accords him an almost divine right. As she says,

> There is no logic in a conceptual system which holds that orgasm is always and everywhere good for you, that vaginal orgasm is impossible, that no moral opprobrium attaches to the expenditure of semen wherever it occurs, that considerable opprobrium attaches to the bearing of unwanted children, *and* at the same time insists that 'normal' heterosexual intercourse should always culminate in ejaculation within the vagina. These are the suppositions which underlie our eagerness to extend the use of modern contraceptives into every society on earth, regardless of its own set of cultural and moral priorities.

Thus through detailed investigation of sexual and reproductive practices, through the history of 'family planning' and its attendant ideologies of eugenics (Marie Stopes apparently thought it was too horrid even that her son should mate with a woman who wore glasses), through an enormous – but never tedious – amount of data on the uses and dangers of modern contraceptives, Greer traces an entire history of imperialism. This is not a different imperialism from the one Marxists write about, but the very same. For capitalism effects a colonization at once global and intimate: those who benefit from its exploitative economy assume the right to tamper with other people's countries and bodies alike. *Sex and Destiny* shows exactly how the economic and the intimate are linked, not through theory but in practice; over and over again Greer shows the specific, individual and local *effects* of schemes that are usually thought of in the West only as sets of *aims* – to be acted out on people whose lives we do not understand and whose values we do not respect. One of the great strengths of her book is the painstaking documentation of many of those lives and values so that the reader can understand them. It actually helps to produce the respect it argues for towards other cultures.

My only criticism of this brilliant and important work is that it has a tendency to treat the dominant, 'Western' culture as homogeneous, whereas it is a very specific culture which has succeeded in dominating worldwide by imposing itself on other traditions here, as well as elsewhere. Greer describes with great warmth the supportive network of Family in other cultures, in contrast to the loneliness of Western individualism and the miseries caused by its imposition on other societies, breaking up long-established ties and holding out the bourgeois nuclear couple as a poor substitute for the community of generations. There is a clear parallel – which Greer does not make – between the Family of Southern, peasant cultures, which she evidently knows a lot about, and traditional Western working-class family networks, about which she perhaps knows less. The same system which tramples the customs and elaborate survival habits of people abroad also destroys and devalues those of its own subordinate class. Many of the aspects of Family life – the involvement of several generations in the care of children, the respect for matriarchal power, the inclusion of unmarried adults in the household, the checking of prospective partners by the whole clan, the assumption of responsibility for the old – have all been established parts of our own working-class Family culture, gradually eroded through the break-up of communities by planners and of community values by modern consumerism.

Ironically, as Greer herself suggests, it is the poor within our own society, whose communal structures have been literally broken up into tower blocks and the like, who support the luxury of the middle class to dabble in imitations of the rural communities destroyed abroad:

> Groups of individuals may attempt to live in the electronic age by the values of an earlier time: they may go back to the land, live in artificial extended families, and give birth at home according to rituals they have learned from anthropology books or from Lamaze and Leboyer, but their freedom to do so is itself dependent upon the wealth created by the workers who live in the mobile nuclear families which the communards despise.

The crucial issue is not the acceptance or rejection of the electronic age, but the politics of harnessing it to improve people's live in ways that *they* want, not in ways that help to maintain our own power.

As Greer frequently points out: if, with all our technology, we could guarantee simply the *survival* of those children born to the poor, if we could promise a healthy future for each child conceived, the poor would be much more willing (for they are perfectly able) to conceive less frequently. But who are we to sterilize parents who well know that few of their offspring may reach adulthood? Who are we to deny them security in old age – since that is what their children provide? Who are we to decide that because we don't want children, they shouldn't either? Who are we to decide what the rest of the world should or should not do? Greer puts the answer most succinctly: 'Let us therefore abandon the rhetoric of crisis, for we *are* the crisis.' One solution to the problem of world resources would be to reduce the numbers not of the poor, but of the rich, who put such a disproportionate strain on the resources not merely of their own countries but of others whose own populations starve while they grow sugar or tobacco for the wealthy.

For ultimately, the key issue with population control as with contraception is what we expect or demand of life itself.

> Whether we believe that the world is overpopulated or not depends to some extent on how we think people should live. If we in the West think that only our kind of life is worth living, then clearly the numbers that the earth supports will have to be substantially reduced. The world could become a vast luxury hotel, complete with recreational space for us to hunt and ski and mountaineer in, but it must not be forgotten that our luxurious lifestyle demands the services of a huge number of helots, who cannot be paid so much that they can afford rooms in the

> hotel for themselves. Like Ricardo, we would like to see the supply of helots kept constant, neither falling so low that we have to take out the trash ourselves or becoming so high that we shake in our shoes fearing insurrection in the compound.

This vivid passage comes right at the end of *Sex and Destiny*, so it is possible that those who feel that Germaine Greer has abandoned a feminist position simply did not get that far in the book. However, if they did, such a response must call into question just what a feminist position might be in global terms. This book *is*, indirectly, a reappraisal of the Western women's movement, but is not so much a reversal as a widening of the frames of reference and a radicalizing of them. It is now clear that in some ways the 'Women's Lib' of the 1970's unwittingly functioned in tandem with both the population control lobby and the chemical manufacturers by providing the ideology of liberation as freedom from conception that seemed to justify their ruthless pursuit of political and economic ends. Feminists today are involved in campaigns against Depo-Provera – the high-dosage contraceptive hormone given in injections almost exclusively to black women – and are learning to question our ethnocentric assumptions, for example, that the veil in Islamic societies inherently degrades women. Reappraisals are definitely taking place, but the issue at stake is no longer just our own 'liberation': it is what, precisely, we mean by that word and whether we have the right to impose our definition of it on the rest of the world.

Education

TEACHING GIRLS SCIENCE

Grazyna Baran

Introduction

In this article a woman teacher, Grazyna Baran, talks about her work as head of the science department in a London girls' school. Her account grew out of conversations with a friend, Pam Linn. First Pam taped an interview in which Grazyna described aspects of her work. Later Grazyna wrote up other areas of her work. Then, in further conversations with Pam, she worked over this material, amplifying and enlarging. Grazyna talked, Pam jotted down and read out, Grazyna amended or clarified. Pam then typed the material, which Grazyna again amended or clarified.

The result is inevitably patchy, with new instances and ideas cropping up in this friendly and discursive process of production. There is nothing novel about this method, as writing usually becomes a social process of referral and amendment, though the image of the lone scribbler dies hard. In fact, Grazyna argues here that school science can have a similar social process, though the convention of school science – as a competitive and individualistic accumulation of disparate facts – dies equally hard.

Becoming a Science Teacher

My first years in teaching were spent in an inner-city working-class girls' school. The pupils showed a complete lack of interest in the physical sciences. I could see why: they were facing similar kinds of abstractions in their science work at school as I had faced in mine at university. They couldn't see the point of it. And at that time there was a shortage of science teachers, which caused some instability as teachers moved from job to job. For most of us, getting on top of classroom control was a goal in itself. I found that it was not enough to prepare lessons in which the content and activities were interesting and relevant to the pupils' lives; I also had to be able to engage with pupils on a social level. I started to learn that control would come from taking the pupils seriously, listening carefully, working on classroom relationships *within the context* of interesting teaching.

But there is also a question of *teacher* confidence here. It is so easy to be undermined, and so easy to slip into liberal woolliness in the process of 'taking children seriously'. If pupils say 'This is boring, Miss', I'll work through with them what they mean by boring and make it clear that there is room for change; what I will not do is to throw away my purposes and sense of what it is we are learning. You can talk as much as you like about relevant content, but you've got to be able to engage with pupils on a social level. It takes time to learn the necessary skills, and often in inner-city schools teachers don't get the chance to get past the first post.

I then moved to another working-class girls' school that so cultivated passivity in the pupils that I had to cultivate techniques to help the girls develop the confidence necessary to engage with me and with each other. I almost had to *undiscipline* them to get some critical work going, as they were used to sitting in rows and copying notes. But the relative quiet did give me breathing space to try out new approaches and to see possibilities.

My next school was an inner-city coeducational school. I didn't know what hit me. In contrast to the girls' schools, physical science was totally taken for granted within the curriculum. Science was taught throughout the school, although it was largely the boys who were doing it. Sexual conflict was ever-present. So was anarchy, chaos, fights, teachers locking themselves in the classroom with their classes. It was a violent male-dominated place. Sexual harassment was seen as *natural*, as part of humdrum day-to-day interaction. What was so shocking about it was that all the rudeness, constant thumping, and teacher collusion – on grounds that 'the girls ask for it' – were not seen to be unacceptable or unusual. Even when I got on well with the boys, it was so easy to get too close; they would immediately respond by emphasizing that I was a woman physics teacher: 'You're too fat.' I had to be very confident about my sexuality. The boys would try to set intellectual traps for me, try to find gaps in my knowledge of physics, and there was a lot of bragging and one-upmanship in the class. It was very intimidating for the girls.

I currently work as head of science in an inner-city London girl's school. A number of minority ethnic groups are represented, with a significant proportion of non-English-speaking Bengali girls as well as Cypriot/Turkish/Greek and Afro-Caribbean girls.

Educating a Science Teacher

When I was at school I was encouraged to do science because I was good at maths. I believed that I was more likely to get a good job, and that science was to do with making things work and having some purchase on the world. I followed the A-level course thinking it was a boring but necessary hurdle to proper science at university. By the time I got to university I realized that most of my optimism was unfounded.

In my first year I found myself immersed in abstractions. Almost everyone else seemed to be doing courses about people and the world – sociology, economics, literature – whilst I was struggling with electrons in potential wells. I suddenly became a 'low-ability' student and was made aware of what it feels like to be so labelled. Even while I understood the scientific words. I couldn't see the *purpose* of what was being taught. Perhaps even if I'd understood the pedagogic purposes of my university teachers, I wouldn't have wanted to take part in those objectives. In university lectures, at least in science departments, the content of courses has been so abstracted from the historical context, the practical circumstances, and even the philosophical debates, that it lacks all the texture and flavour that gives knowledge life. Everything is presented smoothly, as if all problems were solved one after another. All the messiness, all the cultural dimensions get swept away, and with them the meaning for having that bit of knowledge at all. University science teaching is so authoritarian that even asking questions – and they became rebellious questions after a while – just reinforces the view that one is a 'low-ability' student. Seminars are opportunities to show off; the male students do more of the talking; but more to show off what they already know, to assert themselves, than to raise any questioning or oppositional views.

It's a very competitive atmosphere. No wonder science teachers, educated in that environment, find it difficult to engage in open-ended discussions with schoolchildren.

My own disillusionment with science at university led me to believe that science teaching should contain a large element of practical work around technical activities with familiar technological products, rather than around traditional experiments designed to demonstrate abstract principles. For me that implies allowing the messiness back into the process of learning about the world, in the same way as scientific discovery and technological development is actually 'messy'. For example, it takes a lot of time to identify and define the precise nature of a scientific problem during the research period. The same thing applies in the pursuit of any knowledge and therefore to the learning experience for pupils.

In science lessons, children usually have the questions and problems posed *for* them. No wonder large sections of the population accept questions as having validity in themselves, not to be challenged on their content or premises. This attitude is reinforced by rigid assessment and examination systems which render the assessed powerless. To counter all that, teachers should try to avoid getting too anxious if pupils raise problems and issues in ways that don't coincide with the planned teaching schedule. We should be wary of teaching as if knowledge were acquired in a particular set sequence or according to particular hierarchies.

If we look again at the comparison with research and development, we can recognize that it takes a lot of time, thought and knowledge to design and build an experiment. It is impossible to do this without a knowledge of materials, where to get them from, how to put them together effectively – no matter how advanced our concepts of theoretical physics might be. Once we acknowledge this messiness and allow it back into our teaching methods, we need to know what we are doing with it; otherwise we end up with anarchic, purposeless teaching. Making use of messiness, showing the complexity of the world and the knowledge process, has both a class and gender dimension. Let me explain what I mean by that.

Very often what we present in school science is so abstracted that it's actually in contradiction to pupils' own observation and experience. To take complexity on board helps to overcome that problem; to look at the complexity of a situation puts the problematic back into the learning process, gives it an interest and a challenge for the learner. Children who are labelled as 'low-ability', or, more often, as 'bright but she won't get through the exams' very often experience complete frustration because they actually see the problem in a more complicated way. Teachers fail to recognize that.

I've seen working-class children of great intellectual vitality put down because they do not demonstrate the expected behaviours of competence. Often children will ask a question in a way that appears to be garbled, but if you persist in pushing, you often find that they are trying to grasp the complexity. I think as teachers we have to learn to listen to children and this is particularly the case where working-class and girl pupils are concerned. Both boys and middle-class children are expected, and *expect themselves*, to be successful at science. So they are prepared to accept the abstracted account, largely without question.

Girls, particularly working-class and immigrant girls, lack confidence in themselves and their abilities, especially in unfamiliar areas. Having spent a lot of time watching them, I have noticed that girls exert pressures on each other which reinforce this lack of confidence. There is pressure not to brag, 'show yourself up' or make a fuss; otherwise you may be labelled 'big-headed'. Discretion and modesty are valued, while outspokenness and self-assertion are suspect, if not 'punished' by the group (unless they express anti-authoritarianism).

Imagine a girl attempting to formulate a question in a science lesson under such pressures. She is likely to expose her vulnerability in two ways. First, she risks the censure of the whole group. Second, she almost certainly risks being dismissed and thus unintentionally ridiculed by the teacher for failing to pose the question in a sufficiently abstract frame of reference to be recognized by that teacher. In such a context, girls may readily reject scientific knowledge wholesale as being at odds with their own experiences.

The choice of language also comes into play here.

Given differences in socialization of linguistic assertiveness, science teaching can unintentionally turn out to deepen those differences. Often both pupils and teachers mistake the mere use of complex scientific language for a real conceptual understanding.

Rather than centre science teaching upon abstractions in the name of expediency, we should encourage pupils to formulate their own questions or problems for science. In so doing, we will be bringing science teaching closer to the processes followed in the pursuit of knowledge more generally, as well as benefiting girls by turning their self-doubt into a virtue rather than a liability.

Some Current Dilemmas for Science Teachers

Within fairly conventional science teaching there are many problems. When I started teaching, the stress was on lots of practical work and worksheets. But it matters what sort of practical work pupils engage in. I could not help feeling that pupils did not know what they were doing, why they were doing it, nor what use it was going to be to them. There was almost a complicity between teacher and pupils: so long as busy activity around apparatus seemed to be occurring and the correct word or number was filled in on the dotted line, neither teachers nor pupils would rock the boat and ask any questions.

There are major dilemmas which characterize school science teaching, which I, like so many others, pondered. As someone trained in the traditional, academic way, how can I step outside that and start to apply myself to practical, everyday things? If most of my scientific knowledge is abstract, how can I begin to make it relevant? Relevant to what, and for whom? If there is an examination syllabus to follow, do I dare cast it aside and present the required knowledge in a different way? If I spend too much time making things or adapting things, surely the pupils won't have time to cover all the material on the syllabus? And what about the pupils? If they get the least hint that I am not teaching them in the way brothers, sisters, or boyfriends have been taught, won't they revolt and demand to be taught in the orthodox way? And teachers might ask: surely these practical, relevant approaches are supposed to be for the less able? They are supposed to be good with their hands, but the more able have too many intellectual concepts to tackle and can't afford to waste time playing about with things! In addition, as teachers, we have enough to do in keeping up with and perfecting the work we are already engaged in without taking on new ideas, approaches and materials. These are very real problems which have involved me in a long struggle over the past fourteen years.

There have been a number of strategies for dealing with these problems. There are science teachers who seek to make science relevant by tackling topics like science of the motorcar, photography, and personal health. They attempt to weave science into everyday life and, by that means, try to make it more interesting. Other science teachers try to embrace science *and* society issues into their teaching. They look at such topics as nuclear power and environmental issues. These contemporary topics *can* all be tackled in interesting ways. However, it is crucial to stress that the relations of teaching and learning are of central importance. Otherwise these topics can assume the same flat and boring character as the more conventional teaching content.

We live in a society in which 'science' and 'technology' are evoked as important parts of social, political and economic life. Yet so many of our pupils turn away from these subjects well before the end of the fifth year. Girls do so more than boys, although the problem is widespread among working-class pupils as a whole. Changing the content, approach, and teaching materials is a start, but it is not nearly enough. It's important to look at the 'what', but the 'how' is often missing. It's the 'how' that is importantly related to gender, and to class. It is this sense of the problems and priorities of science education which feeds into my current teaching.

One Way of Tackling the Dilemmas

At my present school we run a course on technology. The unit is within the context of a contemporary studies course for fourth- and fifth-year pupils, and is taught by most of the staff in the science department. The course comprises a general introduction and a number of options. The options were added because some of the pupils were resistant to going out of the school to visit other workplaces.

The general introduction starts with the question, 'What do we mean by technology?', and that question is pursued throughout the entire course. As a class we are trying to define some of the problems and areas relevant to that question. Here are some of the things we do during the general introduction:

1. We visit the central Post Office Sorting Office at Mount Pleasant in London. This provides the opportunity to show pupils that, despite the introduction of new technology, much of the mail is sorted by hand. Upstairs we can see new equipment introduced to mechanize sorting. Both mechanical and hand sorting are employed simultaneously, so comparisons are immediately available. It's a useful workplace to visit: as so many sites are either in transition, or are working 'old' or 'new' technology. The Post Office is interesting because the two are running in tandem.

2. In our classes, we try to focus on the division of labour, experience, the production line and skill. To start with, each pupil gets a Lego truck. They are asked to dismantle and construct it, and to time how long they take on construction. They do that again and find that practice improves speed. They are then asked to work in groups of five to make six trucks, in any way they want, as fast as possible. The next stage involves the class dividing into two big groups; they're asked to produce trucks in a production line. We'd hoped to use the experience to provide the basis for discussion on skill and work organization. But it takes a long time, and that makes it difficult to follow up all the details. The danger is that we leave pupils with the impression that the production line is the best way, that there is an inevitability about the fragmentation of work. This demonstrates my earlier point that practical work itself is not enough. It has to be qualified with careful analysis with the students in the class.

It might not be obvious why a science department rather than a sociology department is doing the things I described above. It is important to root an understanding in the concreteness of technical experience, and this can best be handled in science teaching.

I have seen some sociological texts on new technology which do not explore the concrete limitations and possibilities of the particular technologies. What I'm trying to give pupils is some sense of the enormous amounts of work that go into technical artefacts, and of the limitations that follow from that. But even in the science department, this has proved to be the most difficult strand in the course.

Unpacking Technology: the Post Office Example

For example, we try to follow up our Post Office visit with work on some of the automated processes in the Sorting Office. This goes far beyond the knowledge of science teachers, so we've had to call upon people with experience of technical work in industry. For instance, we've tried to give some indication of the limitations of Optical Character Recognition (OCR). When they sort the letters automatically, workers read the post code and type it into the sorting machine. This information is then encoded in a string of dots on the envelope. Since our first visit, the Post office have introduced an OCR machine that eliminates the worker's reading of the post code. But that machine works only on bulk mailings where the addresses are typed uniformly. On the visit the obvious question is 'Why have the workers at all, why not let the computer do it?' But when we do the practical work around OCR, it helps pupils appreciate the limited properties of computer technology. The pupils may assume that machines that can recognize typed text today can read handwritten text tomorrow. What I want to show is how *difficult* that kind of computer applicaton is, how difficult it is to get OCR to recognize handwriting.

This is one of the ways in which we try to show the lengthy efforts (and costly research) required to make a machine do a simple task, like recognizing handwriting, which we take for granted. And I think it is important to demonstrate the limitations of machines. By such means we show that workers use a number of unrecognized skills in their daily activities. If pupils, future workers, do actually believe that machines *are* wonderful, that they can do as well as living workers, then this reinforces the self-deprecation that girls in particular acquire and exercise. This relates to the way that women are prepared to sell their skills cheaply because *they*, and others, negate them and are prepared to believe that they have very little skill at all.

Among the options that are available to the pupils are:

1. A comparative study of the carpentry/furniture-building trade and the rag trade. This involves a consideration of the sex stereotyping of jobs and definitions of skill. One of the reasons why this option arose is that the girls often discuss their own experiences of the rag trade. Many local women are employed in sweat shops and small factories: mothers, grandmothers, sisters, aunties of the girls in our school. Those discussions highlight how little the girls value the skills of women in the rag trade. That has parallels with girls' tendency to undervalue their own achievement and their own skills, and here again the *methods* of pedagogy, the 'how', has to go hand in hand with the project of challenging those negative self-evaluations.

One of the ways I've tried to chip away at that lack of self-confidence is by exploring these stereotypical male and female workplaces. We encourage pupils to observe and to question the different ways in which definitions of skill come about. Just because carpentry doesn't come easy to these girls, they are more willing to accept that carpenters should be paid more. Yet when we look at the two workplaces we find that the length of time it takes to learn a job is not necessarily related to how much recognition that skill gets. It's more related to *who* is doing it.

2. Other options include an investigation into the technology London Transport use to control the underground and buses: some examination of the skills and work of people who are employed at the school – laboratory technicians, media resource officers, librarians, and school meals workers. Some pupils also look at medical technology, and visit the Well Woman Clinic at the local hospital.

Examining Domestic Technology

We also look at domestic labour. We started with an old picture of a kitchen, with a maid in it. I cut out masses of 'ideal home' pictures with wonderful ready-made kitchens – all those upmarket adverts with preposterously clean, empty, and *huge* kitchens.

There was quite a range. There's the initial fact of the predominance of women in the pictures, although there's one with a very upper-class man in an apron. We mounted all the pictures and asked the pupils to think about a whole series of questions. For instance: 'What are the visible and implied differences between the old kitchens and the adverts?' 'What do you know about the history of domestic work, and what kind of kitchens people had in the last century?' and so on. All sorts of discussions can arise out of these questions. One picture had maids in it: who were these people? It's interesting, but their first comment is that the old kitchen is cluttered, whereas the new one is clean. You have

by permission of the University of Reading, Institute of Agricultural History and Museum of English Rural Life

to unpack what they mean by cluttered. They usually mean that there are *people* in the kitchen.

We try to talk about kitchens people have in their homes and *advertisements* of kitchens (making the distinction clear). There are other areas to consider – plumbing, machinery, and so on. When people think about technology in the home, they tend to think about toasters and microwave ovens. And yet much more technology was introduced into the house and kitchen earlier in the twentieth century than has been in the last twenty years. What I'm saying is that some of the domestic technology introduced earlier was, in some ways, much more labour-saving and transformative: consider the difference a plumbed water supply made to houseworkers, or the difference electricity made compared to all the dust and dirt of coal fires. (Moreover, there were huge class differences in that work.) There's plenty for the class to work on. For instance, we can discuss the domestic lives of working-class people in London in the thirties, having a roast dinner only on Sundays, or going to the local baker's to bake Sunday dinner in the big ovens there. All that kind of detail helps to set our present domestic arrangements in a historical perspective and to relate domestic labour to domestic technology. As a contrast with today's technology, we take a recipe book which says: 'This is the cook's list of essential tools.' It lists, *none* of this modern stuff like an electric mixer.

We've got a whole series of questions for the pupils to address. They work in small groups and then we have a discussion afterwards. The discussion isn't always successful, but we try to draw out the class differences, and discuss maids and consumer goods – who are the maids today, so to speak.

We find ourselves trying to do too much. An afternoon session goes really quickly. I'm not certain what the girls get out of that work, but it bustles with activity and thought and involvement. Sometimes that is enough!

Although girls of that age are familiar with aspects of domestic labour, babysitting, warming the beans, they do not have experience or control over the full range of domestic work. Yet what they tend to do is to undervalue the skills that they have already acquired. When I tried this material with a small group of sixth-form girls, one thing was clear; they did not recognize any of their own domestic labour that involved technology. And this was in marked contrast to the high value they attributed to masculine competence with other objects of household machinery.

As I mentioned, for a large part of the course we try to get a grasp on what we are talking about when we discuss 'technology'. What does it mean? So we tackle it from that end. And what were the chores that people used to have to do before they got parcelled out in very different ways today? That's an important thing to try to get across.

Thus, in the housework section of the technology course, we use a questionnaire to get the pupils to think about skill and about what is technology within the home. We choose a lot of consumer artefacts found within homes, ranging from lawn mowers to vacuum cleaners to tin openers, anything. We ask the girls to specify who would be likely to use each implement. Does the use require any skill? Who usually maintains it? Who mends it when it goes wrong? How many people have this kind of thing? (Are there class differences, in other words?)

We've not done much with the *answers*; the useful thing was the process of filling in the questionnaire and thinking it through collectively. In the end the girls decided that everything is an artefact or a product of technology, even if not needing some technological skills to be used. So we've tried to get all those things debated.

To introduce an historical dimension, we tried to provoke some discussion on very early technologies. We used a picture of a stone and a bowl for grinding corn. In the present group there are four Bangladeshi girls. And every time we looked at a piece of 'ancient' technology in these pictures, these girls said, 'That's just like in my village at home, Miss.' 'We do that.' Then we considered how old technology was not necessarily regressive technology and new technology not necessarily advanced. We *had* to take on that discussion. And it reminded us that those 'old and new kitchen' pictures were very ethnocentric. But you can't tackle everything. Fortunately we could take up this issue this time because the girls were there to help us. It certainly helped us to raise questions about technological 'progress'.

In describing these examples, I'm not suggesting that they provide a blueprint for teaching girls science. Our technology course is not entirely typical of the kind of teaching that we do throughout the rest of the science department, nor can science departments in other schools easily create the preconditions for such a course. At the same time, surely there is some place for such examples elsewhere within the science curriculum, wherever that occurs on the timetable?

The nature of our technology course will change radically as we establish our new approach lower down the school. At the moment we are expecting the girls to take far too much on board all at once. The girls in the present fourth and fifth years have not had the benefit of the kinds of lower-school science that we are now providing. In a couple of years' time the fourth-year girls will have had far more experience in designing and making things, more opportunities to develop confidence and power over some aspects of the physical world, and more understanding of the historical context out of which the technologies arise. I hope that the cuts in educational resources don't stop us from retaining a core of teachers who can develop this way of working across all years.

Conclusion

I would like to remind the reader of the Introduction describing how this article was put together. A series of discussions like the ones Pam and I held will inevitably result in the kind of 'messiness' that I referred to later on. Under these circumstances I find it difficult to write a conclusion without opening up new areas for further discussion. So here I would like to take the opportunity to widen the debate around the relationship between science and gender at school level.

Publicly, that debate has largely centred on 'equal opportunities' – that is, encouraging more girls to enter the scientific and technical professions. At government, management and political levels, the issue is seen as one of a lot of talent going to waste, when this section of the labour market is suffering from a shortage of skilled labour. Within the feminist movement, various positions have been taken up, ranging from an uncritical complicity with the 'equal opportunities' approach, to a complete rejection of anything scientific or technical; the latter position doesn't want to subject more women to such a male domain – brutalizing, mechanical and alienating. Both extreme positions are completely understandable, and there is plenty of evidence to support each.

Both positions, however, ignore two important points. First, people's sense of alienation from science and technology runs along race and class lines as well as gender lines. At the same time, this country has consistently had difficulty in recruiting pupils and students into the scientific and technical workforce from all class backgrounds. This difficulty is related to the elitist and specialized way in which science teaching has been approached – related, in turn, to the history of our education system.

Second, most people express some kind of fear, ignorance or deference to things scientific or technological, either totally or partly – that is, through specializing in only one particular aspect and thus lacking an overall view. Unless we overcome the poverty of science teaching, decision-making around controversial issues will continue to be portrayed as a matter of technical expertise. This ensures that most people see themselves as unentitled or powerless to engage with these issues, much less to redefine what counts as the problem. And this is why we should be encouraging all girls to maintain an interest in science throughout their schooling.

How should we do that? What are the pitfalls? We need to recognize that girls express interest in certain areas of science (e.g. biology). We must also look at the framework within which the whole of science teaching is currently presented. Mere cosmetic changes to the science curriculum will not succeed. For example, current teaching materials tend to treat 'relevance' as simply a move from the abstract to the concrete, e.g. from pure optical experiments to photography as an application, or from prescribed experiments to 'problem-solving' experiments. Although these moves are an improvement, they still fail to engage with any of the purposes of photography or problem-solving, much less girls' purposes.

It is so tempting to be prescriptive in our teaching methods.

After all, we as science teachers have been the products of this kind of teaching. Prescriptive teaching gives us the security of 'knowing the answers' and covering the work faster. However, such an approach is likely to reinforce the powerlessness felt by pupils, especially girls, with their relative lack of confidence.

Lastly I should mention that the current trend of official thinking is for science education to emphasize process rather than factual memorization. This is a welcome development. Yet it is alarming to see certain groups already seeking ways in which such 'process' can be assessed. There is the inevitable danger that this will result in fragmentation of pupil activities and the kind of prescriptiveness that will yet again render the pupil powerless to engage with the issues.

These are just some of the pitfalls we must avoid in order to overcome race, class and gender divisions in school science. The aim isn't simply to give equal access to the excluded, but to transform what we mean by science and technology.

LABOURING TO LEARN
Women in Adult Education

Mary Kennedy

Women in adult education experience an acute tension between public and private knowledge. They ask for, and are presented with, publicly legitimated knowledge, at the same time as they are engaged in a learning process producing knowledge which receives little recognition. Both forms of knowledge are powerful.

The struggles and changes that have been going on in adult education since the 1970s reflect to some degree the changes in the influence of feminism which has permeated British society. They have involved issues of the power relationships, past and present, between women and men, as well as the changing focus between teaching and learning. The tension is not only between the tradition of authority and specialist knowledge contrasted with student passivity. It also concerns educational methodologies – the teaching and transmission of publicly organized bodies of knowledge, and the informal practices of democratic group learning which start from student experience to work outwards to theoretical understanding. For so long women have heard the injunction of St Paul repeated through the centuries – 'Let your women be silent' – that we have remained muted in public, or tentative, caught in the 'maybe' syndrome, in committee and classroom. Although we have difficulty in projecting authority in public, at the private level we are aware of our own skills and knowledge. Over the last twelve years through women's studies – research, teaching and writing – feminists have begun the process of questioning the differently perceived and received expertise and experience of women and men. This essay will discuss these gender issues within the context of adult education in the belief that such education should be a bridge between the academic and working worlds of women.

Adult Education Provision

In Britain the mainly state-funded adult education service is the chief provider of post-school education ranging from basic literacy, sport, languages, domestic and mechanical skills, the arts and crafts up to university-taught subjects. It is distinct from higher and further education provision because it has open access for all students and, apart from the Open University and a few university diplomas, its courses are non-examined. The ideal is life long, continuing and flexible education at low or no fees which adults can freely enter and leave, to study at all sorts of levels in a wide variety of subjects. The theory is that the different kinds of provision will be a vital lifeline for extending learning opportunities both collectively and individually for mature students, as well as for re-educating them for changes both inside and outside employment. Most adult educators believe that their education is open to change because it responds flexibly to student demand and invites student participation in devising courses. Indeed, many believe passionately in education as a motor for change in society and in the individual.

Yet the reality is somewhat different. The provision is fragmented by a variety of providers – the Local Education Authorities (LEAs), the Workers Educational Association (WEA), university extramural and adult education departments, as well as voluntary organizations. The provision also varies greatly from region to region, as do the types and levels of classes on offer. Adult education lacks a strong power base, despite an annual turnover of nearly two million students, because only 0.66 per cent of the national education budget is spent on the service (*TES*). It is not only squeezed by the big battalions in the politics of education – the large school sector, the status of the universities and polytechnics in higher education, and the expansion of further education colleges; it is also under-resourced and lacks any well-researched methodology of its own.

Historically, adult education is burdened by the contradiction between its leisure-recreation image, its utilitarian vocationalism and its missionary educational aspirations of a service open to all. This contradiction can lead to confused aims and ineffective provision. Currently there is a struggle going on between the philosophy of an open-access education service committed to providing a variety of subjects at low fees for all adults and the vocational training policy of a government which treats education in the commercial terms of the needs of the labour market and a return on investment. Such government policy is curtailing extension academic education, as provided by the Open University, the university adult education and extramural departments and the WEA; it has also skewed the broad adult education provision in the local authority sector – the main provider. We are now in a situation where the main trunk is being starved of funding at the roots and many branches cut off, while certain new branches, carefully shaped and controlled – adult literacy, courses for the unemployed, specified technology training and skills-based courses, etc. – are funded and allowed to flourish through special and temporary support which can be lopped off at any arbitrary point as decided by the choppers in the Department of Education and Science. The result is an increasing bureaucratization with complicated formulas for state funding based on a sliding scale of payment by results for 'innovatory work among the disadvantaged' as long as the fees are raised for the ordinary student. This may provide full-time employment for the grey-suited, grey-minded desk organizers, but does little for the average adult student, who is not wealthy, highly educated nor necessarily working in an upwardly mobile career structure.

Women in Adult Education

Within the adult education service women are to be found predominantly in middle management rather than at the principal or head of department levels, whilst they make up the majority among part-time tutors who do most of the teaching. Women are also a majority of the students, reversing their situation in further and higher education. In 1981–2 there were an estimated 1.5 million students in LEA adult education and youth centres in England and Wales, of whom 1 million (65 per cent) were women. In addition 173,682 (58 per cent) students studying in university extramural departments were women; and women made up 59 per cent of the 122,001 students studying in WEA classes in the UK (DES). In many respects adult education is a 'women's service' (Keddie, 1981), studented by women, serviced by women and run by men. Yet women are so invisible that the typical student is still invariably described as 'he'.

Truthfully speaking there are no 'typical' students, even though women in particular tend to be lumped together because of their biological and familial roles as seen by education organizers. Thus, although some attention is paid to the economic background of women students, this is defined in terms of their husband's occupational status; the dependency of the unwaged housewife is ignored. Single women or single parents pay their way in fees or are allowed concessions if unemployed or on social security. But all women can be penalized because they get no concessions if they are low waged or doing part-time work. Class and race also tend to be ignored in the philosophy of an education service declaring itself open to all adults and yet denying the political significance of those divisions.

The table presents a general statistical picture of the adult

Adults in continuing non-examination education
England and Wales, 1980
(as percentage of population)

Age	Men %	Women %	Class	Men %	Women %
17–24	20	22	AB	10	23
25–44	14	13	C_1	18	21
45–64	5	10	C_2	7	11
65–75	4	9	D/E	6	5
All	11	13	All	11	13

Note: Figures include the 2% currently in full-time initial education.

Source: ACACE, 1982.

student body in continuing non-examination education in 1980, by age, social class and sex, as a percentage of the total adult population in each grouping. It is important to understand that although the proportions of women and men are fairly equal in the under-forty-five age groups, the figures are deceptive since men are found more commonly on full-time or sandwich courses, in vocationally related courses, or in classes leading to qualifications. Women, in comparison, are more often found in part-time, non-advanced general courses which are not vocationally related, and carry no qualifications. But they outnumber men by more than two to one in part-time, non-vocational education in the over-forty-five age groups, most notably in the pre-retirement stage when some women are being freed from childcare responsibilities and want to develop themselves with new interests, or to return to paid work. The figure of 44 per cent of women students coming from the top three social classes further confirms the fact that at present adult education caters for those who have had the longest initial (school) education and yet have not had easy access to higher or specialist vocational education and training.

This factor of keenness to participate in post-school education does raise the issue of whether women should be considered as a deprived group, regardless of their social class placings, because of their common economic dependency if married, and the lower earning possibilities for most of them. When their efforts to study are dismissed as 'wives trying to catch up with their husbands' (ACACE 1982), there is obviously a credibility gap in failing to take women seriously in their desire for educational improvement.

At the other end of the social scale it is men who make up the majority of adult literacy and numeracy students in basic education classes. The reasons for the lower take-up rate from women are complex. Juliet McCaffery argues that women are not seen to be held back in the same way as men; and that administrative ignorance, poor resourcing (creches, transport, timing, etc.), and lack of interest reflect the low importance attached to women's education both by men and by women themselves. It would seem that the image of adult education provision, as well as the language used to advertise courses, particularly skills-based classes of all kinds, fails to overcome women's fears of being publicly exposed as ignorant or incapable. There is little understanding on the part of the policy-makers that, for many undereducated women, to step out of their front doors into a class is a political act of courage. Once they take this step, particularly into one of the generic 'return-to-study' type courses, the majority are exhilarated by the second-chance possibilities and the increase in confidence of the 'it changed my life' variety.

Since 1975 a number of official reports have pointed out the need for wider educational and training opportunities for women, based on the argument that the country cannot afford to neglect the potential of one half of the population on practical grounds. Yet there is a fair amount of evidence to show the mismatch between women's perceptions of their education and training needs, and the opportunities available to them in course provision and employment prospects. One comprehensive government survey published in 1984 revealed that the majority of women want long-term paid employment with only a short career break, and that many also want better training and improved career opportunities (HMSO, 1984). In the *Times Educational Supplement* a reviewer of a 1984 television documentary, *Class of '62*, pertinently remarked: 'What shone through was the women's great longing for education and training. All the concentration, commitment and self-assertion that had been lacking at sixteen was in bud by twenty-six, in full bloom by thirty-six.' This highlights the particular problems of women's different education

Cath Jackson

needs at times different from men within both the school and post-school system.

We still lack in-depth research into the motivational factors in adult learning which might investigate how women and men may be differently connected to the world and to the existing curricula. In so many ways the education of adult women is still restricted by rarely admitted assumptions about the different needs and abilities of men and women, particularly the latter's ties to familial relationships. Given women's generally disadvantaged position in our society, their special needs – such as creches for those with children, flexible timetabling, low or no fees, accessible public transport – are still not considered as normal provision in the same sense that a room, tutor, heating and lighting arc considered to be the essential minimum for all adult classes. Likewise the choice of subjects on offer in the daytime classes, attended mainly by women, are all too often restricted to art, crafts and domestic subjects rather than providing a wider variety of subjects for study, whether academic or skills-based.

The Influence of Feminism

Many of these assumptions and practices have been challenged and modified by small groups of feminists who have led the educational vanguard in the last twelve years to establish a base for women's studies and different kinds of women's education.

They started first in the WEA and university extramural departments, and more recently in the LEA sector. Women's studies have provided an educational environment where women can rediscover women's lives and achievements, and use feminist research to question and reinterpret knowledge afresh. They have also begun the process of introducing a feminist dimension across the curriculum, putting gender considerations into courses as a normal part of adult learning. This feminist dimension, which has to be taken on board by men as well as women tutors, operates at various levels in the curriculum. It means not just putting women back into history, but also examining the relationship between women and men in the past, exploring why women were invisible in certain periods or classes, and what sources have been used. It involves revising accepted ideas about work, as in the debates about housework or the implications of the reality that although women retire from paid employment, they rarely retire from domestic work.

Certainly feminist educators and tutors have promoted a greater awareness of the gender bias in education, and have shifted the emphasis away from methodologies of how to transmit knowledge towards one of process, of shared learning in groups. But that 'perspective transformation' is not yet firmly grounded; nor are the power relationships between women and men altered radically within the education institutions. Feminists have struggled to introduce organizational change through collective strategies such as women's networks and equal opportunities working groups within institutions and the trade unions. There is a greater awareness now, but the changes are concessionary and piecemeal. Tokenism still rules. In the education of women, as defined by feminists, the aim is to transmit skills and knowledge combined with a critical understanding of the politics of culture, which enable women to have more control over their lives.

Commonly held beliefs about women, seen as somehow deficient males, suppose and impose a gender-biased scale of values, reproduced within adult education[1]. According to Julia Berryman: 'Sex difference research has shown that, whilst there is evidence for differences in intelligence between men and women, these differences are minimal, and in many cases probably caused more by environmental than biological factors. For educational purposes men and women are best regarded as having equal potential.' Yet the old attitudes and divisions persist, such as in the crude derision of the proverbial saying: 'To educate woman is to put a knife in the hand of a monkey', quoted by a working-class woman student on an extramural history course, who was studying despite the scepticism of local friends (*Adult Education*, 1983). This derision is a familiar experience for many women who return to study seriously in adult classes.[2]

What Holds Women Back?

There are, then, heavy psychological barriers as well as institutional restrictions of custom and practice, culturally defined, for women to climb over, to break through, to challenge. The perception of what constitutes special knowledge, skill or expertise is embedded in the division of roles and labour between women and men. Thus the technical expertise of the housewife or her community involvement are not rated, even by her, as special knowledge to be taught formally to others; she may just pass them on informally as tips for survival. Male trade unionists will test a female tutor in industrial studies until she proves her knowledge and authority, but they will accept the teaching of a doctor on health issues without question. It is doubtful that men would fit very happily into a tutorless health study group, as women do, because they would not consider this proper education – just women talking.

The professional tutor is the agent intervening in the educational process to translate internally learned skills and knowledge from the private to the public domain. Because of the dominant ideology, this person can colonize a great deal of knowledge and experience which has not been recognized as valid until it has been removed from the private domestic and unpaid area of women's activities. Quite apart from the current debates on the validation of women's managerial and technical expertise in running a home for entry into higher and further education, most women can and do have a perception of their knowledge which they assess differently from most men. For example, in a study of 'working class housewives and the world of work', Marilyn Porter found that

> many of the others [other housewives], having said that they knew nothing about politics and weren't interested, then went on to include among their interests housing, prices, welfare services, care of children and old people, local amenities and sometimes even things like earthquakes or wars. All these things were described as 'not political' – and that left (effectively) industrial affairs and parliamentary politics . . .

This is a pertinent illustration of the different hierarchies of knowledge as commonly defined by men and women. Politics equals party and trade-union activities, which are men's interests and important. The working-class women here rejected the 'political' label for themselves, yet the issues that interested them are closer to the word's original meaning.

Translated into education provision, this division was highlighted in a recent advertisement by an education institute for a class on motor maintenance 'for ladies of little ability'. (Quite rightly, it did not recruit any students.) Here is an example of an educational institution dutifully trying to put into practice an equal opportunities policy which the adult education organizer felt was inappropriate, since mending cars is traditionally a skill in the masculine sphere. In another sense, the progressive retitling of girls' and women's cookery classes – as domestic science, home economics and now food and nutrition studies (currently called human ecology in the USA) – was an attempt by educational reformers to raise the status of this vocational subject into a 'science'. But this skill, almost universally considered to be domestic, and therefore female, is rife with contradictions: women are cooks (private, domestic, and unpaid), while the few men who study it are chefs (public, recognized, and paid). As a traditional women's subject, it is held in low esteem within the hierarchy of curriculum subjects, yet is one of the main ways of attracting into adult education large numbers of students which help maintain the service. Such classes are in effect women-only classes: often men are actively discouraged from joining them. And yet little is done within them to change the sexual division of labour in the home, such as by positively encouraging women to think about the reasons for their domestic role position, or by encouraging men to learn these skills for themselves.

Despite the fact that women have been using technology inside and outside the home for a long time, they find it difficult in practice to transfer the principles of their domestic expertise across into another sphere. Given the encouragement and shown the links with household budgeting, Second Chance students in women-only classes find they can learn mathematics quite easily. Making visible such an intellectual skill breaks down one barrier so that they feel able to move on to a more advanced level of study. The crucial link in the chain is to find a way of enabling women to cross the divide from personal modesty into public confidence. Karen Alexander, a video worker, describes the process in working with a group of black young mothers in Lewisham:

> I went there and talked to them for weeks before they had enough confidence to make a tape. In the end they decided to make one about the attitudes they found really annoying when they told people they were pregnant. They made the situation quite comic: they took on the roles of their parents, their boyfriends and the doctors, and really exaggerated them. At the same time they were learning how to use the equipment, and then they edited the tape. The whole process took a long time and some of them got bored after a while . . . I think the experience was useful because before that they wouldn't ever have imagined themselves learning to use video equipment and producing a tape . . . (*Feminist Review*)

It is not that women always want to learn different things from men, but that they may want to learn them in different ways. Recent feminist research has shown that girls and women are more interested in the human and social applications of science and technology subjects, that they are not interested in studying a subject in isolation from the environment.[3] Thus women students will join classes to study conservation and the environment, but will shy away from an economics course. Transport studies bore them with techniques and statistics, but in the context of community-based women's education they can learn how to analyse public transport structures and the economic aspects most easily because the approach starts with their knowledge and then works outwards. The Greenham women's example has provided the inspiration for the revival of peace studies, not necessarily on technological grounds alone, but because they have reopened the issue publicly on ethical and emotional grounds – a terrain which is considered to be female and private.

In another sense, more difficult to assess, many women seem to be caught in a trap, lacking the confidence to choose what they think it is important to study, and choosing instead what they think is expected of them. An ACACE Report found that women and men chose the traditional gender-divided areas as new subjects for study: 53 per cent of women chose languages and domestic science as their first two options, compared with 25 per cent of the men; 18 per cent of the men, and only 6 per cent of the women, asked for carpentry and do-it-yourself classes; and only 11 per cent of the men, compared with 16 per cent of the women, said they would like to study creative subjects (art, painting, sculpture and pottery). The report went on to comment on general cultural and creative subject classes, where more women than men participate: 'We do not know, however, whether this genuinely relates to differences in interest or temperament between men and women, or whether men *simply do not have the time* because of the pressing need for work-related courses' (my italics). The implication that it is more necessary for men than for women to take work-related courses is blind like Justice: men already have more professional qualifications than women, yet over 40 per cent of women do paid work. Women seem to feel that if they are attending daytime adult education classes and spending household money (their wages?), they should take work-related (i.e. domestic or practical) subjects themselves. But there is another element. Most women are diffident in tackling subjects new to them or perceived to be masculine, in which they lack either an informal childhood experience of messing about with electronics and machines, or the confidence to articulate ideas in university liberal studies classes for adults. My colleagues have observed that in science and philosophy courses women seem to be inhibited from speaking even when their understanding of the subject is equal to that of the men in the group.

A further difficulty is that even when women are present and keen to learn, this is invisible or just not noticed. The BBC's computer literacy project was set up in the assumption that it would be more relevant to men than to women, and so weighted the test sample accordingly: 62 per cent men compared with 38 per cent women. It turned out that the audience for the Monday night programmes was made up of 47 per cent women and 53 per cent men. The only comment on this unexpected result was a one-liner: that there was 'a slight over-representation of men' (BBC, 1983). Recently there has been a spate of articles and reports expressing concern about the developing tendency to mark computer studies as for boys and men; yet the evidence shows that girls and women, given the opportunity and a sympathetic learning environment, are just as interested and can perform equally intelligently. Of course it is not only the assumptions implying the 'maleness' of computers which can inhibit women from learning how to use them, but also the language used to advertise classes, which can suggest that they are more appropriate to men than to women. According to the 1982 ACACE Report, only 1 per cent of women compared with 6 per cent of men had taken computer studies courses.

These are some of the contributory cultural and psychological factors which inhibit women. They are compounded by other obstacles: the different patterns of learning needs at different times from men, part-time tutors' dependence on next year's contract, their powerlessness to make radical changes in the curriculum, the question of fees, access to classes, poor child-care facilities, and lack of transport. Thus we can begin to understand some of the major difficulties of women within adult education. The question is: what is to be done?

Processes for Change

When education undervalues women's experiential knowledge, this reflects the way the world works outside. Of course it is impossible for educationalists alone to transform society. But adult educators open to change can begin by radically rethinking the curriculum, the provision of courses, the methodology; they can also alter the power structures to reflect the reality that women make up some 60 per cent of the student body and a high proportion of the teaching staff in the lower grades.

Because it would be unrealistic to expect men voluntarily to give up their power and control of resources, women will have to push for the changes by themselves most of time. And we will find that we are pushing not only against power networks, but also against the conservative inertia of the tried system and the traditional subject: 'It works all right, so why bother with all this business of change and upheaval?' One person's balance is another's bias. The problem is that there are plenty of education workers, both women and men, who, while acknowledging some injustices in the system and bias in the knowledge, would prefer to stay within the confines of a knowledge they know, where they are safely accepted, provided they keep to their station in the hierarchy, rather than risk responsibility for the unknown and the contentious.

Such attitudes are perpetuated by the acceptable educational provision of classes, laid on by men in the majority of cases, for women and taught by women. These are the traditional female fashion, beauty care and household crafts in the local education authority sector. One-third of all classes, this was the largest type of provision in the late 1970s (Mee and Wiltshire), and the situation has not greatly changed since then. Feminist critics have had to tread a delicate path here, because it was and is important not to devalue the special expertise and knowledge that women already have. The struggle has been on two fronts. One strategy is to raise the status of such subjects within the overall curriculum, so that domestic production and reproduction and its arts are valued as equally important contributions to society's well-being as are industrial production and 'high' art. It is also a question of developing the tutors of these skills into educators: to encourage their professional expertise, often painfully acquired with little family support, and to raise their awareness as teachers about taking their subject skills into broader educational territories.

The other strategy has concentrated on extending the educational content of these subjects, so that not only are so-called 'neutral' skills being taught, but also a critical understanding of the context of the subject matter: the economics of marketing in the food and the fashion trades, the cultural and class content of cookery in our own and other societies; an examination of the chemical properties of beauty-care products and what conditions women to use them. The aim is to encourage and extend thinking rather than a compliant acceptance of received knowledge.

There have been extensions also into the so-called 'male' subject areas as feminist educators strive to demystify manual and mechanical skills in which women have normally not had much practice. Often women lack the confidence to tackle them because they could find themselves lone intruders in an environment in which both tutors and students disapprove of their presence; also, because they have to prove themselves competitively in order to be accepted, women tend to drop out. In such courses women are coming from a different learning experience and may need intensive priming; this is one reason for women-only classes taught by women tutors. Classes for women in bricklaying, plumbing, electronics, DIY, car maintenance, woodwork, welding and mathematics are examples of such work. They have been taught successfully in women's workshops or centres such as those in East Leeds, Haringey and Lambeth, in courses initiated by the Women in the Manual Trades group, and in various adult education institutes. But they have been less successful on the now-extinct TOPS schemes or in skills-based courses run by the MSC, where there has been official resistance to providing women-only classes, child-care facilities or flexible timetabling to suit women's responsibilities and needs.

It is indicative of the barriers women face that such women-only classes have to be specially designated as 'training' by the Department of Employment under the law; if not so designated, then, in practice, similar classes must be on offer for men alongside them. Furthermore, as is also the case with technology and computer studies, funding is often hard to find within the scarce adult education resources, so a great deal of time has to be devoted to negotiating grants from various organizations. There is a question mark over whether these courses are education or training. Furthermore, many women may have difficulty in finding jobs in the skills in which they have trained and which they enjoy practising.

If employers are reluctant to admit them to skilled jobs, and if skilled male workers protect their monopoly, then women remain marginalized on the edges of skilled work.

Since the mid-1970s there have been a number of reports and training programmes concerned to get women into science, engineering and technology, often on the grounds that we cannot afford not to train them and make use of their abilities. There have therefore been some particular 'intervention' policies – such as the UN Decade for Women 1975–85, the recent Women into Science and Engineering (WISE) year, as well as the special public funding of women's groups such as Women and Computing (Microsyster), the Women's Technology Scheme in Liverpool, the MSC/Open University 'women in technology' scheme (updating for returners), and the Haringey Women's Training and Education Centre courses in microelectronics and computing, as well as preparatory courses in the construction trade. Though mature women students enjoy learning such skills and gaining confidence in managing the new technologies, women have found difficulty in getting employment. Their training and expectations are not matched by employers' willingness to accommodate women's needs and timetables.

But there is also a danger that this fashionable emphasis on vocational training may become restricted to behavioural training and operational skills, at the expense of the broader and critical understanding which education should impart. Thus when Margaret Bruce and Gill Kirkup discuss retraining programmes for clerical workers and assembly-line factory workers, the deskilled areas where women work, they argue that 'the uncritical provision of retraining courses for women in these areas simply reinforces the gendered nature of the work, and women's own perception of themselves as "untechnical".'

By this they mean that most such courses prepare women only for specific jobs which are already classified and segregrated as women's work, even if the technology may be new or different. Such training is concerned more with achieving an automatic technical skill than with providing an understanding of the effects of the technology on the organization of the work or the decreasing spaces left for personal initiative and responsibility. Rather than being a training for life, it is a training to fit into the system.

Conversely, there is a failure of equal opportunities policies to include 'a campaign to help men to learn the skills required for domestic responsibilities, caring, secretarial and other support and service jobs, located in female gendered terrain' (Cockburn). Certainly this is an area of female expertise where adult education in general has hardly moved at all in extending the education and training of men, except in the few men's studies classes which started in 1982, and sometimes in psychology classes on 'Changing roles of men and women', or the training of a few men as child-care workers. It is the familiar story of offering women access to 'men's work' by training them for another job skill to fit the economy's needs, whilst not relieving them of their customary household and child-rearing responsibilities – the double burden. *Plus ça change, plus c'est la même chose.*

Strategies for Change

Women's educational confidence and awareness has been raised by the innovatory approaches being developed around the areas of experiential learning. Many of these have evolved out of women's liberation movement groups on consciousness-raising; some are adaptations of Paolo Freire's 'conscientization' process in Brazil and Chile, where teachers and learners worked together, drawing upon their own experience to make their own educational materials, develop an awareness of their own oppression, and learn how to overcome it.

Somewhat similar approaches are being used in the development of new methodologies, adapted from the USA, to identify positively the learned life-skills of women, which can then be validated in a form acceptable for entry into further or higher education, or just used to help women improve their concept of self or self-confidence. The only residential government-funded college for adult women in the UK, Hillcroft College, has since 1983 run several short courses for local women called 'Valuing your Experience'. Working in a supportive group environment with tutors as counsellors, women can examine their life and work experiences, analyse these positively in terms of the learning (skills, knowledge, qualities) they have acquired, and then move on to consider the restraints on their lives and how they might begin to develop practical strategies for their personal educational or career development (Hartree and Marum). In the process of re-evaluating their prior learning experience, the students also learn to look critically at traditional categories of evaluation – jobs, money, status and the paraphernalia of success.

This is a philosophy concentrating on women's strengths and making publicly visible, first to themselves and then to others, the breadth of their expertise in the management of home and family and other unpaid, uncertificated areas of living. The New Directions for Older Women, New Opportunities for Women, Fresh Horizons, Fresh Start, Second Chance, Return-to-Study are other examples of courses for women offering space and support for study and communication skills, educational and work reassessment, and refresher courses in literature, history, sociology, mathematics, and the sciences. Some of these kinds of short courses also help on interview skills, and how to write curricula vitae. In one example of good practice, at a Greenwich unemployed women's class, the group redesigned a job application form so that the applicant could explain her life and work experience (i.e. knowledge) as a single parent and voluntary community worker in relationship to what she could offer; not whether she had been in HM Forces or got 'O' levels which did not fit her life and work experience. She got the job.

In a similar mould, assertion training classes have proliferated in recent years, as have self-defence classes for women. When, in London in the early 1980s, the demands for self-defence classes began because of violence against women, it seemed as though the structures and regulations of the Inner London Education Authority (ILEA) would not be able to respond. It was a non-subject as far as the College of Physical Education was concerned – only training in one of the four recognized martial arts was appropriate. Besides, there were no recognized tutors to teach it. The women's self-defence groups had developed an interdisciplinary approach combining the teaching of physical techniques with experiential learning based upon students' discussion of their fears and attitudes and practical strategies, such as how to joke your way out of a threatening situation; yet they were outside the educational structures. Women worked together with the new Women's Studies inspector, who was able to negotiate with the Physical Education inspectorate, to develop a new form of group validation. Prospective tutors came together with women experienced in self-defence in small supportive groups to define their individual training needs and to evaluate whether they were ready to teach, to become co-tutors, or to have more training. By the end of the summer of 1982 there were enough tutors to start the new classes in the autumn, although the demand outran the numbers of tutors available (ILEA *Contact*). More importantly the process, the group training and interdisciplinary ethos made visible a radical and practical way of developing women's skills educationally and co-operatively, by finding a way of validating women's knowledge without relying on the authority of the inspectorate for approval.

Another interesting model, at a more academic level, is the recent Technology Assessment method developed at the Open University for the 'Changing Experience of Women' summer school. It was unusual in that it was an input into a social sciences and arts summer course, so the tutors had to design material which students with no technological background could respond to and learn from quickly. There were three aims:

> First we wanted to demonstrate that technology is not value-free, and that patterns of technological change in society depend upon a combination of social factors and historical circumstances so that changes in society are related to changes in technology, and that women are more alienated from the technology they experience than are men. Second, we wanted to teach a few basic skills of technology assessment and attempt to develop criteria for evaluating the impact of technology on women. Finally we wanted to build confidence in the women students, so that they could use the assessment skills and their own experience to evaluate, and ultimately influence, aspects of technology that are specially relevant to them.

The groups examined contraceptive technology and transport technology using a mixture of shared-group brainstorming to demystify the technological aspects, and the charting of first-, second- and third-order effects of the subjects, which collectively contributed to a critical understanding of the gendered nature of these technologies (Bruce *et al.*, 1984). This is another way of helping students to have the confidence through co-operative group study, to understand how certain technologies affect them, how these technologies have developed, and how with this knowledge they can be better understood, if not controlled by the users.

Such participatory processes in women's studies classes make academic and scientific knowledge less abstract, less alienating, because the tutor and students together control the pace of how and what to learn, which is tested against both the individual and group experience in a non-competitive way. This process transfers mixed skills contributed by the group in a learning situation, and transforms them by analytical processes into a critical understanding of the subject being studied. It is a positive way of working educationally which draws women out because it uses their knowledge and experience concretely, and moves from the personal outwards to the theoretical.

Of course, we are still in the midst of continuing debates about the hierarchies of knowledge as well as the processes of learning. There is resistance and there is movement, but the reconciliation between public and private forms of knowledge, particularly for women, has not yet been reached.

Notes

Many thanks to members of the editorial collective – especially Pam Linn, Les Levidow and Maureen McNeil – for their helpful and constructive criticism, and their patience.

1. Jean Baker Miller points to one understanding of the way in which the concepts and cultural knowledge of our society are formed:

   A dominant group, inevitably, has the greatest influence in determining a culture's overall outlook – its philosophy, morality, social theory, and even its science. The dominant group, thus, legitimizes the unequal relationship and incorporates it into society's guiding concepts. The social outlook, then, obscures the true nature of this relationship – that is, the very existence of inequality. The culture explains the events that take place in terms of other premises, premises that are inevitably false, such as racial or sexual inferiority . . .' (p. 8).

2. ACACE, in this national survey, deduced that 15 per cent of women compared with 7 per cent of men had not been able to do full-time study because 'the

family objected'; the figures for part-time study were 8 per cent and 2 per cent respectively.

3. See amongst others: Women's National Commission, *The Other Half of Our Future*, 1985; *Times Higher Education Supplement*, 8 November 1985.

References

ACACE, Advisory Council for Adult and Continuing Education, *Adults: Their Educational Experience and Needs*, 1982.

Karen Alexander, 'Video Worker', interviewed by Mica Nava in *Feminist Review* 18 (Winter 1984).

Sarah Bayliss, *Times Educational Supplement*, 3 December 1982.

Julia Berryman, *Sex Differences in Behaviour: Their Relevance for Adult Educators*, University of Nottingham 1981.

BBC, *The Computer Literacy Project: An Evaluation*, 1983.

Cynthia Brown, 'Confessions of an Autodidact', *Adult Education 56*, 3 (December 1983)

Margaret Bruce and Gill Kirkup, 'Post-Experience Courses in Technology for Women', *Adult Education*, *58*, 1 (June 1985).

Margaret Bruce *et al.*, *Teaching Technology Assessment to Women*, Open University, 1984.

Cynthia Cockburn, 'Teaching Technology', unpublished BSA Conference paper, April 1984, quoted by Bruce and Kirkup.

Department of Education and Science Statistics, 1982.

HMSO, *A Lifetime Perspective*, 1984.

Mary Hughes and Mary Kennedy, *New Futures: Changing Women's Education*, Routledge & Kegan Paul, 1985.

ILEA, the Inner London Education Authority, *Contact*, 7 May 1982.

Anne Hartree, and Maggie Marum, *Valuing your Experience: a Tutor's Handbook*, Hillcroft College/Manpower Services Commission, 1985.

Nell Keddie, unpublished paper, 1982.

Juliet McCaffery, 'Women in Literacy and Basic Adult Education: Barriers to Access', in Hughes and Kennedy, *New Futures: Changing Women's Education*, Routledge & Kegan Paul, 1985.

Joan Baker Miller, *Towards a New Psychology of Women*, Penguin, 1976.

L. G. Mee, and H. C. Wiltshire, *Structure and Performance in Adult Education*, Longman, 1978.

Marilyn Porter, 'Standing on the Edge: Working Class Housewives and the World of Work', in Jackie West, *Women, Work and the Labour Market*, Routledge & Kegan Paul, 1982.

Jane Thompson, *Learning Liberation: Women's Responses to Men's Education*, Croom Helm, 1983.

Times Educational Supplement, 'Is it too late for the class of '62?', 3 February 1984.

Technology

GENDER STEREOTYPES, TECHNOLOGY STEREOTYPES

Pam Linn

Referring to the absence of women in high-status jobs, a friend offered an explanation: 'Women don't get offered jobs because they have babies.'

This kindly socialist would not be persuaded by argument: women do not have babies all the time, sometimes not at all, childbirth does not necessarily imply extensive time off, child-bearing is distinct from child-rearing, men have a greater propensity to change jobs, and on and on. He would not accept that – from the point of view of the employer – 'women have babies' is an irrational basis for choice, that it does not make sense to give this priority over other social characteristics; it seems like a fact, yet for an individual employer it is no more or less a fact than the instability of young people. Do employers reject all fifty-year-old men on grounds of heart disease? Again and again he returned to the fixed fact, 'But women have babies!' Such an argument, appealing to an apparent biological certainty, may dissolve on inspection, although biological 'facts' may take some dissolving. I did not deny the biological part of his argument, but I tried to show how the operation of prejudice – sexist employment practices – comes from giving pre-eminence to one bit of biology out of the mass of other social factors.

Referring to the forms of domination and control associated with technology, another friend offered his scepticism: 'I've read all that stuff in *Radical Science* about science and technology as a labour process, but there are real bits of technology. You might say they are embodiments of past labour, but they are real; you can't just define them away!'

This friend also presented an apparently irrefutable fact, a fixed point of departure for debate and political action. I did not deny the material science part of his argument, but tried to show how his argument was as partial as the biologism of 'women have babies'. How a focus on the *hardware* of technology gives pre-eminence to material science, out of a mass of other social factors. I tried to show how such technicism was as selective in its data and as discriminatory in its consequences as biologism. 'Women have babies' is well-trodden feminist ground. 'Technology is about things' is a hard substance to dissolve. The following pages attempt to do this.

The discussion runs as follows: the first section discusses definitions of technological practice from a class perspective, and the second section from a gender perspective; thirdly I describe the difficulties encountered in generating a practical definition of technology.

'Capital's Technology'

Technology is presented in contradictory ways: here used by capitalist management to control and exploit labour; there an instrument of male power; and there again holding out the promise of liberating people from day-to-day labour. How can socialists and feminists achieve a subversive grasp on this many-headed phenomenon?

The rise and rise of labour-process analysis has brought technology firmly on to the socialist agenda (see, for example, Marx, Braverman, Zimbalist, Wood, Thompson). Braverman and successive writers have seen the technology of production as a weapon wielded by capitalist management to discipline paid labour. I believe the political consequences of considering technology in this way have been disastrous. Technology has been held responsible for deskilling, job-killing, worsening health and safety conditions, increases in the pacing, control and surveillance of workers, and so on. The focus has been on technology, on hardware, on fixed capital. But there is more to technology than hardware, more than inert matter. On its own, matter is nothing at all. For us it never exists in that asocial sense. It is always constituted in the social practices of language and other forms of representation, in traditions of use, with associated techniques and training procedures, in domains of knowledge, and in relations of production and consumption. In short, technology is a cultural product.

Radical Science readers may object to this. They may argue that some cultural practices are more fixed than others. Whilst they may agree that the apparent immutability of technology may be dissolved into related practices – all of which are historically embedded and resistant to change – some may well argue that there is a clear distinction to be made between *physical* embodiments of past labour and other expressions of past labour (a training programme, say, or a way of speaking about particular technologies). And I do recognize that there is something particularly certain and rigid about a *physical technological product*. The appearance of a completed product makes a compelling statement about its inevitable effects. But *Radical Science* has always tried to reintroduce mutability into things that appear to be given: the certainties of physical products are as amenable to critique as any other social phenomenon.

The central concepts of the Marxian labour process are those of dead labour and living labour. In purposeful work, people (living labour) use tools and materials (dead labour) for useful production. Braverman and his followers have paid little attention to the relations *between* dead and living labour, except in so far as they emphasize the oppressive and determining ways in which capital's technology acts on living labour. But there is more to the dead/living distinction than that. Acted upon by living labour, the same technological products can both empower *and* constrain purposeful work. Only living labour can set purposes, reflect, reconsider, and reset purposes for productive work because only living labour, only consciousness, has the power to respond to the variabilities of the social world.

Labour-process writers, and their industrial relations colleagues, have focused narrowly on the taken-for-granted technical. The assembly line looms large in Braverman and in much industrial relations literature. Heavily masculine and physicalist, seen as a linear string of minute labour processes, the line has become a metaphor for capital's control and degradation of work. The experience of assembly-line work *is* surely one of rigidity and lack of autonomy.

But there is a broader context: an assembly line can only be *one* part of a productive enterprise: even in the most line-focused industries there are probably as many people off the line as on it. The assembly line is not the only site where technological products are produced and consumed. Most people do not work on visible assembly lines, and other workplaces exert similar kinds of compulsion without capital's technology. When I worked as a temporary teacher in an inner-city school I would pray for the clock to tick over to 3.30 p.m. Nurses and early-morning cleaners are similarly bound to their work by forces other than fixed capital. Is it not technicist to attribute the social relations entirely to the assembly line? I do not want to dispute the physical existence of the assembly line, but to draw attention to the ways in which one bit of physics (itself open to contest) gets given priority out of a mass of other social factors.

What makes the totality of a technological product? Not the physical product alone, not solely those workers who play a visible part in its manufacture, not only those workers – paid and unpaid – who add their labour to consume the product, to release its usefulness. There are other sets of workers who play an equally constitutive role: market researchers and copy-writers who commodify the product, journalists and teachers whose representational work contributes to the ideological character of particular forms of fixed capital.

There are parallels here with film criticism. No one would suppose that film consisted entirely of celluloid or of actors and film crew. Financiers, audiences, critics and the wider ideological context are all seen as constitutive of the filmic phenomenon. The domestic car provides another example. The product of capital's oppressive technology of production, the car is firmly seen as technological. Yet there is more to cars than pressed metal. More than a tool and product for men and women workers, more than an expression of multi- and trans-national capital, the car acts also as a symbol of sexuality, executive and company status, family norms, prudence, or levity. Agitation around the issue of lead-free petrol, increases in road tax, and the uncertainties of the oil market have, however slightly, caused a shift in attitudes towards this cultural product. The car is constituted by circumstances outside the control of General Motors.

It seems daft to narrow down possible areas of political action merely by using a taken-for-granted conception of technology. It is the very given-ness of the technology which awards it its power. The *representation* of what passes for technology occurs in many workplaces and becomes integral to how we, as producers and consumers, experience the artefact.

For some time I was puzzled by the phenomenon of New Technology. It was not *that* new and, in any case, had all the predictable limitations of fixed capital. Then I realized; the 'gee-whiz' representation *is* new. The computer-on-a-chip, robots-ruling-the-world rhetoric *is* the novelty. Such images provide a modern version of 'automation', self-acting technology. And the extent to which the rhetoric of automation has seduced politicians, civil servants, academics, industrialists, bankers – all heralding a new technological dawn – is a testimony to the power of those representations.

Revealingly, such representations usually suggest that technology is self acting. Many advertisements for the technology of domestic production – cars, food mixers, hi-fi, soap powder – present these commodities as objects of desire, but in a way that renders living labour invisible. The one-who-desires (and is, in turn, desired) is separated from the labourer necessary to make the products useful. The promotion of personal computers, however, takes this further; advertisements presume a fearfulness of new technology and offer the reassurance of the 'user-friendly' characterization. The user *does* appear but, with a curious shift of transitivity, as one-who-will-be-made-effective by the new technology, not as necessary and purposeful living labour.

More – paid and unpaid workers – are involved in technological practice than at first appears. That *should* suggest that more people, other groups of workers, have powers to influence the constitution of those practices. The physical existence of capital's technology is not in doubt. Women do sometimes have babies. But we must beware of the tendency to attribute fixed consequences to those certainties.

'Men's Technology'

If, as I have hinted, class analysis of technology fetishizes the product, then what of feminist analysis? The conventional assumption is that women are estranged from technological practice, certainly they are largely excluded from status-rich sites of technological design and manufacture. Yet *cultural products* are constructed in a number of different workplaces, both waged and unwaged. What influence can women wield in the constitution of technological products? And to what extent can an emphasis on the gender dimensions of technological practice help to subvert the rigidity of technological products?

With few exceptions, the literature on women and technology is uninspiring. Women *do* appear to have low levels of participation in the production and consumption of the technology of paid production. And women are certainly absent from high-status science and engineering jobs, as they are from all other high-status jobs. That is not in question, but the explanations given for those low participation levels *are* open to debate.

Feminist writers have given very diverse accounts of women's exclusion from technology. Here are some examples:

– Women are denied access to techniques, to schooling and to training programmes, to the formal and informal means of becoming familiar with technology.

– Women are denied access by men (both management and workers) to the paid workplaces of scientific and technological production.

– Technology is designed by and for men to oppress women.

– The domains of scientific and technical knowledge have developed both a positivist and masculinist character, thereby excluding women from conceptual participation.

– The history of technology neglects women as inventors of technology.

– Women are denied recognition for the technical skills they *do have*.

Others simply assume that women are disinclined towards technology, do not take the opportunities available to them, and have insufficient strength to engage in some forms of technologically related work. Still others argue that women have separate but distinctly different technical skills and aptitudes. The examples are usually drawn from home, child care or medicine. The pseudo-essentialist association of women and nature is often evoked in this context.

Only the last of these approaches questions the *concept* of technology at all, and then substitutes another concept taken for granted – nature.

The prevailing assumption again is that technology is hardware. Here, too, the *products* of technological work are taken to be the sum total of 'technology'. The network of relations in which the cultural product is embedded is neglected in favour of the artefacts, the dead labour. And the political consequence is again to accept unchallenged the claimed efficacy of the product. I want to argue that here, too, fixed facts dissolve on inspection into sets of practices which *can* be influenced, though not always in circumstances of our own choosing. But here there is a double problem: on the one hand the complexity of the category 'woman'; on the other, the ambiguity of 'technology'.

At a recent conference on the theme of representations of women in the media, I heard about the concerns of mothers, single mothers, lesbians, lesbian mothers, black women, older women, women in journalism and international feminists (who found it difficult to reconcile their sisterhood with Sinn Fein women and the Catholic homophobia of these Irish sisters). At the end of the day I was left wondering: these are all significant groups with particular forms of oppression, yet what is the commonality here? 'Woman' is evoked as an economic category, a familial category, a status and subjective category, quite apart from race, class and age differences. Participants wanted more 'women's issues' covered in the media; what *isn't* a women's issue? All women occupy and suffer various inferior status positions. But the specificities and relativities of these inferiorities are so diverse that the commonality of 'women' keeps slipping away, with only a resort to biology as a defining difference. The categories of male and female are constantly changing, from context to context, and through time. We can have no fixed taken-for-granted assumptions about these constructs, yet they act upon us with the apparent certainties of physical laws. In practice – in this article and in everyday discourse – it is difficult to maintain a distinction between the apparent rigidities of sex categories which derive from their cultural embeddedness and those which simply refer to biology for their legitimation.

'Women', a cluster of social categories, is a difficult topic to grasp. Who makes 'woman'? And the ascription 'technology' is full of paradox. Why, for example, are the chemical processes, stainless steel tools and electrical gadgetry of hairdresshing not often seen as technology, when television repair *is* associated with technology? And yet, relative to the routinized procedures of TV repair men, hairdressers need to exercise more decision-making and problem-solving in their work. Consider two workers in a factory: one operating an industrial sewing machine, one an industrial sanding machine. Only the latter is seen to be working in a technical area. Why are some forms of dead labour designated as technical?

At a conference of educationalists in Washington, a university director of studies explained how his work was impeded because 'we haven't yet developed adequate technology'. He meant a test, a questionnaire to evaluate and assess particular areas of student skill. Educationalists are at the bottom of everybody's academic hierarchy. Can it be that the description 'technology' is an enhancer of status? But this, too, has its class and gender limitations; engineers are concerned with the technical, yet characteristically bemoan their *lack* of status relative to traditional professionals.

It does not seem possible to distinguish technology by reference to the complexity, power or usefulness of the artefact. And what things get *called* is not the heart of the matter. The approval in the label 'technology' has more to do with who is using it, in what statused context. It has been argued that jobs are skilled because men do them (Phillips and Taylor). Is dead labour made 'technology' when men use it? The constitution of 'woman' and of 'technology' are not separate practices; similar, even congruent, power relations obtain. Men's work is often defined as technical, technical work is seen as men's work. And the obverse: women's work is often defined as non-technical, non-technical work is seen as women's work. What practices sustain the definitional power of 'technical men'?

Perhaps it is less useful to ask what gets called technology, and more important to look at what constitutes a *challenge* to definitions of technology. The work of feminist movements in all spheres of social life can be seen as challenging the absolutes of biological givens. Dissolving sex differences into relations of gender – which are open to contest and campaign – has occurred in technology-related practices as it has elsewhere. Feminists have fought for girls' and women's access to curricular choice in schools and colleges; for women-only training programmes; for greater feminization of scientific and technological employment; and have challenged stereotypical representations of sexual divisions of technological labour.

Rather than consider questions of *access* to taken-for-granted areas of technological practice, here I want to concentrate on those feminists who appear to challenge the *definitions* of technological practice. One such challenge comes from feminist science fiction. Most writers in this genre assume that when men are in charge of technology, the abuse of power and destruction is the outcome. Where male science fiction puts emphasis on *human* abuse of science and technology, feminist storytellers presuppose *male* abuse of the instruments of production and destruction. Feminist writers also show how women are controlled by men being in control of technology. For example, in Zöe Fairbairn's *Benefits*, control of women is secured by contraceptive implantation.

Most conventional science fiction focuses on future hardware whilst retaining the relationships of the white middle class, described by Joanna Russ as 'intergalactic suburbia'. Feminist writers largely focus on different modes of *relating*; hardware remains in the background. (See Ursula Le Guin's *The Left Hand of Darkness*, for example.)

Women writers speculating about a technological future take one of the following positions. First, they entirely reject existing and future technology because it is tainted by male control. In an imagined primitivism, where life is lived 'close to nature', a version of alternative technology frequently appears: women characters have telepathic powers, talk with rocks and the wind, sometimes communicate with animals, and are generally in blissful harmony with nature. Such worlds explicitly develop the supposedly feminine qualities of caring, sharing and loving and, in the process, attempt a vehement critique of man's use and abuse of technology.

The dangers of biological determinism are evident. In feminist science fiction the frequent appearance of telepathy as a form of technology is related to the presumed intimacy between women and nature, to ideas of female creativity, and to its suppression by the domination of patriarchal technology. The concept of patriarchal technology slips quickly from gender relations into the biologism of men-as-a-class; yet it is often difficult to specify the character and extent of men's *conscious* or conspiratorial control over technological practice.

The second mode of feminist science fiction confers control upon women and extrapolates to technological forms which make life more comfortable. For example, in Sandi Hall's *The Godmother*, a group of women use computers to challenge the interests of a big business corporation. In Susy Charnas' *Motherlines* – a story of women survivors in the wilderness – a group of women perfect a technique to reproduce without men. They do, however, need the assistance of horses. The difficulties of this approach are that taking control of technology requires an ahistorical leap, and even if bizarre events provided the conditions for some women to be powerful in a particular technological area, taking control does not dissolve the structuring historicity of existing technique.

The third kind of feminist science fiction offers an oppositional view of technological practice. In *Woman on the Edge of Time*, Marge Piercy offers a critique of male-controlled medical technology and the race and class dimensions of its constitution and use. This critique is integrated into a utopian vision of technological development and production for usefulness within non-hierarchical social relations. Piercy's other world – a federation of villages with decentralized agriculture and industry – combines harmony with the physical world with a related spirituality in daily life. Her Utopia embodies high-tech gadgetry (for necessary, repetitive jobs) with low-tech methods of ecological conservation.

This computer works faster than a speeding bullet! ROCC claims to turn a mild-mannered company executive into a comic book superhero who has got everything under control – at home and at work.

Neither *Woman on the Edge of Time*, nor the similar *Dreamsnake* by Vonda McIntyre, offers a vision of technology entirely under the control of women. They present societies where gender relations are relations of equality. This provides a more satisfactory solution to the issue of power; power is transformed rather than reversed to women-centredness (Interestingly, the notion that 'women have babies' occupies even these thoughtful writers. Piercy opts for extra-uterine gestation and male and female lactation.)

Of course, feminist science fiction is not intended to be a programmatic blueprint for a more equal society. Essentially and importantly, this genre provides visions to question the taken-for-granted and to nourish the possibility for transforming existing technological practice.

Changing Relations of Technological Training

Other feminists have taken more practical initiatives to contest masculine strongholds in manual skills and technical training.

A fragile network of women's workshops has opened around the country, attempting to train women in such areas as carpentry and joinery, plumbing, painting and decorating, and electronics and computing. The explicit thrust of women's training workshops is twofold to enable women to enter areas of paid work and to gain access to men's rates of pay; and to empower women by enabling them to acquire practical skills to minimize dependency on men with technical experience.

Such initiatives come closest to *reconstituting* relations of technological practice, even though the explicit purpose is to give women entry to skills. Workshop syllabi are usually traditional. Yet the means of recruitment, pedagogy and working relations are certainly not. Child care, group and individual support, training and travel allowance, flexible hours, and the importance of relevant practical experience have all been seen as integral to the teaching and learning process – a far cry from the technical training experiences of young men. Yet if such initiatives do not grasp the implications of their feminist practices, their changed relations of production, then women trainers will be limited in how far they can transform definitions of technology. Setting up a women's workshop is no mean achievement. Funding, staffing, premises and continuity are well-nigh impossible to achieve. Understanding the broad range of social practices which contribute to 'the technological' would enable women trainers to recognize the subversive worth of their work and to challenge, further, technicist definitions of technology.

For some time I have been associated with a more explicit attempt to change the definitional practices of technology. That small attempt – a technology network – confirms the deeply gendered domination of products over processes in technological work.

Changing Technology: a Technology Network

A while ago, in *RSJ* 13, I wrote a letter describing some of the difficulties faced in setting up a Technology Network based alongside a London polytechnic. Technology Networks are part of the socialist initiative of the Greater London Council (GLC), part of the general attempt to develop London's local economies, to combat London's high levels of working-class unemployment, and to counter the 'necessary' austerity of the Conservative government by providing some positive examples of what a people-centred Labour administration could do. It should be noted that these aims carry their own contradictions, trying to be all things to all men, they seek to achieve success in both wealth-generating and 'community' production terms. At a local level these contradictions manifest themselves as differences between individuals. We were concerned to provide an alternative to unemployment, to facilitate community access to productive facilities, and to put GLC funds to good use. Our concerns are largely expressed through the ups and downs of day-to-day working relationships. In my last letter, in *RSJ* 13, I wanted to counter the abstractions of the Left Scientism issue by concretely detailing a few of the rigidities which are apparent in specific settings. Setting up the Technology Network meant facing a number of apparently immovable objects – for instance, not enough time/money/space, patronizing/conservative/uninterested attitudes by key people;

and the conceptual and practical uncertainties surrounding how to work towards changed technological practice. Here's a review of our efforts so far.

The inspiration to set up half a dozen technology networks came from Mike Cooley, famous for his work in co-ordinating the Alternative Plan at Lucas Aerospace – an accomplishment which eventually lost him his job. At the Greater London Enterprise Board (GLEB), a wing of the GLC, Cooley's intention was to give Londoners some means of access to the accumulated technical expertise in the universities and polytechnics around London, and some practical means to give expression to the technical creativity of local people. Some Networks are technically specific, focusing on new technology or energy, whilst others are geographically specific to north-east or south-east London. Each Network has necessarily taken on a particularity influenced by local circumstances.

Our Network attempts to provide conditions within which local people, consumers and producers of technology, can work together as equals. This is done by a combination of community work – to identify groups, individuals, projects – and development work. Project groups are given access to people with relevant skills and experience; these may be marketing or legal people, technicians, designers, engineers, accountants, and others. Often polytechnic students become involved in projects; at other times polytechnic lecturers share their experience with project groups. Being conducted under benign (although temporary)[1] circumstances, this attempt involves some of the most favourable conditions within which less exclusive processes of production might flourish. Benign though the circumstances are, they are not without constraint. Our Network is being developed within many already-existing structuring relationships, amongst which gender and expertise feature prominently.

From the start the Network was conceived of as a practical reconsideration of the processes of technological production and consumption. We began our initial proposal with the firm statement.

> This proposal rests on two premises:
> Firstly, the social conditions within which goods are produced shapes their final usefulness.
> Secondly, that the human resource of many workers, both paid and unpaid, in and out of employment, is needlessly cramped and confined within the rigidities of the social division of labour.
> Thus more equal working relations between makers, and between makers and users, can produce more useful products.

This initiating document then went on to describe the means by which we intended to foster collaborative modes of product generation: to bring together people with needs, and people with skills, with enabling plant and expertise.

In my last account I tried to point to the relations between socialist vision and practical compromise, and detailed some of the constraints and contingencies involved in getting the Network started at all. If the opening statement above sounds hopelessly naive and utopian, let me counter that by saying that a strong, recognizably socialist design was a necessary part of getting approval and funding from GLEB. This had several positive consequences. It meant that a fairly explicit socialist critique of the exclusions and domination of technological production and consumption could be used to give an overall coherence to the proposal. The socialism of the initial proposal also provided a useful touchstone and source of legitimacy in later disputes about the direction of the Network's activities. In addition, the Network provides a practical opportunity to explore some of the debates in radical science.

During the two years or so since the proposal was accepted, we have engaged in the usual start-up activities: moved into new premises, recruited staff, formalized our legal status, developed systematic procedures for handling aspects of the Network, tried to establish some public image through publicity, and have met a wide number of local groups. I do not suppose that we are any different from other projects in these particulars. In what respects, then, could we claim that the workings of our Technology Network was in any sense socialist, or was in any way contributing to our understanding of oppositional technological practices? In the next two sections I try to detail some of the gender dimensions of technological production at the Network: first in terms of the relentless focus on products rather than processes; secondly, in terms of the work processes, the differential recognition awarded to the labours of men and women employees.

What Does a Technology Network Do?

According to the initial GLEB concept, networks are supposed to focus on 'socially useful products'. That is not a simple matter. The concept of a 'socially useful product' is difficult to realize. Some people see 'social usefulness' in aids for disabled people or in play materials for children. Some see usefulness in resource-saving projects, for instance in recycling glass or generating compost. None of these forms of usefulness is clear-cut. A technical fix for underprivileged groups or an appeal to 'resource saving' (independent of whose resources are saved) are ambiguous areas for socialist action. It is not at all clear for whom the product is supposed to be useful, or under what circumstances. And, in any case, how can usefulness inhere in a product? We thought that usefulness would be more likely to derive from making the *purposes* of consumption a central constitutive feature in the processes of production. The work of production requires umpteen detailed decisions. And usually people who consume things do not get the opportunity to contribute to those constitutive decisions. By making the *purposes* of consumption a decision touchstone, we hoped to bring producers and consumers together as people, to dispel the anonymity of the commodity marketplace and, in the process, to change both relations of production *and* products. We have tried to do this, but probably underestimated the power of existing notions of production and of technology.

The uncertainties and ambiguities of the original GLEB conception of technology networking made life difficult. But a more pervasive danger is the tendency to see the Technology Network in entrepreneurial terms. New events are interpreted in terms of the old, and the network is often treated as if it were simply an enterprise agency for small businesses, or an R&D service for inventors. But technology is never just about hardware. A visit to our Network by GLC potentates threw contrasting views of technology into sharp relief.

Our visitors were Mike Cooley, the inspiration of the original network idea, and Robin Murray, University of Sussex don and chief economic adviser to the GLC. Mike Cooley has long experience, both theoretical and agitational, of thinking about technology from a socialist perspective. Robin Murray is chief architect of the GLC's London Industrial Strategy.

The workers outlined some of the projects being developed: a compost maker, a mobile vascular monitoring unit, and glass and scrap recycling projects. Initially, discussion focused on these differing forms of project work as products. When Jane, a project development worker, described a visit by a redundant silk-screen printer, she spoke of her 'brokering' role – putting the printer in touch with a wide range of available expertise, in marketing, training, financing, among others. Robin Murray asked, 'What's technological about that?' Unaware of the diversity of technological work, the VIPs were concerned about only two things other than hardware: publicity and property relations. They were concerned about generating 'the big project' as a showcase for GLEB promotional work; and establishing matters of patenting, licensing, and sole ownership over designs generated within the Network. It did not seem to occur to our visitors that technological production involves many workplaces, many skills. A product takes shape from many hands. Unless the GLEB theorists and funders realize this, they will continue to work with taken-for-granted notions of technology – notions which are characterized by hierarchy and the physicality of masculine production.

In contrast, the major concerns of the workers are immediate and practical:

– How to relate the productive resources of the Network to the needs of individuals and groups within local communities. If the intention is to democratize technological production, then it is important not to offer local people a technical fix.

– How to process enquiries through a whole range of experience and expertise – marketing, engineering, financial, advertising, patenting, etc. – to provide realistic help whilst not intimidating with 'experts' or making the project seem too complex or out of the control of the project group.

– How to work as a team across community and workshop divisions of labour to provide advice and guidance on development, management, and product control for fledgling groups.

– How to devise practical criteria against which to evaluate both new proposals and the development of the Network as a whole.

– How to contain the frequent and changing demands from GLEB for financial reports and all the paraphernalia and criteria of conventional accounting.

The visitors heard about a number of developing projects at the Network. But their enquiries were grounded in assumptions about the product, and the Good Idea. It has been difficult to convey to these, and our many other visitors, a sense of the many divisions of labour and experience which constitute the process of project development. Questions always revolve around the kinds of machinery we have, the engineering technicalities of the product, the novelty of the design. Here are three examples of network projects:

1) One of the community team met Bob, a redundant sheet-metal worker. Like many other people, Bob had a friend who had been injured in a road accident with an unlighted rubbish skip (a large metal container, delivered by lorry and parked by the side of the road). Bob wanted to develop his design for a skip lighting device. The Network provided design advice, facilities for prototype construction, arranged for a product and market survey to be done by students in collaboration with Bob, helped Bob take out patent rights, and negotiated for the local council to test and buy the lighting clamp for all their municipal skips. Whenever other experience – legal, financial, mechanical – has been called for, Bob has been party to all negotiations and at all stages of development.

2) As a result of meeting with tenants' groups, one worker started talking with a local woman who has skill as a Caribbean cook. A group of friends and relatives got together and moved into the canteen on Network premises. Members of the group had found it difficult to find good cheap Caribbean food, especially takeaway. They wanted to work together to provide that service,

as well as 'meals on wheels' lunches to workers in local offices and factories. Translating their experienced need into practical provision called for great organization. A lot of balls had to be kept in the air at the same time: finding cheap and reliable suppliers of fresh and preserved food, devising ways of working together, discovering which dishes are popular, devising and costing menus, finding ways of packing and transporting hot food, doing a market survey and targeted advertising. All this was in addition to questions of cash flow, indemnity insurance, finding out about health and safety legislation and laws relating to the preparation of food for sale, forming a limited company, creating procedures for stock control and wages . . . These are ordinary working-class people – black men and women whose considerable organizational skills have never been given public recognition, either in paid work or in educational qualification. The challenge, the task in hand for the Network, lies not only in helping to set up a Caribbean cookshop, but also in the practical validation of experience. That is one way in which the Network attempts to subvert expertise, to change relations of production; but our visitors' talk, their questions, always return to the thickness of metal, the best kind of clamp or cutting tool, or the computer configuration. These aspects of the work are necessary but insufficient. Too often our questioners stop there.

3) A local man with severe physical disabilities has been working with a group of mechanical engineering students to develop a Reacher, an electronically controlled mobile device to pick objects from the floor and place them at an appropriate height for a wheel chair user. This is a good example of different kinds of experience coming together in the process of development. Yet again and again visitors have asked about the rotational mechanism, or the simple electronics. Hardly ever have those questions been related to the modes of *use* envisaged by the disabled worker, let alone recognized the centrality of his part in the development process.

These projects – and the many others in the Network – came about as the result of a number of already existing skills, experience, and knowledge of local needs. It is all too easy to see 'a good idea' as a starting point, and to see project development solely in terms of a physical product. The drift is interminably towards products rather than processes. It is an uphill struggle to keep people to the fore. It is almost as if technological change were merely a matter of a different *design* or production technique – rather than a consequence of changed working relations. Focusing on the narrow technicalities of the product makes the real work invisible. The *product* is only the tip of an iceberg. Like football programmes on television that focus on goals (and neglect, for example, practice and training, the market in players, and the constitutive effects of sponsorship), an emphasis on hardware ignores the efforts of those involved in setting up a particular project. Whatever the project, someone has to work at developing relationships, ensuring that everyone has the information, tools and materials they need, keeping the impetus going – the kinds of invisible work with people and processes that women workers have learned, from the cradle, to do so well. An exclusive focus on the physical product reinforces the apparent rigidity and immutability of technical work. At the same time those who do essential work, across and between technical labour processes, are structured out of the productive account. They are given no recognition.

The next section provides some extracts from an interview with one such worker, the longest-serving, most highly qualified and committed worker in the Technology Network. They point to the high personal costs of challenging taken-for-granted definitions and relations of technological work. More generally the following extracts re-pose the questions running through the previous pages.

What is the relation between *product*-focused tendencies and the practical, everyday inequalities of gender relations? *Product*-focused conceptions work to make both class and gender exclusions. Such a focus minimizes or negates the many kinds of necessary but low-status production work which working-class people, and especially women workers, are required to do.

Who has the power to validate experience? Certain kinds of experience are recognized as technological and, when certificated, such experience is transformed into expertise – with all the added material power that legitimation brings. Why are men's experiences more likely to be seen as technological?

Working in a Technology Network

There are now eleven permanent workers in the Technology Network. In addition to an accountant, two clerical workers and a cleaner, there are two teams: the workshop team and the community team. In principle both the workshop team (three men and one woman) and the community team (two women and one man) engage in project development work with individuals and groups of local people. In practice the workload is borne overwhelmingly by the community team and the clerical workers. Of the eleven workers there are six black workers, both men and women. Jane is the co-ordinator of the community team; she works with Janet and John. Paul is the co-ordinator of the workshop team; he works with Sandra, Alan and George.

JANE: Gender relations shape all our work, not only the projects but also the general running of the Network. We're trying to break down the barriers. Yet we have two teams, one classified as the technical, which is male-dominated, and one classified as the community team, which is female-dominated. And yet, when you actually look at what the two teams do (and this is obviously biased because I'm in one of the team), I think the two teams each do just as much technical work. In fact if you look at the whole of this Network – and in that you include the clerical workers – you find technical work all around.

When we had to run a computer course for people who wanted to set up in co-ops, it wasn't Alan [the computer man in the workshop team] that did it. It was Sandra [electronics, workshop team] and Valerie [clerical] that ran the whole course; set it up, did all the technical side of it. And if anything goes wrong with the computers, or if anything goes wrong with any of our electrical items, it's always Sandra that sorts them out. When we moved to the downstairs office, we had George coming round saying, 'Let me put that up!' Janet and I just ignored him, but John had to say to him eventually, 'The community team can pick up a few nails, you know!' It's always that sort of simple thing, they always consider them to be men's jobs. It's not really the technical things – mending plugs, we can all do that. That's not the problem. If you look at what the workshop team *does* do – sorting out the photocopier is considered the technical, the men's job, like fixing the toilet seat on or sorting the locks out. But for instance, the alarm system – we've now got alarms on all our exit doors. It was Sandra that organized all that. And right at the end Paul came along and gave alarm keys to all the men.

PL: Why are you thinking about the photocopier, the word processor, computing and mechanical things as the technical?

JANE: I'm not really, but that's how Paul and George view it, with a hardware focus. That's the whole point about the Network, people only look at the hardware. I really have tried to push it the other way and to make it the people thing. There was an example of that today. You know I have been working with Donald [a man with considerable nursing experience who has been working on a prototype for a pelvic bath]. While I was away, Donald met with Sandra and Alan. I usually go to those meetings with him to give him a bit of support, although Sandra wouldn't oppress him. Donald said to me, 'Alan just won't listen to me. When I try to give him technical points he gets all shirty and angry as if I didn't know what I was talking about!' I said, 'Donald, the whole idea of the Network is exactly that people should develop their own projects, give *us* ideas, tell *us* what they want and what they think, and we take them on board.' The account shocked me. This has obviously been going on and we just don't realize; in that face-to-face small-scale way, people are being intimidated, or having control taken away by the technical men. Of course, Donald does talk a lot and you have to cope with that, but he's enthusiastic about his project, and he should be.

PL: What worries me is the illusion, delusion, that there is something called the technical. All you've said assumes that, yet your examples are about oppressive behaviour with *people*. Can you tell me about a project that doesn't involve the technical men? How would the technical be enacted there?

JANE: Let me tell you about Belinda. She's a Jamaican woman with a lot of experience in dressmaking. She's not been involved with the workshop team at all. Her project is concerned with designing and producing clothes for larger women.

The technical side is taken on by her and me. We're working

together on the whole project. Anything that goes wrong with her machine, we'll mend ourselves. Pattern cutting, costing, layout are all done by her and me. Belinda does have a lot of experience, she had a business in Jamaica. She was running it with her sister, but her sister died tragically and Belinda had a divorce, so everything went wrong for her and so she decided to leave. When she first came to the Network, we went up to her house and picked up all her equipment to install her here. We carried it all and didn't need a man's help, and we didn't ask any man for help. We carried these heavy machines, took them in and set them up at the Network. She just has a small machine now at home which she uses in the evenings when she gets her daughter off to sleep. If anything went wrong with her machine, obviously she'd try to mend it herself, because she does have the experience of working with machines, or if it's something really drastic, she'll call in a maintenance person. The only technical contact she's had at the Network is Paul giving her a copy of the agreement to say she'd comply with the health and safety rules.

PL: I can see that Belinda's work is marginalized by the workshop team, but they aren't all technical men. Can you tell me a little about Sandra? How does a woman get on in the workshop team?

JANE: The workshop team see John as an oddity. The thing about Sandra is that she is very technically competent but very unassuming about the whole thing, so she can be quiet and gentle with project people but has confidence in her own judgement to tell them when she thinks it won't work. If she's trying to explain something, she can do so without using too many technical words. We get a lot of phone calls for *Mr* Abbott, and I say 'I'm sorry, it's Ms Abbott.' And then when they meet her and find she is black as well, it's great. I think her strength comes because she knows she is technically competent and confident in her abilities. Confident not only that she can draw up a circuit and then produce it, but confident in the fact that she can communicate, that she can express her ideas, and that she can actually do the other side as well. She is the only one in the workshop team who can put their ideas down on paper. She can give you a written report that is accessible.

These are *selected* extracts from a much longer conversation. They are included here not to 'tell it like it is'; nor to suggest that I have an impartial role at the Network. Jane's account has been included as part of an attempt to put some particular flesh on the more general questions about the divisions of labour which contribute towards definitions of the technological.

Jane's account confirms the ambiguity which surrounds definitions of the technical. Her definition moves between that imposed by the men in the workshop team, and a more general sense of the technical being related to machinery. Either way, 'technical' work is men's work. The distinction within the Network between the technical team and the community team further confirms the association of men's work and definitions of the technical. The introduction of the Caribbean cookshop into Network premises did much to challenge people's preconceived notions of technical work. The oily rag/soldering iron image of technical work has been, in part, undermined by delicious Jamaican food and by Belinda's elegant dress designs. But those projects are seen as 'soft' by most of the men working at the Network and certainly by the funders of the Network. Even when women like Belinda do develop skills in a 'soft' area, they cannot win. As the brief account here illustrates, familial relations constrain and prescribe opportunities for paid work. Part of the feminization of technological work (from hard to soft) is the process of production changes necessary to accommodate other conflicting responsibilities, for instance having to work on a small machine at home. Even when such women struggle to achieve competence, and perhaps some financial independence and stability, the associated cost is low status.

Even when projects fall indisputably into a 'technological' area of work, it is difficult to gain recognition for the 'soft' work that necessarily accompanies the project. 'Soft' work is largely women's work. It is not defined as technical. Trying to gain recognition for that work is part of the challenge to definitions of technology, part of the attempt to chip away at the dominating myth that production consists of a string of tasks, starting with specialized conceptual work and ending with a physical product. That account makes a mockery of the real work of production, and particularly excludes the work largely undertaken by women workers at the Network, including those women with technological training.

Just as gender stereotypes rest upon biology for legitimation, so technology stereotypes rest upon an equally partial view of production. In identifying, and challenging, the power of gender relations, feminists have tried to wobble the whole creaking edifice balanced on the claim that 'Women are different, women have babies!' A similar effort is required to challenge technological relations – the certainties of objects and the powerful forms of recognition associated with technical work.

Note

1. Our funding comes from GLEB, which in turn originally received its money from the GLC. Fearing too much socialist success, Mrs Thatcher has engineered the abolition of the GLC and other Metropolitan Authorities, as of spring 1986. Like thousands of other projects, we have had to work fast to show results before the money dries up.

References

Harry Braverman, *Labour and Monopoly Capital: The Degradation of Work in the Twentieth Century*, Monthly Review Press, 1974.

Susy M. Charnas, *Motherlines*, Berkeley, 1979.

Zöe Fairbairns, *Benefits*, Virago, 1979.

Sandi Hall, *The Godmothers*, Women's Press, 1982.

Pam Linn, 'Working with People', *Radical Science Journal* 13 (1983), 100–104.

Ursula Le Guin, *The Left Hand of Darkness*, Macdonald, 1969, Futura, 1981.

Vonda N. McIntyre, *Dreamsnake*, NY, Dell, 1979.

Karl Marx, *Capital: A Critique of Political Economy*, vol. 1, Penguin, 1976.

Marge Piercy, *Woman on the Edge of Time*, Women's Press, 1979.

Paul Thompson, *The Nature of Work*, Macmillan, 1983.

Stephen Wood, ed., *The Degradation of Work? Skill, De-skilling and the Labour Process*, Hutchinson, 1982.

Andrew Zimbalist, ed., *Case Studies in the Labour Process*, Monthly Review Press, 1979.

GENDER, SCIENCE AND CREATIVITY

L. J. Jordanova

Review of Brian Easlea, *Fathering the Unthinkable; Masculinity, Scientists and the Nuclear Arms Race*, Pluto, 1983, £5.95.

Writing a book is a complicated business. Authors have both conscious and unconscious reasons for writing, and there are conscious and unconscious strategies at work in all texts. Easlea's book is dense with purposes, motives and intentions which are by no means transparent. On the surface, the book is a highly political one in the sense that it seeks to persuade people to think in a certain way about nuclear weapons. What Easlea offers is therefore an elaborate attempt to cajole readers into accepting a number of basic propositions about the history of science in order to command their assent when he explains the development of the atomic bomb in terms of the masculinity of science. Having offered this analysis to readers, he clearly wishes them to reject nuclear weapons, and masculine science, in favour of some vague alternative in which there would be more sharing of child-rearing responsibilities and a generally more 'feminine' approach to nature. Nature, he implies, would thereby be less subjected to the rape of science. In saying this, Easlea draws on the old opposition between nature and artifice, using it in his argument as if it were quite unproblematic.

It should be clear from this thumbnail sketch that *Fathering the Unthinkable* is a highly polemical book. Part of the polemical strategy is to present several distinct, though presumably related arguments. The early part of the book begins with the Scientific Revolution, concentrating particularly on Bacon, and offers a feminist analysis of science as a form of domination of both nature and woman, since woman and nature are identified with one another. Using Mary Shelley's *Frankenstein* (1818), he outlines the 'wrong' approach to knowledge by describing the main activities of her 'hero'. A supplementary thesis introduced early in the book is that during the Scientific Revolution natural philosophers ceased to see nature as mother and came to view 'her' instead as a virgin, thereby giving themselves *carte blanche* to penetrate and even gang-rape her. Unfortunately Easlea does not explore the notion of virginity (frequently associated with strong sexual taboos), of motherhood (evidently complex, given the pervasiveness of the Oedipus myth) or of femininity (notably polymorphous in theory and practice).

The argument then shifts to an enitrely different plane when Easlea takes up the story of the discovery of radioactivity and the development of the atomic bomb. This is narrated with great vigour, and makes exciting reading. He deftly reveals the political use of the bomb at the end of the Second World War and convincingly shows the ruthless manipulation of nuclear weapons in the dealings between the Great Powers. At the very end of the book yet a further level is introduced in the form of a brief discussion of alternative approaches to childbirth as a mini-paradigm of the larger problem the book addresses. These different narrative levels were presumably carefully chosen for their emotional impact on the reader, but they do not, in fact, fit very well together. The long middle section of the book on the genesis of the bomb is by far the most successful because it vividly conveys the excitement felt by those working on the bomb and the political machinations surrounding its development in sufficient detail to be persuasive.

Easlea's introduction makes it clear that he expects to be criticized; he has some elaborate defensive tactics. He seems to feel vulnerable in his decision to look at the rhetoric of science and at the images and metaphors scientists use about their work. There is no need for him to feel defensive – his approach is wholly justified and requires no special pleading. He also takes pains to tell us that he is not saying that all women are good, all men bad. There *is* a romanticization of the feminine in the book, aided in part by the fact that he never defines femininity, instead allowing it to remain that which is raped by the masculine.

In his attempt to fight on many fronts, to draw all manner of things into his argument and to present an all-encompassing perspective, Easlea has lost a lot of depth. All the expected references and ideas are there, while new analytical strands are absent. The book does, however, serve as an excellent introduction to an alternative approach to the production and deployment of scientific knowledge. It would also be a good book for teaching sixth-form modern history, for it offers a radical alternative to the generally received perspective. In this sense, *Fathering the Unthinkable* is a successful piece of political polemic, and should be warmly praised as such.

Yet there is another dimension to political writing in addition to persuasion. It can, and should, shift the level of discussion and analysis, so that our understanding of science is deepened. *Fathering the Unthinkable* does not do this second job at all. As a result, the disparate ideas Easlea draws upon and the various elements of which the book is composed sit uncomfortably together; they are juxtaposed, rather than being welded together analytically. For instance, although Easlea connects changing ideas of women and of nature with the forms of political power gained by science, he does not extend this to a consideration of political power itself, the transformations this underwent, and the resulting implications for both sexual relations and the natural sciences. He could, for example, have turned to Jean Elshtain's inspiring work on women and political theory and in particular to her analysis of the implications of the history of the public/private dichotomy for gender. The public/private distinction was of fundamental importance in the development of science as a distinctively masculine realm – an issue worth detailed exploration. This is only one of at least three ways in which a thesis about masculinity and science could have been extended.

In using *Frankenstein* and alluding to Faust in passing, Easlea evokes a long-standing Western literary tradition of 'overreaching'. While the classic overreacher was someone who desired more knowledge of (and hence power over) nature than human beings are supposed to have, there is no specific connection with *science*, that is of the modern, Western variety. This prompts us to investigate what is specific to the period following the Scientific

Revolution, and the ways in which this relates to the more general human dilemma conventionally designated as hubris. A more extensive foray into illegitimate knowledge of all kinds would have significantly broadened our understanding of power over, and knowledge of, nature.

Another issue is the history of feminism. Easlea makes the point that masculine science used rationality as a cover for its irrationality, invoking reason to legitimate quite unreasonable activities. He has some interesting and pertinent things to say in this connection about the role of philosophy of science in perpetuating the notion of science as (genuinely) rational at its core. Readers of *Radical Science* will certainly be familiar with this approach to science. What Easlea does not explore, however, is the extent to which attacks on the veiling of irrationality by an apparent, yet ultimately spurious rationality was an established part of feminist critiques of male power, particularly in the Enlightenment. The vigorous pamphlet published in 1739, 'Woman not Inferior to Man' by 'Sophia', is an excellent example of such critiques. Here, as was the case with overreachers, the arguments were applied to *all* forms of male power, not just to science. Significantly, these were wide-ranging political debates. We must now ask to what precise extent science has participated in already established alignments of power and/or forged its own distinctive forms of authority. Whatever the answers – and they are bound to be complex – it is crucial to look at the accretion of power by specific social groups, and at the ways in which the masculinization of science was bound up with broader processes of social change and of class formation in particular.

To go, as Easlea does, from the Scientific Revolution to nuclear physics is quite a jump when the social processes which connected them remain unspecified; without a sense of historical process, the overall analysis remains weak. For him, it is the lineage of ideas which stands at the core of the natural sciences; hence he pays little attention to the ways in which scientific ideas are mediations of social relations. Investigating these mediations is important, difficult and politically vital. Easlea's book lacks a feel for social processes and for the mediations which connect apparently disparate historical phenomena. This is in part because it operates at a number of different levels, which remain distinct, as I mentioned earlier. For example, Easlea uses *Frankenstein* as a tool, a metaphor through which another story can be told. This may be a convenient expository device, but it leaves readers with a number of different narrative elements rather than offering them an integrated sense of wholeness. Parables, I suspect, often tell half-truths.

One possible reason for writing the book in this way is that it avoids the tricky question of the nature of human creativity. At the beginning Easlea says that men envy women their capacity to bear children, and consequently most of what they do is a substitute for their lack of feminine procreative power – 'womb envy'. There is, of course, an element of truth in this, but the comment is also somewhat facile. Human creativity is considerably more complex than such remarks imply. The interesting questions are how and why creativity of all kinds has been defined in a gender-specific way, and what implications this has for power relations. Several times Easlea admits that an individual scientist was highly imaginative in his thought. It is this creative power – whether it is applied to science, art, literature or music – which has preoccupied Western society since its inception. By historical processes, those exhibiting *scientific* creativity have acquired certain rights and privileges, but not those exhibiting other types of creativity, at least not in our society; yet Easlea does not explore how this came about. There was, for instance, an opportunity here to reconceptualize the extensive literature on the sociology of the professions which addresses itself to the collective mobility of a variety of social groups.

Another route which the argument could have taken is a consideration of women's capacity for creativity. This might have considered those people who connected female intellectual power with a life of celibacy on a religious model in which sexuality was repudiated in favour of the cultivation of mind and spirit. (The late-seventeenth-century writer Mary Astell is an interesting example of this.) Yet other strands of feminist thought totally rejected an implied separation of the lives of the mind and the body, claiming full public rights for women on the grounds that procreation, child-rearing and other forms of achievement were mutually enhancing. ('Sophia's' pamphlet mentioned earlier takes this view.) From this we can conclude, at the very least, that there have been concrete struggles over these issues which need to be examined before we can pronounce upon the relationship between science and masculinity.

These suggestions of ways in which an examination of science and gender could be extended reveal both the strengths and weaknesses of *Fathering the Unthinkable*. The book raises some important and exciting questions, and indicates the considerable potential for further work in the area. As it stands, it is an excellent introduction to the main issues surrounding science, power and gender. In the last analysis, however, it fails to be really thought-provoking and conceptually satisfying and so does not offer new tools with which to examine science or change the ways in which we think about it. None the less, if it stimulates others to think harder about the questions Easlea raises, it will have performed a useful service.

References

Mary Astell, *A serious proposal to the ladies*, London, 1694.

Mary Astell, *Reflections on marriage*, London, 1700.

Jean Bethke Elshtain, *Public Man, Private Woman, Women in Social and Political Thought,* Princeton, 1981.

B. Hill, ed., *The First English Feminist: Reflections upon Marriage and other writings by Mary Astell*, London, 1986.

Carol MacCormack and Marilyn Strathern, eds, *Nature, Culture and Gender,* Cambridge, 1980.

'Sophia', *Woman Not Inferior to Man: or, A short and modest Vindication of the Natural Right of the FAIR-SEX to a perfect Equality of Power, Dignity, and Esteem, with the Men*, London, 1739.

RECENT FEMINIST APPROACHES TO WOMEN AND TECHNOLOGY

Anne Karpf

An analysis of women and technology can easily turn into a discussion of the very basis of the sexual division of labour. But it should not surprise us that, to talk convincingly about technology, we need to talk about what is not considered technology. The areas which a society demarcates as 'technological' help to shape what is defined as beyond technology, such as the domain of emotion and intimacy. It is hardly surprising that the subject generates a multitude of divergent positions, even among feminists.

In this essay I do not attempt a systematic discussion of the division of labour. Rather, I draw critically upon some relevant writings, in particular two books about women and technology, one American and the other British (see Rothschild, and Faulkner and Arnold, in References). In so doing I evaluate some current ideas about the relationship between technology and women, and the effects of technology on women's lives.

As edited collections of essays, neither of the books offers a single, coherent, sustained theoretical position. Indeed, they often address quite different issues and rest on diverse conceptions of what technology actually is. So while one essay is virtually an apology for more benign management (Martha Moore Trescott in Rothschild), another proposes that we cannot currently justify the use of any tool (Sally M. Gearhart, also in Rothschild). The papers in *Smothered By Invention* in particular, although its opening editorial manifesto enjoins us to distinguish carefully between 'techniques' and 'technologies', often slip too easily between the two. Neither book raises the fundamental question: Can we usefully talk about 'women and technology' as a general category? What connections can we draw between, say, the ways in which birth-control techniques are developed and used, and women as production-line assemblers of microprocessors, beyond generalities? Can we analyse women's problems with technology as producers and consumers in the same way?

These difficult questions hover behind the debates in these books but rarely put in a front-of-house appearance. Instead, the books draw together a plurality of often conflicting voices, reflecting the current diversity of thinking within the women's movement, from ecofeminist to Marxist-feminist. My own position is to move away from formulations of technology as a wholly oppressive or liberating force in women's lives. I try instead to see technology as a network of forces and relations which affects us differently according to where we are positioned in the production and reproduction of labour. As a result. I am interested in how Marxist analyses of technology can be amplified and enriched to consider the effects of technology not only on class relations but also on gender relations. I also try to identify briefly how women's relationship with technology has changed historically in concert with changing ideological and economic forces.

I want to start by seeing if there is any common ground among feminist analyses of technology. Most would agree that women are largely absent from the institutions which define and create technology. Women rarely design technology or are its high-tech, high-skilled constructors. Often the assemblers of technological components, women most of all are the users of technology, entering the chain at the point of consumption.

The effect of male control of technology – and women's exclusion and alienation from it – is that the technologies produced for use by women may be highly inappropriate to women's needs and even pernicious (e.g. the Pill), as well as embodying male ideologies of how women should live. What passes for women's control is largely a mirage of the market – the exercise of preference (within financial, geographical, cultural, and time constraints) and with the negative sanction of refusing to buy, although as consumers women have also to some extent resisted and modified the technologies offered to them.

But even these limited criticisms of technology are contested.

There are those who argue that it is not so much that women are excluded from the creation and production of technology, but that women's technological achievements are socially unrecognized and the technologies which women have produced are defined – by dint of the gender of the producers – as non-technological.

This is the 'hidden from history' argument, which usefully and often inspiringly reclaims women's hitherto invisible expertise. Examples of women written out of the records abound: the cotton gin was invented by Catherine Green, but her employee Eli Whitney got his name on the patent because Green would have been subjected to ridicule as a female inventor. Autumn Stanley (in Rothschild) has suggested that herbal medicines are classified as 'domestic inventions' when invented by women, but as medicine or drugs when invented by men. Again and again we find that the very definition of what is technology is problematic, reflecting the gendered values of the definers.

Technophoria

While that argument examines women's contributions to technology, another position explores technology's contributions to women's lives. Thalidomide, pollution and other major techno-scares notwithstanding, there is an enduring and resilient strain of technophoria which holds that technology has liberated – or has the capacity to liberate – women. Some would argue that the Pill has freed women from child-bearing, the 'appliance revolution' has liberated women from housework, convenience foods have removed the tyranny of cooking, and the typewriter brought women into the labour market.

You do not have to be the chairman of a multinational company to hold such views. Shulamith Firestone is a celebrated feminist believer in the liberating power of technology: she argued that reproductive technologies would free women from what she saw as the biological imperatives of childbirth. (Today, her views resonate with the affluent optimism of the 1960s, a variant of Harold Wilson's 'white heat of technology'. Feminists in the gloomy 1980s recession are more likely to side with Jalna Hanmer (in Rothschild) that reproductive technologies, as presently developing, extend male medical and professional control over women.)

Technophoria does not, however, survive careful scrutiny; there is much evidence that the time women spend on housework has not declined significantly in the last fifty years, despite the increased availability of appliances. Though utilities – like hot and cold running water, electricity and gas – eliminated many taxing and time-consuming tasks, and vacuum cleaners, washing machines and the like have also eased domestic labour, they have not challenged the sexual division of labour or social relations within the family. As Joan Rothschild argues. 'A technologized household within a technologized society thus has liberated women to perform new kinds of household labour' (p. 84), partly because of the rising standards of housework propagated by the domestic science movement which followed in the wake of the new appliances and which helped to sell them.

The historical evidence suggests that while the transformation and growth of tools and techniques have had a great impact on women's lives, those products and processes do not of themselves have the power to change women's social roles, upon which their oppression rests. The result of new appliances was that domestic work changed rather than shrank. As Rothschild notes, instead of polishing, scrubbing and scouring, women spend more time as consumer shopper, chauffeur, family counsellor, social arranger and hostess. As with other forms of labour, it is argued that housework has become 'deskilled' with the new technologies: traditional skills like soap-making became redundant, and the status of housework declined. Yet here we face one of the many contradictions of the 'women and technology' debate. The skills which may have had higher status were also experienced as burdens on women's times and energies. And are the new skills any less valuable, though they are less visible and do not run on motors or use elbow grease?

Use/Abuse Model

While that debate asks whether technology has improved women's lives or simply reinforced the existing division of labour, the use/

abuse model argues that technology itself is neutral, without intrinsic good or bad moral or political values: it is the human application of technology which abuses or misuses it. Those who take this line also see technology as ungendered: we need more women in key positions of employment in technology in order for technology to be used and experienced in a more benign and convivial way.

This approach is not without its attractions. It is true that we fetishize technology, imbuing products with the intentionality that belongs to their creators and users. Feminists have done this too – when considering childbirth technology, for example. But Frances Evans (in Faulkner and Arnold), in a survey of women who had had babies, found that they were more disturbed by the social relations within which technology is organized than by its use *per se*. The point is, who controls the technology? So is it not legitimate to ask: could not women change the applications of technologies in healthy ways?

I would suggest that there is a key confusion in this argument. Yes, technology is socially produced and shaped by people: the hormonal technology for making oral contraceptives existed by 1938, for example, but popular morality and pronatalist policies precluded the development of the Pill until the 1950s. It *is* people and social forces which create technologies, but the resulting products both bear the imprimatur of their social context and themselves reinforce it: technology is constituted by, but also helps to constitute, social relations. To see nuclear weapons as neutral (a 'deterrent') is a classic use of the use/abuse fallacy; but to expect disarmament without a change in capitalist and patriarchal social relations is to fetishize technology. Nuclear weapons are both the product of the military-industrial complex and patriarchal culture, and a stimulant of masculine military aggression.

While Marxist analyses of the labour process challenge the notion of a neutral technology, they share with the use/abuse model a 'gender-blind' approach to technology. Critics such as Braverman examine the deskilling and loss of autonomy which result from automation and new technologies, but fail to explore their differential effects of men and women. Mechanization does not ripple uniformly through the workplace. As Feldberg and

Glenn (in Rothschild) show, in the case of the generally unfavourable effects of office automation on women clerical workers, technological transformations of work affect workers differently, depending on where they are positioned in the workforce. Women's work has proved peculiarly vulnerable to deskilling, reflecting hierarchical relations within the workplace. The introduction of word processing in offices, for example, has not eliminated boring, repetitive tasks on the scale predicted but has helped to fragment women's work, to increase its intensity and often to increase managerial supervision. As the Science Policy Research Unit argues (in Faulkner and Arnold), 'there is a systematic relationship between the adoption of microelectronics, job losses for women who work low in organizational hierarchies and the creation of new, technical jobs which are generally taken up by men' (p. 217).

Yet their paper does not acknowledge sufficiently the problematic nature of concepts of skill and 'deskilling'. As Anne Phillips and Barbara Taylor have argued, 'Far from being an objective economic fact, skill is often an ideological category imposed on certain types of work by virtue of the sex and power of the workers who perform it.' In other words, there is nothing intrinsic about skill: it is a category to be contested and negotiated, as revealed by the American and more recently British campaigns over 'comparable worth' (see Feldberg).

EcoFeminism

A powerful response to the gender-blindness of Marxist analyses of technology has come from ecofeminism. This marriage of ecology and feminism rests on the 'female principle', the notion that women are closer to nature than men and that the technologies men have created are based on the domination of nature in the same way that they seek to dominate women: both women and nature have become objectified into the Other to be exploited, coerced and ravaged.

From ideas inspired originally by the writings of Simone de Beauvoir and developed more recently by Susan Griffin and many radical-feminist groups, ecofeminists believe that patriarchal violence against women and against nature must be non-violently resisted and replaced by a more loving, intuitive, natural female ecological praxis, which recognizes the interconnectedness of people and their environment. For those ecofeminists who have recognized that such an analysis has mired them into the nature/culture dualism, reinforcing stereotypes of women as inherently pacifist and nurturing, and who find this problematic, it is quite hard to extricate themselves. Ynestra King (in Rothschild), for example, recognizes that the notion that women are closer to nature is a socialized perspective and reinforces the subjugation of women, and that the nature/culture opposition is itself the product of culture. And yet she still posits nature as 'natural' and hopes that feminists can 'consciously choose not to sever the woman-nature connections by joining male culture' (p. 123), thus perpetuating the very dualism which she acknowledges as oppressive to women.

How do we get out of this corner? Can we not recognize – with the ecofeminists – the similarities in the ways in which women and the environment are damaged in our society without having to subscribe to the idea of women as natural geysers of nurturance, bubbling away with peaceful love?

As Dot Griffiths (in Faulkner and Arnold) cogently argues, certainly it is true that women both reject and have been rejected by the masculinity of technology. They are passively excluded from it because of its social image as an activity inappropriate for women. And women who have the choice have actively rejected its goals and values of control, such as the development of weapons of destruction and dehumanizing work processes and products. But while much feminist (like Marxist) literature has offered a critique of the production process with its alienated labour and socially harmful products, most women have no choice over where they sell their labour and do not realistically expect to be anything other than alienated.

Myth of Masculinity

Is there a way of accounting for the cultural opposition between women and technology which does not lapse into ecofeminism?

One of the most exhilarating papers addressing this theme comes from Evelyn Fox Keller (in Rothschild). Keller argues that the belief in the intrinsic masculinity of scientific thought is probably the most single powerful impediment confronting women in science. Although this is perhaps an overestimation, since there are also material conditions which block women's advance through science, she suggests that a cluster of related notions – science is impersonal, women are personal, science deals with things, women favour softness and subjectivity – constitutes a potent mythology, with an ideological function.

Both gender and science are socially contructed, Keller reminds us: this alone should warn us of the need to unpick the dominant ideologies that she has identified. And science as hard, objective, split-off knowledge? Whatever happened to Kuhn? Kuhn and the sociologists of science argued that science is not conducted in an ideological vacuum, untouched by culture, as the community of scientists exerts its own norms and values which determine how science is done. But in analysing women and science, both scientists and non-scientists (ecofeminists included) have fallen, Keller argues, for the ideology of science. In suggesting that technologies are developed in ways removed from personal knowledge and the self, impelled only by logical and impersonal imperatives, we are buying all the baggage of science as a privileged discourse. It is as if suddenly, when we talk of gender and technology, we have forgotten all that we once realized about science being determined by its social context – which includes personal ambition, interpersonal work relations, institutional influences and rivalries. What is that if not subjective? Except, of course, that what we label 'subjective' experience is also shaped by larger social and material forces. In other words, Keller leads us to challenge the apparently rigid boundaries between objectivity and subjectivity from which science derives much of its power, and which it simultaneously reinforces.

Where do these mythologies come from, and why are they so potent that even unswerving feminists and socialists unthinkingly lapse into them? In trying to answer this, Keller turns to our earliest psychological experiences. As boys individuate and learn to distinguish their self from other, compared with girls they have a double job of separation to do, a twofold 'dis-identification from mother' to establish not just a self, but a male gender identity. To cope with the anxiety of this process, boys may adopt postures of exaggerated and rigid masculinity and autonomy. 'In this way, the very act of separating subject from object, objectivity itself, comes to be associated with masculinity' (p. 137).

Public/Private Split

Whether or not Keller's explanation is convincing, the split way in which social roles and emotions are distributed and attributed lies at the heart of the gender and technology debate. There are both material and psychological reasons for the polarization of the public (male) sphere and the domestic (female) sphere. Zaretsky has shown how personal life got split off from productive life: the post-feudal early bourgeois family was an economic, productive unit, but the development of large-scale industrial production – culminating in the nineteenth century in England and the United States – shifted production from the property-owning family to the factory with its wage-labour, and brought with it the notion of the family wage. 'Society divided and the family became the realm of "private life" . . . On one side appeared "society" – the capitalist economy, the state, the fixed social core that has no space in it for the individual; on the other, the personal identity, no longer defined by its place in the social division of labour' (p. 57).

Subjectivity and the home were seen as the antithesis of technology and big business. These dualisms remain prevalent today, although of course domestic labour and household technology are intimately connected with the exchange relations of capitalism, with women's labour contributing to the reproduction of labour power. And men do not cease to experience the world emotionally when they are subsumed into their occupational roles.

As Jean Baker Miller observes, women have become the 'carriers' for society for certain aspects of the total human experience, such as vulnerability, weakness, dependency – essential parts of men's experience too, which are problematic and 'therefore . . . unacknowledged, unexplored, and denied' (p. 23). It is as if men have become emptied of subjectivity and are seen as symbols of the material world, while women have become defined as pure subjectivity, beyond the reach of material forces. Perhaps the most fascinating aspect of the splitting of social roles between the domestic and public domains is the way the boundaries get redrawn over time: tasks and activities are removed from the home, or reallocated to it, according to the needs of the production process, the development of new technologies, and the dominant ideology.

So, with the Industrial Revolution, tasks which had previously been performed in the home entered the economic sphere of mass production: husbands' (or single women's) wages for factory work now paid for commodities (like beer, butter, buttons, starch and bread) and processes (like textile bleaching) that their wives or the whole family used to produce or do before. The shift to mass production helped to exclude women from certain kinds of technological tasks and occupations. It has been argued that the creation of childhood – the extension of the period in which children were considered dependent and in need of nurturing – helped to fill the so-called domestic void.

The displacement of tasks from the home is now happening, to some extent, in reverse: the state is pushing for many activities and processes hitherto conducted in the public sector to return to the domestic domain. Stereos, videos, and the growing use of the home computer are individualizing and privatizing leisure. Jobs which women formerly did for a wage – the care of old people, the cooking of school dinners – they are now doing increasingly unpaid, in private. Even shopping has changed, with supermarkets making larger profits (and helping to drive out the corner shop) partly by transferring the work of collecting goods off the shelves from paid shopworkers to unpaid shoppers. As 'caring' and 'servicing' tasks are pushed back into the home or the private sphere by the erosion of public services and employment, as is happening now, they lose their status even if they are technology – or appliance-aided. They are done for love, they are part of the 'natural' world of family relationships. And this is very problematic for many women: for, while they understand that this is part of the state's ideological apparatus to naturalize women's labour, and thus to get it free, they also do not feel happy with 'Wages for Housework' campaigns or attempts to reduce all social experiences purely to the exchange relations of capitalism.

Assessing Possibilities

Such questions may not appear especially germane to the debate about women and technology, but they inevitably spill out from it and are a reminder of the difficulties of shaping practical campaigns round theoretical contradictions. In practice, how can technology become less alienating to women (and to many men)? There is a prevalent strand of pessimism exemplified by the 'you can't uninvent the bomb' line, but this implies that technologies follow an inevitable trajectory, whatever their effects, and conceals the social decisions made about their production. Yet there is evidence that societies have decided – albeit slowly, reluctantly, and after campaigns, boycotts, and other forms of social pressure – to abandon a process or product with harmful social effects (e.g. the Dalkon Shield and certain kinds of asbestos). But, as Dot Griffiths says, 'Changing the direction of technology is a long-term project involving a radical restructuring of the social order' (p. 71)

Corlann Gee Bush, in a stimulating chapter 1, speaks of how we can set about assessing technologies. She argues that what is more striking than women's ignorance of technology is men's ignorance of the context within which technology operates. She identifies four contexts: the design or development context, the user context, the environmental context, and the cultural context. She suggests that in Western culture, more is known – presumably by those who have the power to initiate and develop technology, though she does not specify this – about the first than about the other three put together. She argues compellingly for an equity analysis of technology which would examine the benefits and risks to different parts of the population of products and processes within each of these contexts. She does not explicitly say who would assess those benefits and risks. I would suggest that it is only when women's own evaluations of the benefits and risks to them of new technologies are considered legitimate that an equity analysis could be a useful tool in challenging dominant ideas about technology. Moreover, this means different evaluations from women positioned differently within the work force, whether through class, race, age, disability, etc.

But the appeal of her argument – and of others in these two books – is that she acknowledges the complex effects of technologies and avoids a knee-jerk 'technology is bad' approach. Since technologies affect different cultures and groups of workers and users differently, we need these kinds of rich and complex analyses of the influence of technology. In this regard it is unfortunate that both books ignore the dimension of First World–Third World relations, except for Ann Whitehead's rigorous analysis of how the Green Revolution has affected women's work (in Faulkner and Arnold).

At times, *Smothered by Invention* reads a little drily and densely, ranging perhaps too wide. As I suggested at the start, both books suffer – but also perhaps benefit – from the perennial complaint about anthologies. It sometimes seems as if *each* author has simply trodden her own path, addressing different questions, while some chapters – those on medical technologies, for instance – offer little new thinking and are theoretically underdeveloped. Still, they contain some convincing and stimulating work, and the two chapters on domestic technology are especially interesting.

Machina Ex Dea, ostensibly a more scholarly book (with its American origins evident), is eclectic though often exciting to read. In general *Smothered by Invention* engages more realistically with how women can and have challenged existing technologies. By contrast, in *Machina Ex Dea*, although several of the chapters acknowledge the economic and material determinants of technology, there is a tendency to fail to identify the ways in which technology differentially affects women of different social classes, races, and ablebodiedness. In the weakest chapters, this has the effect of transforming women almost into an ideal type, a cultural category which owes more to ideology than lived experience.

None the less both books make us think about what a feminist technology might be like, about how the relationship between technologies and people, and between production and use, could be different. They invite us to fantasize about socially useful technologies, in the manner of feminist Utopias sketched out by some science fiction. In the spaces between their well-argued critique, they offer a prefigurative dream. Together these two books make an important contribution to the debate about technology and gender,

Acknowledgements

My thanks to members of the Radical Science Collective, particularly Maureen McNeil and Pam Linn, for their helpful comments and suggestions over this essay.

References

Simone de Beauvoir, *The Second Sex*, Random House, 1968.

Harry Braverman, *Labor and Monopoly Capitalism*, Monthly Review Press, 1974.

Wendy Faulkner and Erik Arnold, eds, *Smothered by Invention: Technology in Women's Lives,* Pluto, 1985.

Roslyn L. Feldberg, 'Comparable Worth: Towards Theory and Practice in the United States', *Signs, 10*, 2 (Winter 1984), University of Chicago Press.

Susan Griffin, *Women and Nature*, Harper & Row, 1978.

Jean Baker Miller, *Towards a New Psychology of Women*, Penguin, 1978.

Anne Phillips and Barbara Taylor, 'Sex and Skill: Notes Towards a Feminist Economics', *Feminist Review* 6 (1980), 79–88.

Joan Rothschild, ed., *Machina Ex Dea: Feminist Perspectives on Technology,* Pergamon Press, 1983.

Eli Zaretsky, *Capitalism, the Family and Personal Life*, Pluto, 1976.

Work

GENDER RELATIONS IN THE CONSTRUCTION OF JOBS

Sonia Liff

Essay review of A. Game and R. Pringle, *Gender at Work*, Pluto, 1984, £3.95.

Even five years ago a feminist review of recent literature on technical change and employment could begin by pointing to the lack of consideration of women workers. The current situation is not so straightforward. It is now far easier to find studies of women workers from both a 'labour-process' perspective and from the broader field of industrial sociology (see reviews by Wajcman and Beechey). In addition, the majority of new general texts on work, from both radical and mainstream perspectives, now include sections on women workers. It is of course still true that most of the research focuses on male workers and that special sections on women workers, when no comparable sections exist on men, show that men still form the model for the 'typical' worker. In this sense, earlier criticisms are still valid. However, the increasing attention paid to women workers should also provide us with the opportunity to move on to examine what questions and concerns may have been overlooked by the particular direction taken by the literature.

The appearance of *Gender at Work*, a book by Australian researchers Ann Game and Rosemary Pringle, marks an important change in approaches to women and work; thus it provides a useful focus for a broader discussion of feminist perspectives. The most obvious difference from previous feminist writing is that this book is not only a study of women workers. As the authors say in their introduction:

> . . . when we talk about the sexual division of labour it is often assumed

> that we are just interested in women's work. What we are in fact concerned with is the historical relationship between 'men's' jobs and 'women's' jobs. (p. 15)

Through a series of case studies, the authors examine the ways in which this relationship has been restructured through the recent period of recession and technical change. The approach taken by Game and Pringle, and the findings of their research, highlight the advantages of moving from a focus on 'women' to one on 'gender'.

Through a review of *Gender at Work* this article attempts to assess what a gender perspective can offer to those analysing technical change in the workplace. It is useful to begin by delineating the main aspects of the approaches that have most often been adopted by those studying women workers.

Women's Work Rather than Women as Workers

Despite the apparent association between the growth in the numbers of studies of women workers and the post-Braverman revival of interest in Marxist studies of work, most analyses have had relatively little to say about the way in which 'women's jobs' fit into the overall work process. For the most part, feminists have not attempted to reinterpret analyses of the development and structure of the labour process. Instead, they have concentrated on redressing the existing imbalance in workplace studies by providing descriptions of women workers' lives, including what is involved in doing a 'woman's job' and how work is fitted around domestic commitments. Or they have concentrated on the ways in which women become channelled into the 'worst' jobs – those which are low-paid, defined as unskilled, and provide only limited opportunities for upward mobility.

To a large extent, the first concern has determined the form taken by the second. Once one focuses on providing an account of women within one particular workplace, it is difficult *not* to take the current structure of jobs as given. The question becomes, 'How do women come to be seen as appropriate for certain types of jobs?' Little attention is given to questions about how jobs come to be created with, or perceived as having, certain characteristics. In this sense, the literature can be seen as primarily about women as workers rather than about women's work.

Understandable as this development is, it has created a number of difficulties. It assumes, at least implicitly, that considerations relating to gender played no role in the development of occupational structures, forms of technical change, workplace practices such as supervision and many other issues. Equally importantly, and perhaps less explicably, this approach fails to examine the signficance of patterns of work organization in the creation and perpetuation of gender difference. As Cynthia Cockburn says in her introduction to Game and Pringle's book:

> The gender issue at work is not just a matter of inequality, of unequal pay and unequal chances. It is a matter of the creation and defence of male enclaves among the occupations, where young males learn to be men, and the complementary establishment of dead-end female ghettos, with very little crossing of the boundaries between. (p. 9)

These difficulties are further compounded by the way in which the specificity of women workers' situation is analysed. The tendency has been to see workplace relations as flowing from the domestic division of labour. It is women's distinctive position within the home which is seen as disadvantaging them, both in their search for jobs and in terms of what they can achieve within the workplace. An increasingly familiar picture emerges from most studies of women with working patterns disrupted by periods out of the labour force for child-bearing; or by part-time work with few responsibilities so that they can cope with home demands; or of older women with little confidence in their ability to take up new areas of work because of their lack of experience outside the home. These circumstances are taken as the reasons why women are concentrated in a narrower, and inferior, set of jobs than men. One does not need to deny the significance of these factors to ask whether gender relations within the workplace might also provide part of the explanation.

For example, it is clear from most studies that male workers and managers behave in ways that are unequivocably gender-specific. Generally no explanation of this is provided and it is very difficult to see how such behaviour could be explained in terms of domestic relations. This again leads to abdicating an area of theory to those who would analyse relations between sections of the workforce without any significant reference to gender. At least as importantly, it makes it very difficult for feminists to develop political strategies to improve women workers' situation which move beyond better child-care and related provisions. While such facilities are undoubtedly important, it is far from obvious that they would, in themselves, guarantee women's access to a wider range of work or change their relationships with male workers.

There are thus a number of issues concerning the significance of the organization of work for the construction of gender relations, and conversely the role of gender relations in shaping the development of the labour process and workplace practices, which have not been analysed very effectively by those studying 'women at work'. It is possible to see how analyses which did encompass these perspectives might develop, and what they might offer, by considering the approach taken by *Gender at Work*.

Occupational Segregation by Sex

One of the most distinctive features of Game and Pringle's book is its explicit focus on occupatonal segregation. This is rare within feminist studies, despite the fact that it is frequently cited as a reason for women's inferior position in the workplace. *Gender at Work* also replaces an approach based on domestic circumstances with one which analyses the ways in which technical change restructures work and workplace gender relations redefine men's and women's work through this process.

It is common to find management, and indeed workers, justifying occupational segregation in terms of the suitability of men and women for particular types of work. Sex-typing is thus seen as the outcome of a process of rationally matching workers' abilities to job requirements. Such approaches fail to examine how jobs come to be constructed in ways which require certain characteristics. Moreover, they fail to demonstrate that skills are held exclusively on the basis of sex, or that all jobs require skills which are sex-typed in one direction. Finally, there is a problem of retrospectively attributing a cause to the observed outcome. That is, observing a match between workers' abilities and job requirements does not prove that jobs were allocated on this basis. Most feminist writers have been content to point to some obvious counter-examples – such as dextrous male brain surgeons – to dismiss such approaches, without developing alternative analyses.

In contrast, Game and Pringle argue that the nature of the work is relatively insignificant. What is important is firstly that men and women should be doing different types of work, and secondly, that men should do work which is seen as empowering, at least in relation to 'women's work'. In this way, occupational segregation is established as a crucial factor in the creation of gender identity and of power relations based on gender.

Each of the case studies within *Gender at Work* raises slightly different issues. It is therefore worthwhile summarizing their findings briefly. Within the domestic appliance industry, Game and Pringle argue, technical change has led to most jobs becoming more like 'women's jobs' as traditionally characterized. For example, they are becoming less skilled, lighter and cleaner. However, instead of women taking up new jobs, the distinction between men's and women's work is reconstructed along a technical/non-technical division, even where this involves moving women off jobs they have been doing satisfactorily for years. Thus, men retain the best-paid and most interesting of those jobs that remain. In banking the number and proportion of women workers has increased dramatically in the postwar period, paralleling two other processes: a massive expansion and diversification in bank services, and a routinization and automation of banking activities. Jobs were opened up to women at the same time that the career structure was being dismantled. By increasing the proportion of women in the industry, this process was obscured since they occupied the low-level jobs, allowing men to continue to have career opportunities.

In their examination of retailing, Game and Pringle point to increasing self-service provisions which have led to overall job losses as well as a routinization and casualization of work. Women are employed in all but managerial positions. The existence of a strong sexual division of labour in the new industries associated with computing is seen as proof that segregation is not simply a hangover of outdated forms of organization. As with banking, women are being drawn into low-level jobs at the same time as these jobs are being automated and career opportunities are becoming restricted.

In hospitals some of the rigid sexual divisions between nurses and doctors are breaking down. This has exposed the extent to which authority relations are based on gender. Female doctors are not able to exert control over nurses in the same way as men can. Doctors are discomforted by male nurses whom they cannot treat in the same way that they would women. In consequence, the male nurses often advance quickly into administrative grades. The chapter on consumption focuses on the different ways in which men and women experience the home/work divide. In contrast to most approaches, Game and Pringle argue that women are forced to make a very rigid distinction between home and work, both in order to be treated as 'equals' in the workplace and to pre-empt arguments about their employment damaging the performance of their domestic duties.

The importance and novelty of a focus on occupational segregation has already been mentioned. One can, of course, find descriptive accounts of the types of jobs within which women are concentrated. However, Game and Pringle contrast the *flexibility* of the form taken by occupational segregation by sex with the *persistence* of its existence. They point out that a situation rooted in biological differences between men and women would lead to a stability in both aspects. An economic analysis might lead one to expect sex-typing to disappear completely. All the case studies within *Gender at Work* suggest that the maintenance of an hierarchical distinction between men and women's work is more important than the particular form it takes. This approach also stresses the significance of periods of technical change and work organization for the study of gender relations.

Gender at Work contains a critique of the more simplistic labour-process analysis. The authors point to the extent to which deskilling is the only aspect of technical change in which Marxists have been interested. This focus, they argue, is irrelevant to those whose work has never been defined as skilled. They also question the common assumption that the entry of women into an area will lead to deskilling. The case studies present a much more complex picture. In manufacturing, deskilling of craft work occurred but men were keen to retain 'their' restructured jobs, since they were still the best of those available. In banking and retailing they argue that feminization *followed* the deskilling of white-collar and semi-skilled service work. In computing, both processes can be seen to be at work, with women drawn into routinized areas of work but men retaining operators jobs even after deskilling. Rather than draw general principles from these examples, Game and Pringle prefer to stress the importance of undertaking specific studies.

Sexuality

It is rare to find explicit treatments of sexuality within studies of women workers. There are some references to sexually coercive styles of supervision and some (although surprisingly few) to sexual harassment. Marxist analyses do not have a specific perspective on gender: women workers are distinguished from men only in so far as they do different jobs and have different domestic responsibilities. Beginning with an examination of gender at work provides a better starting point for understanding the position of women workers.

Game and Pringle consider the role that certain types of work play in confirming sexual identity. For men this ranges from the 'macho' aspects of powerful machines to the threat to their identity as 'real men' if they do 'women's work'. For example, they say that the commonly accepted view of men entering nursing in the early 1970s was that they were all homosexuals. Times of technical change and work reorganization 'frequently provoke anxiety in men about the loss of power or the gaining of power by women to which they are not entitled. Power and sexuality are integral to work relations' (p. 16).

For women the issues are somewhat different. It is frequently suggested by management that women would not want to work alongside men. This raises, at least implicitly, the threat of sexual harassment and its role as one mechanism for keeping women out of the preserves men claim as their own. One consequence of this is that women who are determined to take up such jobs may not only have to deal with the reality of harassment but may also be considered sexually promiscuous by both men and women. Notions of sexuality are, of course, class-bound. Often a woman who succeeds professionally is considered to have done so either by 'sleeping her way to the top' or by rejecting relationships and families. Thus, women's work identity is seen as inextricably linked to their sexuality. Some of the case studies also suggest that, whereas sexual hierarchies can be used to reinforce workplace power relations, management may at times see sexuality as a potentially disruptive force. For example, in retailing, 'The night fillers were initially men . . . Management were reluctant to employ women because of the "hanky panky" they imagined would go on in the dark!' (p. 67).

The Dynamics of Technical Change

There are, nevertheless, some difficulties with Game and Pringle's approach. In their introductory remark about technical change they say: 'Technology does not have an inherent dynamic of its own but is designed in the interests of particular social groups, and against the interests of others.' They argue that this has been considered only from a class perspective: 'We take this further by considering the gender context of the implementation of technology . . . Not only are there conflicts between management and the workforce over machines: but there are also conflicts between men and women over machines; over who, for example, is to operate them' (p. 17).

All that is undoubtedly important, but is still only part of the story. In considering only the 'gender context' of change, Game and Pringle appear to be giving technical developments an autonomy denied by their initial assertion. The case studies also tend to suggest that technical change is determined by managerial goals – including moving into new markets, cutting costs or increasing control over the workforce. A pattern of occupational segregation by sex, based on its own principles, then takes shape around these restructured jobs. This approach is an advance over most Marxist studies, which suggest that gender divisions are something imposed by management simply to divide the work-force or divert attention from the deskilling aspects of technical change. This type of simple functional analysis is rejected by Game and Pringle. Instead, they see occupational segregation as having a strategic role in the reproduction of gender relations. This leaves open the relationship between gender relations and the reproduction of capitalism. They also consider that it does not make sense to talk about divisions being imposed on the workforce since these are generally considered to be 'natural' forms of organization.

What is missing from their analysis, however, is any sense of gender as a dynamic in the design or adoption of technology. For example, historical analyses of the print industry by Cockburn, and of the textile industry by Lazonick, point to instances when machines were designed and marketed with the specific intention of allowing women to be employed on previously male jobs. Cockburn also points to aspects of equipment which were designed around the average abilities of healthy men in ways which would tend to exclude many women. For Game and Pringle capitalism is inherently 'patriarchal', so in stressing the social aspects of technological developments they presumably do assume a gender dimension. But this is never concretely explored.

Explanations for the Pattern of Sex-Typing

A recurrent ambivalence in feminist writings on work is how to treat the types of justification given for women's occupancy of particular jobs. As mentioned earlier explanations based on 'women's nimble fingers' are usually dismissed by reference to counter-examples (although not always, c.f. Elson and Pearson). But it is not clear where this leaves such 'explanations'. Are they entirely bogus? In which case, where do they come from and why are they so widely accepted? Or are they partial truths? If so, what parts are true and how do they become extended beyond this base?

A focus on gender relations in the workplace provides part of an explanation by showing the significance of types of work in the construction of masculinity and femininity. As both Cockburn and Game and Pringle stress, masculinity and femininity are defined in opposition to each other; so that characteristics and abilities associated with one are, by definition, not associated with the other. Examinations of wartime attempts to draw women into non-traditional jobs have shown that by stressing slightly different aspects of the type of skills needed, jobs always considered as 'men's' can be made to appear perfectly suited to women. It is further the case that the occupancy of a job, say by men, is likely to reinforce the perception of that job as requiring masculine characteristics and, conversely, of masculinity involving the type of abilities needed to do that job.

But alongside this apparently arbitrary (or at least socially constructed) basis for allocating jobs between men and women, there lies another account. Game and Pringle seem to be suggesting that there is a new, rational basis for allocation. They come close to arguing that there was some basis for the characterization of men's jobs as skilled, heavy and so on, but that this has been undermined by technical change. The new division of labour is based on men retaining jobs connected with machines and new technology, since these are the 'best' and most 'powerful'. Of course it is not difficult to think of cases where women do work with machines. Game and Pringle counter such examples by arguing that a typewriter or sewing machine is not a 'powerful machine' in the way a computer is.

There are a number of difficulties with this approach. Power does not reside in machines but rather in relationships between people. Thus, what we need to understand is whether the form taken by the labour process – a particular configuration of people and machines – contributes to the power some groups have over others. It may be the case that some types of machine embody characteristics which make them more likely to be used in this way than others; but this is something which needs to be investigated in particular cases rather than assumed on the basis of the imagery associated with them. It is also important to consider the different types of interaction workers can have with the same machine. For example, Cockburn suggests that what is important is understanding power in the workplace is not who works on or with machines, but who designs and maintains them. She describes the situation which often pertains as one in which women are 'lent' technology by men.

To say that men retain the best jobs, even if one can be fairly specific about which those are, thus begs more questions than it answers. What is it that makes a job a 'good job?' Do jobs associated with high technology really have these characteristics, and if so why? What are the processes by which men acquire and retain these jobs?

There are answers to these questions, and they are far more accessible to those with a gender perspective than to those with a more conventional 'women's studies' approach. However, they are ones which Game and Pringle's account neglects. In part, this is because they do not fully integrate their gender perspective into their analysis of the development of new technology as discussed earlier. To an extent, the way in which they focus on the technical/non-technical division is an expression of this. The connection between machines and masculinity is presented in largely symbolic terms; this prevents them examining how the technology came to be like that or what it is about jobs associated with it that provides men with such a power base. They seem to wish to demonstrate that a restructured pattern of occupational sex-typing still complies with certain principles of gender relations; for example, they imply that it was the desire for such an outcome that brought about this result. The case studies are primarily located within a historical account of changing production methods and occupational structures at the level of the sector. As a result, what is crucially missing is the injection of a gender perspective into more traditional labour-process accounts of how workers maintain or lose power through periods of technical change.

Male Power in the Workplace

Most work from a labour-process perspective has concentrated on craft workers and the threat posed to their form of organization by technical change. Before Cockburn's study of print workers, research made at best passing reference to the fact that these workers were usually men. Most research on women workers refers to this fact only negatively – noting that women's jobs do not offer them the control strategies available to male workers. What is important is to turn this insight around – to recognize that skilled men do not just have advantages because of the jobs they do but, rather, that craft unionism is a male control strategy. The significance of this is that gender becomes more than something that simply needs to be taken into account when women's position is analysed. Instead, it must be taken on board by all those analysing technical change in the workplace. Such a perspective begins to overcome the separation apparent in most work – Game and Pringle's included – between the construction of jobs and the different power bases that these afford men and women.

It is not possible here to do more than suggest what such a perspective might involve. What is needed is an investigation of how certain groups of men have established power bases around a certain set of skills and how women have generally failed to do so. One point which seems to be important is that, in contrast to male craft workers, women tend to carry out only very limited parts of production processes. Those parts from which they are excluded usually include design, organization and maintenance. The significance of this seems to be that the particular skills and jobs to which men have been able to lay claim allow them to influence the construction of the division of labour. Labour-process work has stressed this element of craft work as that which has aided male resistance to some of the more damaging effects of the types of technical change management have wished to initiate. It is equally possible to see this as the base from which men have been able to defend their position *vis-à-vis* women. Rather than seeing men as somehow being able to assert the value and importance of whatever skills/jobs they take up within a particular division of labour, this approach begins to make links between specific types of skills, their utility as power bases in certain circumstances, and the maintenance of male power through these conjunctures.

While this form of analysis is missing from Game and Pringle's account, there are elements of their account of male power which are important and which may well be missed by those stressing the approach outlined above. These relate to the degree of consensus that exists between management, male and female workers about gender relations. The association of masculinity and femininity with certain types of competencies, ways of behaving, forms of work, and relations of power are not things over which there are continual conflicts. It is therefore important that a gender analysis should consider not only how conflicts are resolved but also the processes which often prevent conflict explicitly emerging. For this form of analysis we have to look much more carefully at the details of equipment design, employment practices, and workers' perceptions of their own abilities and aspirations than most labour process work has been prepared to do.

Thus the main strength of *Gender at Work* is that by focusing attention on relations between men and women within the workplace it provides a way of moving on from an analysis of where women 'fit in' to one which considers the role of gender relations in the construction of jobs. Equally importantly – particularly since it is a perspective completely absent from analyses which define women in terms of their domestic roles – Game and Pringle establish the significance of workplace relations in the construction of gender. Technical change provides an invaluable focus for this study, but ultimately its treatment of technology is its greatest weakness. Their account becomes confused about the relationship between the characteristics commonly attributed to machines and the productive relationships which give rise to these associations. Furthermore, descriptive accounts of the outcome of a process of change substitute for an analysis of the process itself. Talking about men's monopoly of 'powerful machines' may appear to be simply a convenient shorthand, but it betrays a failure to unpack a series of relationships and processes which are crucial to our understanding of gender at work. Those developing Marxist analyses of technical change could contribute to this analysis, but instead their work has tended to perpetuate the split between labour-process and women's studies approaches. By asserting that women's work deserves as much consideration as women workers, *Gender at Work* should force a reconsideration of this position.

References

V. Beechey, 'What's So Special about Women's Employment? A review of some recent studies of women's paid work', *Feminist Review* 15 (1983), 23–46.

D. Elson and R. Pearson, 'Nimble Fingers Make Cheap Workers': An analysis of Women's Employment in Third World Export Manufacturing', *Feminist Review* 7, (1981) 87–107.

C. Cockburn, 'The Material of Male Power', *Feminist Review* 9 (1981), 41–59.

C. Cockburn, *Brothers: Male Dominance and Technological Change*, Pluto Press, 1983.

W. Lazonick, 'Industrial Relations and Technical Change: The Case of the Self-acting Mule', *Cambridge Journal of Economics*, *3* (1979), 231–62.

J. Wajcman, 'Working Women', *Capital and Class* 18 (1983), 135–51.

'IT'S A MAN'S WORLD'

Maureen McNeil

Review of Cynthia Cockburn, *Machinery of Dominance: Women, Men and Technical Know-How*, Pluto, 1985, Pp. 282, pbk £5.95.

> Let us examine somewhat more closely the fact that machinery more and more supersedes the work of men. The human labour, involved in both spinning and weaving, consists chiefly in piecing broken threads, as the machine does all the rest. This work requires no muscular strength, but only flexibility of finger. Men are, therefore, not only not needed for it, but actually, by reason of the greater muscular development of the hand, less fit for it than women and children, and are, therefore, naturally almost superseded by them. Hence, the more the use of arms, the expenditure of strength, can be transferred to steam- or water-power, the fewer men need be employed; and as women and children work more cheaply, and in these branches better than men, they take their places.
> Friedrich Engels, *The Condition of the Working Class in England* (in Marx and Engels, pp. 434–5)

The preceding quotation is one rendering of the pattern of the changing sexual division of labour which Marx and Engles considered to be typical in the cotton industry, which was in the vanguard of technological change during the first Industrial Revolution. For Marx and Engels, and many of their followers, technological innovation was the *sine qua non* for women's entry into production. This interpretation took on even further significance when Engels (in *The Origin of the Family, Private Property and the State*, 1884, revised 1891) identified women's entry into production as the first step towards female emancipation. This review considers how a contemporary research project builds on and yet challenges some of the parameters of Marx's and Engels' perspectives on the sexual division of labour.

Technology as a Medium of Power

So here we are now, in the midst of what many consider to be a third technological revolution, which promises the transformation of production via electronic technology. At this point Cynthia Cockburn, a socialist-feminist living in Britain in the 1980s, set out on a series of investigations which, like Engels' analysis, look at the relationship between technological change and the sexual division of labour.

The microelectronic revolution is a much more diversified and diffused phenomena than the original Industrial Revolution. Thus, while Marx and Engels were primarily concerned with developments in the cotton industry, Cockburn recognized that studying gender relations and technological change now required research at different sites. Her investigations involved four case studies of the effect of technological change: (1) in the pattern-making and cutting processes of the clothing industry; (2) in goods handling in the warehouses of mail-order firms; (3) on tomography scanning in the radiography departments of hospitals; (4) developments 'upstream' in computer engineering firms which were providing the technology for innovations in other work settings.[1]

Unlike Marx and Engels, Cockburn is a professional researcher and her project was financed by the Equal Opportunities Commission and the Economic and Social Research Council. She made contact with eleven firms, and used both formal and open-ended discursive interviews (196 in total, 113 with men and 83 with women). These were supplemented by informal contacts, as well as surveys and postal questionnaires on new technology.

Machinery of Dominance is organized around these four case studies. The introduction and first chapter set the stage for the presentation of the research. 'Technology is a medium of power' is the stark premise from which Cockburn begins, mapping from there the two relationships of power mediated by technology: 'owning tools, equipment and machinery and putting other people to work on them' and the possession of 'special knowledge and competence with technology' (p. 6). As she points out, it is men who dominate these two types of relationship to technology and women, who thereby are dispossessed of this channel to power.

The framing of the Introduction is slightly confusing on one point. She explains that 'the particular context within which technology is considered' in the book '*is the sexual division of labour*' (p. 8) and 'that means we are not immediately concerned with military technology nor with technologies of contraception, genetics or housework'. The area of concern is further designated by the label '*technologies of production*' (p. 8, italics in original). While there are reasons for confining the study to the technologies of paid employment, I feel that it is unfortunate and misleading to operate with a notion of the sexual division of labour excluding housework. This definition seems to contradict references elsewhere in the book to 'rocking the cradle' as a very significant component in the sexual division of labour. (Her label of 'technologies of production' similarly fudges the much-debated issue of whether or not housework is productive.)

The first chapter provides the historical background for the research. In a sweeping historical review, Cockburn claims that it was in the late Neolithic period that women's position as technologists was usurped by men (pp 20–1). From that point forward, she claims, technological skills became both 'a cause and an effect of male supremacy' (p. 24). This history of sexual domination is interwoven with a sketch of the struggles of craftsmen and then technologists to retain control of their skills. The maintenance of these positions of power was always a precarious struggle, which seems to have involved the privileged sectors of the working class in creating underlings with whom they could be favourably compared. As Cockburn succinctly puts it: 'The technologists' close identification with the machinery and those that owned it was always in danger of standing between them and other workers' (p. 34). From the period of the Industrial Revolution, when women began entering into industrial production, they became a particular target of such strategies of skilled men: 'It is the most damning indictment of skilled working-class men and their unions that they have excluded women from membership and prevented them gaining competences that could have secured them a decent living' (p. 39).

The next four chapters (2–5) examine each of the case studies in turn. In looking at the clothing industry (ch. 2), Cockburn focuses on 'the work processes of cutting and pattern rooms' which 'had for a long while defied innovation' (p. 46). However, as a result of computer-aided design, these labour processes were changing. For while some firms continued with traditional production processes, others were computerizing pattern-making and, in some instances, cutting. Hand in hand with these innovations had come the feminization of the pattern room and the current 'moment of transition' (p. 69) in the cutting room when women and men were working side by side. The 'deskilling' and fragmentation had guaranteed an 'entirely female' destiny for these jobs, in Cockburn's assessment. Nevertheless, she does provide some riders to her prediction on grounds that the requirement of night-shift work, the consciences of male management about unemployed lads and the misogynist pride in maintaining a male clothing industry might put some brakes on this feminization. Of course, in the midst of these changes, senior management and skilled technical posts remained men's jobs.

Chapter 4 reports her research on warehousing, where there is an employment pyramid with mainly married women at the bottom of the hierarchy primarily as part-time workers, and men at the top. Computerization had precipitated a deterioration of the women's conditions of work as their jobs became increasingly machine-paced repetitive and confined to one location. Robotics posed a further threat in that it could eliminate women's jobs in the picking area. However, at the moment, women made up the bulk of the workforce – harassed, pressured and rendered immobile by new technology in warehousing; while the few men in the industry are characterized by their own and management's sense of physical and technological competence and a degree of influence over women's work processes.

Of the X-ray technician, Cockburn comments: 'Probably this occupation involves women in a higher level of technologcal knowledge and competence than any other female-stereotyped work' (p. 112). This is one of the most interesting case studies. Computer axial tomography is the new ingredient in this labour process. In using the new equipment, technicians are 'gaining an additional skill and responsibility only to lose the ability to practise those they already possess' (p. 124). Although defined as a mainly female profession, radiography has a clear sexual division of labour, with men tending to specialize in diagnostic rather than therapeutic work (pp. 127–31) or feeling that they should be more interested in the technological side of the work (pp. 139–40). The new technology presented many women in the profession with a dilemma, as they were 'reluctant to sacrifice closeness to the patients in order to get close to technology or to climb the career ladder' (pp. 140–1).

The final empirical reference point is the British electronic industry, which contributes – on a limited basis, as much of this industry is located abroad – to the innovations noted earlier in the book. In moving 'upstream' to the sources of changes in the mode of production, Cockburn finds only one woman engineer 'who surfaced in person or by reference' (p. 156). Having added this final component to her sketch of workplace technological change in Britain, Cockburn changes gear. While the first half of the book is mainly descriptive, the second half is far more analytical. The analysis springs from her reflections that her research on three new technologies and some of their supplier firms has yielded a picture of women functioning almost exclusively as 'operators'.

Taking Technology at Face Value

Thus the focus is shifted to explanations and strategies for change. Chapter 5, on the engineering industry, is followed by two chapters which examine 'the ideological processes that help sustain divisions and inequalities between men and women, especially enabling them to tide over the crisis of technological change' (p. 170). That is done through interviews with men (ch. 6) and women (ch. 7). The concluding chapter (ch. 8) reflects on strategies for change.

Taking my cue from Cockburn, I shall shift from a descriptive to a more analytical mode and, treating the remainder of the book as a unit, highlight the features of her prognosis on contemporary gender relations and technology at the workplace. I think that it is also helpful to refer back to Marx's and Engels' ideas about the earlier technological revolution with which I began.

Perhaps Cockburn's greatest achievement is a thorough debunking of the presumption – of Marx and Engels and many others – that technological innovation opens doors for women. The sexual division of labour is changing but persistent and, as Cockburn stresses, underpinned by the fact that: (1) '*both people and occupations are gendered*', and (2) '*workplaces tend to be hierarchically structured*, with many different grades and levels, while *work processes are subject to continual redefinition, subdivision and fragmentation*' (p. 231, italics in original). This dual process of gendering and subdivision (and as this book makes clear, the two interact) serves to reproduce male dominance. To go back to Engels' quotation, women did not and do not 'take their [men's] places' in any instance of technological change. For what Engels and Cockburn are looking at, time and time again, are *new niches* in the division of labour. When women *appear* to be replacing men, you can almost always be sure the job has been redesigned and devalued (in pay, status, conditions) in some way.

Engels and Marx opened the way for examinations of women's waged labour and for complex analyses of the economic devaluation of female labour (see Beechey, Anthias). Nevertheless, as Michèle Barrett has suggested, their perspective was very much that of the *male* working class. The quotations above naturalize both the sexual division of labour ('Men . . . by reason of the greater muscular development of the hand, . . . are, therefore, *naturally* almost superseded by them [women and children] and the lower rates of pay for women ('women and children work more cheaply').[2] Cockburn denaturalizes both the gendered nature of skills and pay differentials as products of the social and political relations between men and women, for example in the exclusionist policies of male trade unions and professions.

Despite these achievements, I felt uneasy about some features of Cockburn's interpretation of the gender dynamics of technological change in labour processes. My dissatisfactions could be clustered together under the label of 'taking technology at face value'. Here I have in mind that, again echoing Marx and Engels and many subsequent socialists, Cockburn occasionally espouses a belief in technological progress: 'New technology is continually pushing up the minimum level of technical know-how that is saleable. Women have not yet got access to last year's knowledge, let alone next year's' (p. 162). As Braverman made clear, demands for qualifications do not necessarily mean that greater skills are actually required in areas of technological innovation. New technology is immersed in ideological representations in which progress is the watchword and, at minimum, it would seem advisable to avoid notions that knowledge can be packaged as 'last year's' or 'next year's'.

To my mind there is also a gender issue in these ideological representations. Cockburn seems to accept too quickly the assumption that women are, relative to men, technologically ignorant and incompetent. As early as the Introduction, she states that 'women possess an all-but-invisible fraction of its [the world's] technological know-how and technical jobs'. Then she refers to 'the technical competence that men as a sex possess and women as a sex lack. . . .' (p. 7). Some formulations are even more solidly packed: 'Feminity is incompatible with technological competence. . . .' (p. 12). Others portray women as passive victims of technology: 'Women were actively excluded from technological knowledge, *acted upon by technology* and not interactive with it' (p. 9, my emphasis).

As Cockburn herself acknowledges, we are steeped in a culture which posits women as an anathema to technology: 'In masculine ideology women are represented as non-technological, as incompatible with machinery. . .' (p. 197). Here debates about the ideological dimensions of the definitions of skill might be a relevant reference point. As Anne Phillips and Barbara Taylor have argued, it is often the fact that particular work is done by women, rather than any intrinsic features of the work itself, which earns it the label 'unskilled' (see Phillips and Taylor). Is there not a parallel danger of assuming that what women do and know is not 'technological'?

This book's presumptions about technological progress, and that women lack technological knowledge, tend to reinforce each other. What I am suggesting is that it is important to begin with a healthy scepticism about both presumptions. Here I am reminded of some lovely bits of Diane Harpwood's *Tea and Tranquillizers*. Janet, the housewife and narrator, reflects on her husband's reading: 'I've been reading David's science fiction library books. I've found them all terribly disappointing and unimaginative. David looks supercilious and puts my uninformed opinion down to a feminine obsession with emotions rather than technical details' (Harpwood, pp. 62–3). She also muses on his skills: 'A fully grown adult male who considers himself able to manage the production in a factory should be able to cope with pressing his own clothes' (Harpwood, p. 119).

In describing Cockburn as taking technology at face value, I also have in mind the fact that she attributes much to technology. Anthropomorphic descriptions pop up: 'cleverness' in the computer (p. 55) or 'very much more clever and comprehensive computer programmes' (p. 68). Such formulations render human labour (where cleverness *can* be witnessed) invisible and the commodity (the clever computer or programme) unchangeable. Elsewhere, Cockburn interprets sexual harassment at work as 'the clearest expression that men wish to maintain rights in technology as men's private property' (p. 203). Again, this would seem to exaggerate the significance of technology, for sexual harassment is not confined to technological workplaces. These various hints that much is being attributed to technology come together in her general evaluation: 'A grasp of technology is personally empowering' (p. 228)'. Such a statement is simply too sweeping. Couldn't the obsessional knowledge of some working-class lads who are car buffs, or of some of the avid readers of mechanics or computer magazines, be interpreted as evidence of impotence?

I am merely suggesting that the relationship between knowledge, power and technology is far more complex than this statement indicates. A place to begin might be with a distinction between the *representations* and *realizations* of power.[3] There is no doubt that in our culture technology *represents* the promise of power. Computer advertisements, and Reagan's statements of faith in the space programme to the American people after the Challenger disaster, revolve around that promise of power. The role of the space programme in Reagan's campaign to solidify American power might be debated. Nevertheless, it is clear that many home computer owners (no doubt, like many working-class Americans who 'believe' in the American space programme) will never realize the promise of technology. Similarly, distinctions can and should be made between the *status* and *effectivity* of different kinds of knowledge.

My final point takes me back to Engels' picture of the cotton industry during the Industrial Revlution. For Marx and Engels, women were the pawns of greedy capitalist entrepreneurs. By contrast, looking at men at the forefront of the current technological revolution, Cockburn observes that the romance with technology ensnares men into new forms of self-exploitation: 'Many of the men I met worked very long and irregular hours' (p. 181). 'Capital exploits men by means of their masculine identity. Men destroy each other' (p. 184). 'Many of the male engineers and managers I met worked phenomenal hours of overtime' (p. 212). Obviously many women also work long hours, both inside and outside the home, for limited rewards. Nevertheless, clichés about 'labour of love' do package Utopian aspirations for patriarchal purposes and do denote a resistance to the motivations which sustain capitalism. This is well illustrated in Cockburn's own example of the dilemmas of female radiographers who were unwilling to sacrifice involvement with patients for technological knowledge and career advancement. Moreover, in a world in which technological work increasingly means military work, or eliminating or intensifying the labour of others, women's resistances to jumping on the technological bandwagon would seem to be quite sane and healthy. Again, Cockburn acknowledges this along the way: 'Technology and the relations of technical work have to change before most women will choose to engage with them' (p. 13). Unfortunately, the concluding reflections on strategy are a bit vague about alternatives and positive moments of female resistances. The contrast with Engels' picture of the first Industrial Revolution is sharp when she warns: 'Women have somehow to avoid becoming accessories to exploitation as they become technologists.' But too quickly she closes the consideration of these dilemmas: 'It is only by getting inside it [technological knowledge] that women have a chance of succeeding.' (p. 254).

In a sense Cockburn's is a late-twentieth-century response to Engels' call to 'examine somewhat more closely the fact that machinery more and more supersedes the work of men'. For Cockburn this means a much sharper analysis of gender *relationships* at the workplace. The sophistication of her picture, relative to that of Marx and Engels, is linked partly to the complexities of twentieth-century capitalism. But it is also due to the fact that Cockburn pushes the analysis of the sexual divisions of labour much further than Marx and Engels did. She refuses any form of naturalization of these divisions and she is concerned with the power which working-class men, *as well as* capitalists can accrue from them. Thus, unlike Marx and Engels, she never takes the sexual division of labour for granted. However, she is sometimes too willing to take technology at face value, which sometimes undermines this very important book.

Notes

1. To describe such technologies as 'upstream' is to take a somewhat technologically determinist interpretation of the organization of production. Moreover, it tends to naturalize a rather complex picture of production, the division of labour and the history of technology. I am grateful to Pam Linn and Tony Solomonides for bringing this to my attention.
2. See Barrett for a very interesting examination of the work of Marx from the vantage point of gender relations. Her argument supports my own reading of Marx and Engels on the Industrial Revolution – that they are primarily concerned with the replacement of male labour and that their accounts are very much from the perspective of the *male* working class.
3. The linking of knowledge and power, literally in the concept of 'power/knowledge', is a very important concept developed by Foucault. However, this can lead to rather dangerous simpliciations of the relationship between power and knowledge. See Foucault.

References

F. Anthias, 'Women and the Reserve Army Of Labour: A Critique of Veronica Beechey', *Capital and Class* 10 (Spring 1980), 50–63.

M. Barrett, 'Marxist-Feminism and the Work of Karl Marx' in B. Matthews, ed., *Marx 100 Years On,* Lawrence & Wishart, 1983, pp. 199–219.

V. Beechey, 'Some Notes on Female Wage Labour', *Capital and Class* 3 (1977), 45–66.

H. Braverman, *Labour and Monopoly Capital; The Degradation of Work in the Twentieth Century,* New York and London, Monthly Review Press, 1974.

F. Engels, *The Condition of the Working Class in England,* in *Karl Marx Frederick Engels: Collected Works*, vol. 4, 1844–1845, Lawrence & Wishart, 1975.

F. Engels, *The Origin of the Family, Private Property and the State* (1891), introduced by M. Barrett, Harmondsworth, Penguin, 1985.

M. Foucault, *Power/Knowledge,* Brighton, Harvester, 1980.

D. Harpwood, *Tea and Tranquillizers: The Diary of a Happy Housewife*, Virago, 1982.

A. Phillips and B. Taylor, 'Sex and Skill: Notes Towards a Feminist Economics', *Feminist Review* 6 (1980), 79–88.

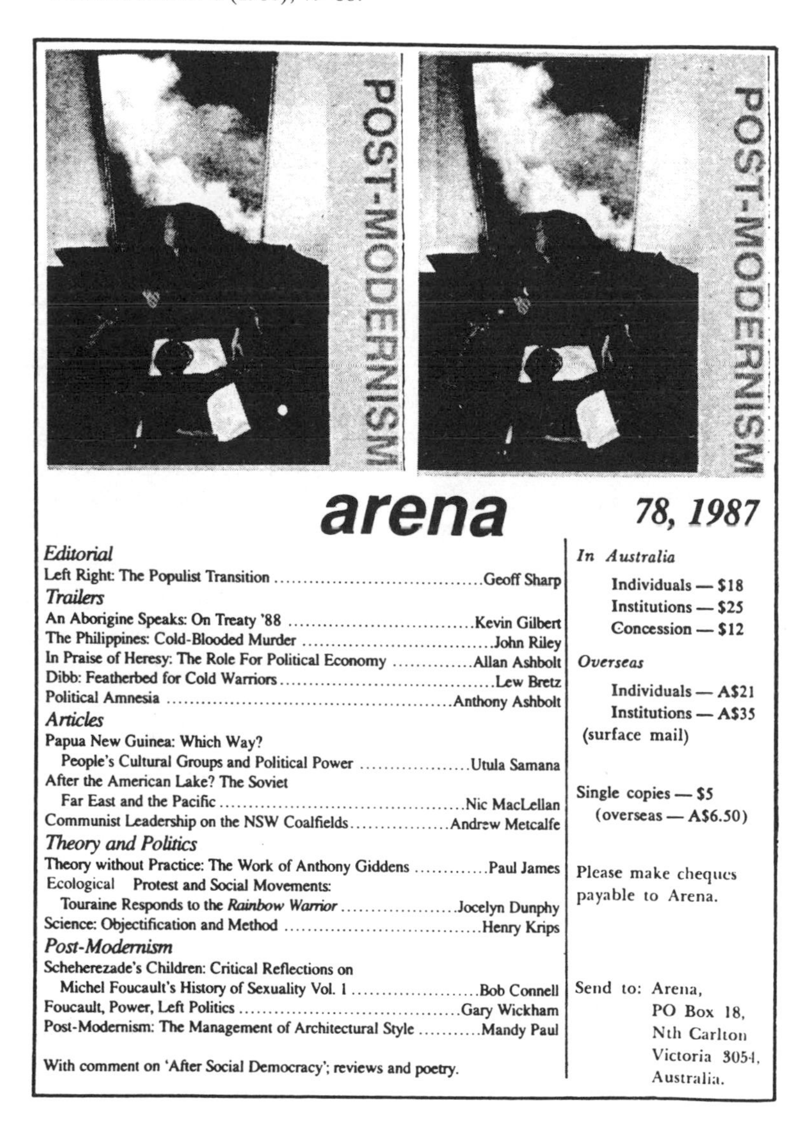

HOUSEWORK AND DOMESTIC TECHNOLOGIES
An Essay Review

Alison Ravetz

The academic study of domestic labour, its evolution and its role in society, are as yet scarcely two decades old. Serious comment by feminists – Mary Wollstonecraft among others – is of course much older, and between 1900 and 1940 British women in the co-operative and labour movements published several classic studies of working-class housewives, which the Virago Press has recently made available to us again.[1] In addition, some facets of domestic labour have been annexed by other fields – ergonomics and child care, for example. However, the totality of work done by women at home has not in general been treated as a legitimate object of serious study; indeed, most women who have persisted in it have their stories of ridicule and dismissal to tell.

There are a good many reasons why this should be so. The primary, and historical, one is that one result of industrialization was that only wage labour outside the home was considered to be work contributing to the national economy. It followed that work in the home must be 'not work'. Another reason is that the essence of domestic labour is to combine many things, usually concurrently. In particular, as well as the more specific tasks of cleaning and cooking, which are what most people consider to be housework, there are the management of resources, of people (in various stages of infancy, old age, sickness and exhaustion), of interpersonal relations, and what some writers aptly refer to as 'tension management'. Many of these are considered to be leisure activities, or simply part of personal life. Domestic science, or the somewhat broader American field of home economics, directed its main focus on cooking and cleaning. That focus was unhelpful, for it considered isolated fragments of the complex and integrated

Metropolis II by Christopher Plowman

task of home domestic labour in order to make them more amenable to government policy, school instruction, time and motion studies, or studies that were intended as guides to consumer behaviour for industry.

In the twentieth century home economics fell for, and indeed actively promoted, the fallacy of 'labour saving': that is, domestic technology and kitchen design that were intended to remove the labour from housework, so releasing the housewife for tasks that were implied to be non-laborious, such as companionship with children or giving hospitality. Swallowing the same argument, housewives then found themselves caught in a web of confusion as their work mysteriously refused to lessen, even though their kitchens were packed with more power than the mills of the early Industrial Revolution. Feminist thinkers were then of little help to them, for the early militants were either ignorant of or in full flight from domestic bondage. Most of their latter-day descendants still regarded housework in this light, and housewifely standards and attitudes as themselves strongly suspect.

It is, therefore, historically no accident that a fresh, sympathetic and analytical attitude to the subject has emerged only since the women's liberation movement of the last fifteen years, when it could derive from two or three different impulses. One was the Marxist perspective on industrial society, as reinterpreted or expanded by feminism, which yielded historical and contemporary studies of the role of housewife.[2] Another was the history of technology, with a broader and less partial treatment than the evolution of domestic appliances had usually been given.[3] Tools and the social relations of work were now considered together, within a broadly Marxist framework.[4] The third impulse, of which two recent books provide outstanding examples,[5] is from the lived experience of being a housewife within a historical setting. Ruth Schwartz Cowan sets her own personal experience as a mother, housewife and professional woman in the American evolution of housewifery, while Meg Luxton uses the experience of three generations of Canadian women to illustrate change during this century.

It may be said at once that, valuable though both these studies are, a vast amount of work still remains to be done in working out the details of the historical development of housewifery. Apart from the obvious allowances that need to be made for social class at any time, the task for all social classes changed over time, with demographic and social policy change affecting things like family size, health, education, and the length of wage-earners' working weeks. Added complications arise from the fact that definitions of the task also changed. Thus, the origins of something like today's role of housewife lay in the nineteenth century – to diffuse up and down the social strata[6] – while in today's world the redefinition of work and leisure, personal and public spheres, must bring further profound changes.

In recent years something of a feminist orthodoxy has been established by scholars of housework, who suggest a solution to the conundrum referred to earlier by postulating that the labour-saving gadgets of this century had an opposite effect to what was expected by introducing new tasks and raising standards. Illuminating though this theory is, in a broad historical sense it needs detail and qualification. Where women had already become multiple-role housewives, for instance, domestic gadgets did undoubtedly lighten their burden – not only the drudgery, which Cowan usefully distinguishes from 'labour', but other parts of their task as well. It is likely that this occurred, in Britain at least, around the midpoint of this century, and in America perhaps rather earlier, with two categories of women: the newly servantless upper middle classes, who tried to maintain their standards unaided or with skeleton daily help, and the upwardly mobile working classes who, with better housing and smaller families, could aspire to middle-class standards. Certainly reformers of many kinds, including women active in the labour movement and propagandists for home economics, welcomed domestic machinery, and in particular the electrification of houses. Their fervour is explicable only if one supposes that they were not wholly misguided about the wants and needs of housewives.

There are other lacunae urgently waiting to be filled, such as housewifery at different stages of the life cycle (notably after children have left the parental home) and change in the balance of the different components of housework at different periods of history. The majority of studies have focused on women in the early and middle stages of family formation, and these two studies are no exception. They do, however, make a point of including very nearly all domestic tasks within their purview – with certain exceptions such as household maintenance and 'DIY' – and acknowledging that these were balanced differently at different times.

More Work for Mother

Cowan covers a long period, looking at four phases: the pre-industrial, beginning any time around 1860 or before; the early industrial between that and the period 1900 to 1940; and the postwar years. Her broad argument is that, before industrialization, domestic tasks were shared between all the family members, including children. Men and women, in fact, could not long survive without each other's labour. The main effect of industrialization – which she traces in the cases of flour, manufactured stoves, cloth and water – was to replace the labour of men and children, for whom the home could then become a refuge from paid work or school, and a place of leisure. Women, however, lost out as they first became isolated in their kitchens, and then had imposed or spontaneously took on new tasks that were more complex or with higher standards. Although piped water might most obviously seem to be a lightener of both drudgery and labour, according to Cowan it laid on women the injunction to 'produce' clean bathrooms.

The now-conventional wisdom is that the most significant historical change in the task of housewives has been from production to consumption, beginning in the last century but climaxing in this (Branca and Davidoff). Like other post-women's-liberation scholars, Cowan broadly agrees, but with the essential proviso that consumption is also laborious. It is an important part of her thesis, however, that not all forms of production have been taken out of the home into commerce. Most particularly, transport, for which pre-industrial women were not responsible, has become almost totally the responsibility of contemporary housewives, as they have to transport goods into the home and convey family members to all services outside the home. This, it might be argued, is a classic example of a task that is generally either ignored altogether or considered as 'not work', in spite of the time and energy it consumes, not to mention its essential role in the national economy.

In a chapter on 'the roads not taken' – which include commercial services, inventions, alternative communities and co-operatives, some of which were in fact followed for various lengths of time – Cowan is concerned with why women should apparently be passively complicit in a process that, if the Marxist-feminists are to be believed, did them so much damage personally, socially and economically. The answer, for her, is that women did indeed know what they were doing: they placed privacy and the autonomy of the family above all other priorities, so proving the Marxist-feminist interpretation wrong. For her, therefore, the way forward for housewives is not fundamental structural change but the sharing of tasks between husbands and wives, accompanied by the relaxation of unnecessarily high standards.

For an English reader, Cowan's interpretation raises many questions of comparison and possible contrast. What she calls pre-industrial is different in many ways from that stage in England – we might rather call hers a frontier stage. In particular, she does not describe a peasant society where the poor worked as domestics of the rich, having little home life of their own to speak of. In contemporary society, English women are nothing like as motorized as their American counterparts and do not have the same standards of perfection in cleaning and laundrywork. It might, then, seem a legitimate question whether lower standards have enabled English housewives to reap the benefits of domestic technology with fewer of the drawbacks.

However, the existence of similar contradictions in the housewife role suggests that there is, after all, something deeply structural about women's role in industrial society at work here. It is true that Cowan's theory that women consciously opted for family autonomy and privacy does receive backing from English research into women's attitudes towards rehousing and suburbanization, most notably through the channel of council housing.[7] Yet at the same time her rather hasty conclusion seems unnecessarily to overlook the fact that many social groups can be taken in by fallacious remedies, especially – in such a materialistic society as our own – where advanced technology is concerned. Housewives are eminently suggestible for various reasons, and they would seem to be vulnerable to the appeal of technologies designed with a limited view of their task and little care for its underlying social relations.

Phrases from two of Luxton's interviewees reflect the dilemma this bestowed on women: 'It took me awhile to figure out what was going on. I was always tired, dragged out and run down.' 'For years I thought it was all my fault, that I was so unhappy and tense so much of the time.' For a generation or more, the failure of technology to deliver the expected liberation could, it seemed, only be the fault of women, who were then classified as lazy, ungrateful or neurotic, according to the standpoint of the onlooker. If we are to take the point of one of the most penetrating indicators of the industrial/domestic system, this was scarcely surprising, for domestic technology was designed in such a way as to control domestic labour and keep it docile, so that the former was a powerful adversary indeed (Rothschild, 1981a). At the same time, in a contradiction or 'irony' clearer than any expressed by Cowan, the development of modern domestic technology became a precondition of the recent women's liberation movement (Rothschild, 1983).

Rather to my regret, Cowan does not here enter into any of these theoretical debates, though her other published writings confirm that she might have done so with distinction.[8] *More Work for Mother* is a historical review and interpretation which aims at a wider than academic audience, as its picture essays and bibliographical guides show. To judge from its frequent personal allusion, it also seeks to rescue from silence and dismissal the labour of middle-class, professional or wage-earning housewives, so justifying their contribution – not least to professional women of earlier generations or childless contemporary feminists. The acknowledged founders and theoreticians of twentieth-century feminism, we may remember, resembled their Victorian predecessors in being unshackled with children and conventional housewifery.[9] Cowan represents and rightly defends a newer generation of liberated women who work in both the domestic and public spheres; among other things, this uniquely qualifies her to expose the myth that housework is an invention of discontented housewives that 'expands to fill the time available'.[10] Any woman working at home would know that it expands, quite simply, with the number of people in the house, including herself.

In Luxton's beautifully lucid and economical study, the three generations of women (1927–39, 1940–59, 1960–77) are all located in the industrial phase, reminding us of the fast and continuously changing development of housewifery. Though hunting and food-gathering, most surprisingly, still played a part in their domestic economy, all three generations were multiple-purpose, isolated housewives, ensconced in the home; but the first came to inhabit tents and shacks in the raw, unpaved mining town of Flin Flon in northern Manitoba. The last were conscious of their progress and wealth of gadgets, although these induced guilt and worry: 'I keep thinking about how much easier things are for me than they were for my mother. Everybody keeps telling me how with all the modern things I have I shouldn't have to work very hard. Is there something wrong with me?'

Whereas, in Cowan's terms, machinery lightened drudgery rather than labour, in Luxton's more deliberately Marxist terms it can shorten labour time but not necessarily production time. 'Production time measures the duration of a task from start to finish; labour time measures the specific period during which a worker is actually expending labour.' Overall, the production time of all that a housewife has to produce still runs 'from sun to sun'.

What does a housewife produce? Luxton expands on the Marxist thesis that her true function is the reproduction of labour, by the conversion of wages into food and other commodities, into 'motherwork' and many varieties of the management of people, in a continuous, fragmented and 'endless barrage of pressure'. Like Cowan's study, this one, based on the reminiscences and first-hand observations of about a hundred women, provides a panegyric to the skills and services of housewives and mothers. Luxton finds that, while its internal dynamics have been reorganized, the work remains the same in its fundamental characteristics of being 'private, isolated, the essential responsibility of women'. Luxton's solution, however, differs from Cowan's, in proposing a raised political consciousness of their state and a deeper commitment to community affairs among women.

Of all things, a company town like Flin Flon is a laboratory-like example of the way housework is tailored to fit the needs and rhythms of industrial work, and it is remarkable how often the words of the women confirm the Marxist interpretation: 'Who says we don't work to the whistle? With us it just doesn't show. We got to have dinner on the table before that whistle blow.' But the peculiar nature of the industrialization of the home was that, unlike work in the mill and factory, this work was not socialized and that, far more than the manual labourer, the housewife was alienated from the technology she used. This was designed by members of the other sex, repaired by them and even paid for by them; as Luxton finds, wives used the strategy of seducing husbands when they wanted some particularly expensive piece of equipment.

These two studies, therefore, make a valuable contribution to women's history, reminding us of their role in helping to build up newly emerging nations, and raising interesting questions and comparisons with the older and different industrial society of Britain. They also contribute to the neglected but important part of the history of technology, where manufactured goods, services and sophisticated tools interact most crucially with personal life. Since this is explored, primarily, with the motive of illuminating the development of housewifery, the authors do not extend their studies with proposals concerning the future of domestic technology; but they will undoubtedly become part of that canon of works concerned with the sensitive interface of technology with people and social organizations.

Notes

1. Maud Pember Reeves, *Round About a Pound a Week* (1913), Virago, 1979. Margery Spring Rice, *Working-class Wives, Their Work and Conditions* (1939), Virago, 1981. Margaret Llewelyn Davies, ed., *Maternity: Letters from Working-Women* (1915), Virago, 1978.
2. Lee Comer, *Wedlocked Women*, Leeds, Feminist Books, 1974. Ann Oakley, *The Sociology of Housework*, Oxford, Blackwell, 1974. Ann Oakley, *Housewife*, Allen Lane, 1974. W. Secombe, 'The Housewife and Her Labour under Capitalism', *New Left Review* 83 (1974), pp. 3–24. Leonore Davidoff, 'The

Rationalization of Housework', in Diana Leonard Barker and Sheila Allen, eds, *Dependence and Exploitation in Work and Marriage*, Longman, 1976. J. Gardiner, 'Political Economy of Domestic Labour in Capitalist Society', in Barker and Allen, eds, *op. cit.* Eli Zaretsky, *Capitalism, the Family and Personal Life*, Pluto, 1976. For reference, see: Nona Glazer-Malbin 'Housework', *Signs: Journal of Women in Culture and Society*, Summer 1976, pp. 905–22, review essay. Peter Rushton, 'Marxism, Domestic Labour and the Capitalist Economy: A Note on Recent Discussions', in Chris Harris, ed., *The Sociology of the Family: New Directions for Britain*, Sociological Review Monograph 28, June 1979.

3. Marjorie and C.H.B. Quennell, *Everyday Things in England*: vols for 1500–1799, 1933–1851, 1851–1914, 1914–1968, Batsford. Lawrence Wright, *Clean and Decent: the Fascinating History of the Bathroom and the W.C.* Routledge & Kegan Paul, 1960. Lawrence Wright, *Home Fires Burning: the History of Domestic Heating and Cooking*, Routledge & Kegan Paul, 1964. See also: Siegfried Giedion, *Mechanization Takes Command: a Contribution to Anonymmous History*, Oxford University Press, 1948, which deals in great detail with invention and diffusion but is not concerned with the social relations of housework. For a specialized study see: Adrian Forty, *The Electric Home: a Case Study of the Domestic Revolution of the Inter-war Years*, Open University, 1975, A 305, 19–20.
4. Sarah Fenstermaker Berk, ed., (1980) *Women and Household Labor*, Sage, 1980. Joan Rothschild, 'Technology, "Women's Work" and the Social Control of Women', in Margherita Rendel, ed., *Women, Power and Political Systems*, Croom Helm, 1981a. Joan Rothschild, 'A Feminist Perspective on Technology and the Future', *Women's Studies International Quarterly*, *4* 1 (1981b), 65–74. Joan Rothschild, 'Technology, Housework, and Women's Liberation: a Theoretical Analysis', in Joan Rothschild, ed., *Machina Ex Dea: Feminist Perspectives on Technology*, NY and Oxford, Pergamon, 1983. Christine Bose, 'Technology and Changes in the Division of Labour in the American Home', *Women's Studies International Quarterly*, *2* (1979), 295–304. Christine E. Bose, Philip L. Bereano, Mary Malloy, 'Household Technology and the Social Construction of Housework', *Technology and Culture* 25 (1984), 53–82. Ursula Huws, 'Domestic Technology – Liberator or Enslaver?', *Scarlet Women, Journal of the Socialist Feminist Current of the Women's Movement* 14 (1982), 35–38. Graham Thomas and Christine Zmroczek Shannon, *Technology and Household Labour: Are the Times A-changing*? Science Policy Research Unit, University of Sussex, March 1982.
5. Ruth Schwartz Cowan, *More Work For Mother: The Ironies of Household Technology from the Open Hearth to the Microwave*, NY, Basic Books, 1983; see also her related essay, 'More Work for Mother: Technology and Housework in the USA', in Les Levidow and Bob Young, eds, *Science, Technology and the Labour Process*, volume 2, Free Association Books, 1985, pp. 88–128. Meg Luxton, *More Than a Labour of Love: Three Generations of Women's Work in the Home*, Toronto, The Women's Press, 1980.

6. Patricia Branca, *Silent Sisterhood: Middle-class Women in the Victorian Home*, Croom Helm, 1975. Leonore Davidoff, *op. cit.* (Note 2).
7. Michael Young and Peter Willmott, *Family and Kinship in East London*, Routledge & Kegan Paul, 1957. Peter Willmott and Michael Young, *Family and Class in a London Suburb*, Routledge & Kegan Paul, 1960.
8. Ruth Schwartz Cowan, 'A Case Study of Technological Change: the Washing Machine and the Working Wife', in Mary S. Hartman and Lois Banner, eds, *Clio's Consciousness Raised, New Perspectives on the History of Women*, Harper & Row, 1974. Ruth Schwartz Cowan, 'The Industrial Revolution in the Home: Household Technology and Social Change in the 20th Century', *Technology and Culture* 17 (1976), 1–23. Ruth Schwartz Cowan, 'Two Washes in the Morning and a Bridge Party at Night: the American Housewife Between the Wars', *Women's Studies* 3 (1976), 147–71. Ruth Schwartz Cowan, 'From Virginia Dare to Virginia Slims: Women and Technology in American Life', *Technology and Culture* 20 (1979).
9. Simone de Beauvoir, *The Second Sex* (1949), Jonathan Cape, 1953. Germaine Greer, *The Female Eunuch*, MacGibbon & Kee, 1970.
10. Betty Friedan, *The Feminine Mystique*, Gollancz, 1963, chapter 10, applying Parkinson's Law to housework.

Biographies

From: Maureen McNeil (ed.), *Gender and Expertise*, London: Free Association Press, 1987.

BARBARA McCLINTOCK What Price Objectivity?

Ania Grobicki

Barbara McClintock won the Nobel Prize for medicine and physiology in 1984. The previous year a book about her life and work, written by Evelyn Fox Keller, had been published. Understandably, it became something of an inspiration for women working within science and technology, feminists and non-feminists alike. The story is heroic, made all the more enjoyable when one knows that there is a happy ending. But beware, because idealized biographies like this one can minimize and obscure the real issues which lie behind one woman's life and work.

McClintock is an astonishing woman in her tenacity and her capacity for self-reliance. She survived setbacks in her career and attacks from her 'scientific colleagues' that would have annihilated (and in fact did annihilate) most women who attempted to do original scientific research in the past sixty years. Her chosen field was cytogenetics, which studies genetic traits by looking at an entire cell and analysing the appearance of the chromosomes.

Through cross-breeding and growing generations of maize plants, and examining their individual cells under a microscope, McClintock gradually developed a unique understanding of the relationship between heredity and environment and of the development of organisms from the embryo. Her work is extraordinarily detailed and complex, yet at the same time she displays a vision which is, as Keller says, 'transcending that of both Lamarck and Darwin' (p. 195).

During most of her sixty years of research she worked alone, without students or technicians to carry out the more routine tasks, and with some long periods of financial insecurity. In her personal life she had few close friends, and we are told that she sought no family ties. For McClintock the dilemma of career versus family was irrelevant: she loved her work and followed it wherever it led her, without planning or making conscious choices. It was her inner conviction and the sheer enjoyment of her research that sustained her throughout. In this respect she was different from most women entering science, who frequently find the conflicts between their work and personal life intolerable, and whose field may stifle rather than reward their creativity.

McClintock was eventually offered a secure tenured position in 1942, after nearly twenty years of contract work. By 1951 she had gained a considerable scientific reputation, very unusual for a woman of that time: she received support from ther colleagues and various academic honours. However, in that year she presented her revolutionary theory of 'transposition' at a major seminar and found herself ridiculed. She had developed a complex explanation of genetic instability, which depended on the ability of chromosomal fragments to move around or 'transpose' on the chromosome at various stages in cell development.

The scientific basis of the work is very clearly explained in Keller's book, and it is well worth the effort of following the arguments. It is astounding to read of the rejection of McClintock's ideas, the rebuffs and insults she received, to the point where she refused to give talks or even publish her research findings. Yet she continued with the work. For many years thereafter her ideas were ignored by the world of genetics, until they were supported by new developments in molecular biology. Some of her theories began to be understood and taken up by workers in the field during the 1970s. The rest, as they say, is history.

Idealized Biography

It is a great pity that McClintock's biographer was not able to draw out of this story the powerful indictment of Western science that it deserves. She contents herself with a narrow, academic analysis. What is ignored becomes more important than what is included. Present throughout the story is the consciousness of a far broader, more complex reality than that being described – the consciousness being McClintock's, not the author's. At the same time the book is well researched, clearly presented, with an elegant structure. In fact it is like a scientific text, with all the omissions and simplifications that implies. One might expect to gain insights into issues of gender and expertise, but they are available in spite of Keller's approach, rather than because of it. The only specific mention of gender in the entire book is in the acknowledgements. Here Keller writes:

> My exploration of McClintock's life has also sharpened my thinking on a subject I have written about elsewhere: the relation of gender to science. In her adamant rejection of female stereotypes, McClintock poses a challenge to any simple notions of a 'feminine' science. Her pursuit of a life in which 'the matter of gender drops away' provides us instead with a glimpse of what a 'gender-free' science might look like. (p. xvii)

It was undoubtedly the fact that McClintock was a woman which marginalized her so thoroughly, and the sheer sexism of her academic environment that enabled her critics to dismiss her as 'mad' (p. 140). Women in research still often walk the tightrope between ridicule and self-betrayal, because the preponderance of men keeps sexist mechanisms firmly in place. In this context McClintock's pride in being a 'maverick' is superb. She freely admits the importance of emotion in her work, in her identification with the plants she studies. In one anecdote she tells how her intense frustration over a problem caused her, after three baffling days, to go for a long walk and 'let the tears roll a little' (p. 115). When she returned to the lab, she found that she understood what she was looking at under the microscope. The pattern had suddenly become apparent.

Thus another (and related) reason for McClintock's isolation within genetics was her holistic approach. Reductionism has been the motivating force behind the Western scientific edifice, which relies on elegant simplification, on the ability to describe reality through numbers and equations. Genetics as a 'true science' took off when molecular biologists finally succeeded in reducing the basis of life, the chromosomes within the cell, into building blocks and formulae. It was many years before the greater complexities of the system began to be understood within mainstream genetics. Yet McClintock had grasped and described such complexities decades before, through her perception of the organism as a coherent whole, capable of undergoing adaptation and development, and through her ability to perceive intricate patterns without having to break them down.

The argument I am presenting here is not that women (as a gender) have access to a more emotional, holistic type of understanding than men. It is not rare for women to confine themselves to rigid, mechanistic modes of thinking, particularly when their careers are at stake. The point is that, within an oppressive patriarchal structure, the women who have the courage to do their work with a deeper consciousness are doubly penalized. Western scientific thought thas been developed almost exclusively by men, within a reductionist mode. Thus women like McClintock are vulnerable both because of being women and being 'unscientific' and they are attacked under the cover of the ever-present claim of 'objectivity'.

Feminist Objectivity?

In *A Feeling for the Organism,* Keller not only ignores these issues but refuses to question the basis of 'objectivity' on which the scientific community operates. Her remarkably insipid analysis touches on the relationship between the individual and the community (both seemingly gender-free) and the role of deviance in generating new ideas. She discusses differences in perception and problems of communication, which leads her to look at modes of discourse. There is even a mention of alterntive modes of thought, since Barbara McClintock has no hesitation in calling herself a mystic and is drawn to some of the Eastern philosophies. She had an active interest in other cultures. However, Keller dismisses these last characteristics as 'oddities' (p. 204).

Even when she is writing in a women's journal under so bold a heading as 'Feminism and Science', Keller displays classic liberal sentiments. She writes from a scientist's perspective first and foremost, depicting science as a single massive 'enterprise' that has certain flaws: 'The lens of feminist politics brings into focus certain masculinist distortions of the scientific enterprise, creating, for those of us who are scientists, a potential dilemma.' She goes so far to say: 'I will suggest that we might even use feminist thought to illuminate and clarify part of the substructure of science (which may have been historically conditioned into distortion) in order to preserve the things that science has taught us, in order to be more objective' (p. 589).

If we look more closely at the concepts used by Keller, we find that she wants 'a science less restrained by the impulse to dominate'. She would like to see the 'scientific project' cleansed of its 'masculinist ideology'. The cornerstone of good, progressive science is its objectivity, which embraces 'critical self-reflection'. The crude realism of most male scientists thus needs to be 'refined'. On the other hand, relativism means a return to feminine (subjective) values, and effectively removes feminist critique from the scientific arena altogether. She warns against the 'intellectual danger' of 'viewing science as pure social product'. Thus true objectivity occupies the middle ground and enables 'us' (as scientists) to make the correct choices, the correct judgements, and develop a science which is unhindered by androcentric bias. (All quotes are taken from the above paper by Keller.)

Such a position is inherently conservative. Objectivity is equated with detached knowledge, which is somehow true and neutral, once it has been critically examined for traces of sexism. Experiences of struggle, however, surely teach us that there is no knowledge, and no scientific practice, which can be divorced from the setting in which it is made or used. The false dichotomy which Keller creates between objectivity and subjectivity, relegating the latter to the realm of feminine values and emotions, blocks a deeper understanding of reality from being expressed. McClintock's life and work was informed by such a deeper understanding. Keller reduces her struggle by confining it to the narrow, 'objective' ground that she so clearly transcended.

In a recent paper devoted solely to the subject of gender and science ('How Does Gender Matter?'), Keller asserts unashamedly:

> Modern science, as we know it, has arisen once and only once in cultural history. . . . We cannot look to other cultures, with other gender systems, and ask how their science is or was different, for the

> simple reason that the knowledge practices of other cultures do not conform to what we call science.

At this point it becomes necessary to look more closely at what it is that Keller calls science. It clearly began only a few hundred years ago with people like Kepler and Newton: it provided the underpinning for the Industrial Revolution; and it takes place largely in Western Europe and North America. Because of the objectivity inherent in it, 'good science' is certain to predominate over bad science, which is crudely biased towards men. Keller interprets the recent vindication of McClintock's work as showing clearly that science has the innate capacity to rectify wrongs, and it 'bears witness to the underlying health of the scientific enterprise' (p. 197).

This naive and dangerous attitude takes no account of the fact that this type of science developed with, and is entrenched within, the capitalist system. It is transformed by the exigencies of that system and is used to manipulate and control people in terms of race, gender and class divisions. Science has defined the parameters of the workplace, to the detriment of the workers therein; and more recently technology for mass consumption has played a large part in shaping whole cultures. Yet Western science is only one way of describing reality, nature and the way things work – a very effective way, certainly, for the production of goods and profits, but unsatisfactory in most other respects. It is an imperialist arrogance which ignores the sciences and insights of other cultures and other times.

In this context, McClintock's eventual triumph is not a vindication of Western science. Rather, it shows how a deeper vision, pursued with courage, integrity, and some financial security, can transform the dominant treatment of reality into a different way of doing things. Despite the powerful interests which attempt to block their development, there are now many avenues, even in Western societies, down which we can look to find alternatives. From the more holistic approaches to medicine, especially that of 'woman-centred gynaecology', to the study of whole systems of social and technological interconnections; from the blurring of boundaries between disciplines, to the growth of 'green ideas' and the Marxist critique of science; there are numerous areas in which change is taking place and in which the nature of gender oppression is becoming well understood. In countries where progressive political change is higher on the agenda than in Britain, there is a particularly urgent task of choosing and developing sciences and technologies which are not oppressive and yet are adequate for people's material needs.

I do not espouse the concept of 'feminist science', but neither would I join with Keller in calling for a 'gender-free science'. Every scientist's work – like any other type of work – reflects in some way her or his gender, background, and class position, together with the structural constraints which society places on that work. Science is not monolithic and it cannot be transformed as if it were. Yet it needs to be entered and used and thought about from within, as well as from without. There may be enormous penalties and constraints, but there are also pleasures and rewards in the struggle, as McClintock's story shows. This is true not only of rarefied research, but also of development work and teaching. Above all, it is important for the people most oppressed by Western science to make use of what resources there are, to acquire skills and confidence, and to keep challenging the orthodox pretensions of 'scientific' hierarchies of power.

References

E. F. Keller, *A Feeling for the Organism: the Life and Work of Barbara McClintock,* New York, W. H. Freeman, 1983.

E. F. Keller, 'Feminism and Science', *Signs*, 7, 3 (1982), 589–602.

E. F. Keller, 'How does Gender Matter?' British Association for the Advancement of Science, Annual Meeting, August 1985.

MARY SEACOLE

Pam Smith

Review of Ziggi Alexander and Audrey Dewjee, *Wonderful Adventures of Mrs Seacole in Many Lands*, Bristol, Falling Wall, 1984, £3.95.

I first learnt of Mary Seacole around 1980 from a *Time Out* review which referred to the 'Roots in Britain' exhibition organized by the editors of her book, Alexander and Dewjee. It surprised and fascinated me that Florence Nightingale had had a black counterpart in the Crimea. It also appalled me that I had gone through nursing training and medical sociology courses and not heard of her. However, on eventually reading Mary Seacole's adventures in order to write this review, I soon realized why she had been hidden from history in general and nursing history in particular. I discuss later some of these reasons, particularly those related to gender, race and class.

Other issues emerged from reading about Mrs Seacole's life and times and led me to reflect upon my own experience as a community nurse teacher in Tanzania and Mozambique during the 1970s. One such issue was the appropriateness of training programmes for health workers in underdeveloped countries; another was the division of labour in the delivery of health care. In other words, many countries continue to train doctors and nurses within a Western model of hospital-based curative health programmes. During colonial times doctors and senior nurses generally came from Europe. They were white and the doctors were usually male. Nursing training and sometimes medical auxiliary courses were offered to the local population. The majority of entrants were men, since few women had the necessary educational qualifications. As education became more widespread, increasing numbers of women were actively recruited for

Mural dedicated to Mary Seacole, Brixton, south London. Photo: Maureen McNeil.

nursing, whilst medical practice by doctors remained mainly a male preserve.

It is true that Tanzania and Mozambique have made great strides in overcoming their colonial heritage in many ways. Health policies have subsequently emphasized primary health care as a more appropriate model for meeting the health needs of a largely rural population, 45 per cent of whom are under fifteen. However, at Independence (1961 for Tanzania, 1975 for Mozambique), both countries inherited large numbers of Western-trained nurses. Many of them, particularly in Mozambique, were undertaking tasks for which they had not been trained. Posted to remote rural areas, they were involved in diagnosing and treating common infectious diseases and malnutrition, rather than nursing patients in hospital beds under the direction of doctors.

Similarly, Mary Seacole's work as a healer and doctress, in contrast to Nightingale's hospital nurses, illustrates the contradiction of nursing training for many Third World situations. Her use of traditional herbs and remedies also highlights the potential of integrating traditional practices into so-called modern health-care systems. The fact that she was from Jamaica and had worked in Central America prepared her for the conditions she was to meet in the Crimea far better than any experience she could have gained in London.

This reminded me of the situation in Tanzania and Mozambique, where foreign health workers were much more effective, certainly in the short term, if they had had appropriate experience and training before coming to work there. In Mozambique, for example, doctor auxiliaries had not been trained during colonial times, as in other African countries. Medical assistants from Tanzania and Guiné-Conakry, who had been specifically trained to work in the health services of their independent countries, adapted quickly and well to working in Mozambique. Particularly interesting were the surgical assistants from Guiné-Conakry who could perform basic surgery in small hospitals rather than having to transfer patients long distances to urban centres. For my own part I found that I drew on my health visitor training rather than my hospital nursing training.

Moreover, getting relevant experience includes exposing trainee health workers to situations they will meet once they are qualified, as well as encouraging them to use the experiences acquired before training. I am thinking, for example, of the field trips in Tanzania, during which student nurses in their final year spent two months in rural health centres and village health posts. During these trips, far away from the capital Dar es Salaam and the teaching hospital where they had acquired most of their training, they were able to use their technical skills. They were also able to use their childhood knowledge of rural life to adapt to village conditions with no electricity or running water and limited foodstuffs.

Indeed, it is a worldwide feature of many forms of technical and general education that students' prior knowledge and experience are neither valued nor utilized during formal training programmes. In addition, professional socialization often results in students suppressing or rejecting knowledge and skills they possessed before starting their formal training. This is particularly frequent in nursing, since it is an occupation which consists of many caring activities that do not require specialist training and are traditionally associated with women. Training programmes therefore tend to emphasize technical nursing and may even routinize care activities into formal procedures. Mary Seacole was unique in the Crimea in that she was able to combine her many talents much more successfully outside the emergent British health-care structure: a structure that was to dominate the future development of health care not only in Britain but also in countries which became British colonies.

Mrs Seacole – The Book

Mrs Seacole's *Wonderful Adventures . . . in Many Lands* was originally written and published in 1857. Mrs Seacole, who was as famous as Florence Nightingale in her lifetime, wrote the book soon after her return from the battlefields of the Crimea. It serves as an account of a unique individual who, despite being female and black, was able to operate as an independent agent in the repressive white male-dominated world of the nineteenth century. The book provides insights into her own and Western society's perception of class, gender and race, as well as describing her skills as a doctress, healer and businesswoman.

Born in 1805 in Kingston, Jamaica, she died in London in 1881. She was married but soon widowed. Although her time in the Crimea spanned only two years (1854–6), it was this period that was to make both Mary Seacole and Florence Nightingale household names in Britain. Significantly, it was the 'lady with the lamp', the epitome of Victorian upper-class womanhood, who took her place in history as the founder of modern nursing. W. H. Russell, *The Times*' war correspondent, wrote in the preface to *Wonderful Adventures*: 'I trust that England will not forget one who nursed her sick', yet Mrs Seacole's class and race militated against memory of her surviving into the twentieth century.

She certainly did not fit the popular image of a nursing leader, neither then nor now, and nursing the sick in the Crimea was just one of her many activities. Mary Seacole worked independently of the medical profession and military authorities. Consequently the scope of her work, coupled with her commercial interests, differed dramatically from that of Florence Nightingale and her nurses. Even though she had left the West Indies for London with the intention of being recruited to nurse with Nightingale in the Crimea, Seacole's personal application was rejected. She therefore resolved to go at her own expense. Her medical skills and commercial experience, gained in the West Indies and Central America, were far beyond the experiences of the British recruits.

It is well known that Nightingale and her nurses faced hostility and opposition to their work, particularly from doctors. In order to overcome these negative reactions, they restricted their activities to the hospitals rather than the battlefields. Their tasks complemented those of doctors. Hence they fed patients, tended their wounds and cared for the dying. This is not to undervalue their important work, but a model was established for the future of nursing in Britain in which nurses received orders from doctors and organized their work accordingly. In the second half of the nineteenth century doctors viewed a nurse as 'a reliable assistant who was constantly on the wards and could be relied upon to distribute the medicine and apply the poultice exactly as desired' (Abel-Smith p. 43).

The Crimea also established a precedent in the recruitment of women from the upper and upper middle classes to become nursing administrators or matrons. In the voluntary hospitals there was the 'reproduction of the wider Victorian class structure based on preconceived notions of the division of labour between the sexes and between women of different classes'. Hence the matron maintained the status quo as ' "lady of the house" whose organization and supervision of the servants (the nurses) complemented rather than subverted the authority of her husband (the doctor)' (Carpenter, p. 92). Mary Seacole did not fit into either mould. Her mother had been a hotelier and doctress in the tradition of many West Indian women. Her father was a Scottish army officer. The editors think this may partly explain some of her enthusiasm for military life and personalities.

Mrs Seacole had run a successful hotel in Central America with scarce resources before going to the Crimea. She also had experience of dealing with cholera epidemics and treating a wide range of other diseases and conditions. Seacole's understanding of the link between hygiene and contagion was advanced for the period. Some years before John Snow's essay 'On the mode of Communication of Cholera' (1855) she describes the sound measures she took for controlling the disease in the Central American community where she was living. She even performed a post-mortem on a child cholera victim to understand better its pathology and hence improve her treatment of the disease. Her skills went far beyond the conventional duties of a nurse. She was in her own right a healer and a doctress of the sort that the British Medical Act (1858) sought to ban in the interests of a newly emerging class of 'professional' male doctors.

Seacole's altruistic impulse to help people, unlike that of the Victorian ladies of means, was tempered by the need to earn a living. She set up what was to become the famous 'British Hotel', which provided hospitality and supplies for both officers and men. The sudden ending to the war, however, resulted in her arriving back in Britain almost penniless. A benefit was organized for her by the military in an attempt to compensate for her losses and in appreciation of the good work she had done as a doctress, nurse and 'sutler' (one who follows an army and sells provisions to the soldiers).

Although Mrs Seacole's style in *Wonderful Adventures* is at times ingratiating and personal, a recent reread of a novel written at that time reminded me that this was a common characteristic of Victorian authorship. It should not be forgotten that Mrs Seacole is addressing her upper- and middle-class contemporaries. Her own views about class and race were often shared, and she was at least as proud of her Scottish ancestry as of her Afro-Caribbean roots.

The editors' introduction provides interesting background information. Although their style is descriptive rather than analytical, this is no major criticism of the important work they have done in reissuing Mary Seacole's *Wonderful Adventures*. They have made an important contribution by giving Mary Seacole a place in women's history, so that she is no longer hidden. Her adventures are pertinent to understanding the interrelationships of race, gender and class, as well as the role of woman as health workers.

References

B. Abel-Smith, *The Hospitals, 1800–1948: A Study in Social Administration in England and Wales*, Heinemann, 1964.

M. Carpenter, 'Managerialism and the Division of Labour in Nursing', in R. Dingwall and J. McIntosh, eds, *Readings in the Sociology of Nursing*, Churchill Livingstone, 1978.

CRITICAL BIBLIOGRAPHY: GENDER AND EXPERTISE

Maureen McNeil

The topic of gender and expertise is so wide-ranging that a bibliography such as this is potentially infinite. This is necessarily a limited one, suggesting some of the most interesting work on various aspects of the issues. As will be obvious from the references below, there has been a flourishing of analysis on this topic recently, so it is rather difficult to keep abreast of the growing literature.

There is also the constant temptation to look for treatments of the 'woman and' or 'women in' variety. To some extent this is unavoidable, as looking at the position of women in various fields of expertise has always been a primary way into gender relations. Yet almost all the literature about diverse fields of expertise could and should be re-read for its revelations about gender relations. For this reason I have also included items which are not particularly focused on women yet where gender relations are crucial (although often untheorised).

The bibliography is arranged thematically. This seemed to be the most useful way of presenting the references. However, many items do not fit exclusively into one category, so occasionally references are repeated where this seemed appropriate. Where whole categories seem rather intertwined I have also suggested that other sections should be consulted. The categories are arranged alphabetically for convenience, except for the listing of special issues of relevant journals at the end; where their contents are not obvious, some explanation is provided. (Publication is in London unless otherwise stated.)

BIOLOGY

Biology has, of course, been a main tool in defining and constructing sex differences. Thus this list includes analyses of both contemporary biology and the history of biology. Bleier's *Science and Gender*, Birke's *Women, Feminism and Biology*, and Fausto-Sterling's *Myths of Gender* are the newest attempts from within feminism to tackle biology. Donna Haraway reviews Sayers' *Biological Politics* in this collection.

Also consult references under: *Primatology, Evolutionary Theory and Sociobiology; Reproductive Medicine, Technology and Politics*.

E. Bartels (1982) 'Biological sex differences and sex stereotyping', in E. Whitelegg *et. al.*, eds *The Changing Experience of Women*, Oxford: Martin Robertson, pp. 254–66.

R. Bleier (1984) *Science and Gender: A Critique of Biology and its Theories on Women*, Oxford: Pergamon.

—(1986) 'Sex differences research: science or belief?', in R. Bleier, ed. *Feminist Approaches to Science*, Oxford: Pergamon, pp. 147–65.

L. Birke (1985) *Women, Feminism and Biology: the Feminist Challenge*, Brighton: Wheatsheaf.

L. Birke and J. Silverton, eds (1984) *More than the Parts: Biology and Politics*, Pluto.

A. Fausto-Sterling (1985) *Myths of Gender: Biological Theories about Women and Men*, New York: Basic.

E. Fee (1980) 'Nineteenth century craniology: the study of the female skull', *Bulletin of the History of Medicine* 53.

—(1983) 'Women's nature and scientific objectivity', in M. Lowe and R. Hubbard, eds *Woman's Nature: Rationalizations of Inequality*, Oxford: Pergamon, pp. 9–28.

N. Goddard and M.S. Henifin (1984) 'A feminist approach to the biology of women', *Women's Studies Quarterly* 12:11–18.

M.J. Goodman and L.E. Goodman (1981) 'Is there a feminist biology?', *International Journal of Women's Studies* 4:393–413.

S. J. Gould (1978) 'Women's brains', *New Scientist* 1127:364–7.

D. Griffiths and E. Saraga (1979) 'Sex differences and cognitive abilities: a sterile field for enquiry?', in O. Hartnett *et al.*, eds *Sex-Role Stereotyping*, Tavistock.

D. Haraway (1981) 'In the beginning was the word: the genesis of biological theory', *Signs* 6:469–82.

K. Harstrup (1978) 'The semantics of biology: virginity', in S. Ardener, ed. *Defining Females*, Croom Helm.

R. Hubbard (1981) 'The emperor doesn't wear any clothes: the impact of feminism on biology', in D. Spender, ed. *Men's Studies Modified*, Oxford: Pergamon, pp. 213–35.

R. Hubbard, M.S. Henifin and B. Fried eds (1979) *Women Look at Biology Looking at Women*, Cambridge, Mass: Schenkman.

—(1982) *Biological Woman, the Convenient Myth*, Cambridge, Mass: Schenkman.

R. Hubbard and M. Lowe eds (1978) *Genes and Gender II: Pitfalls in Research on Sex and Gender*, New York: Gordian.

L.J. Jordanova (1986) 'Naturalizing the family: literature and the bio-medical sciences in the late eighteenth century', in L.J. Jordanova, ed. *Languages of Nature*, Free Association, pp. 86–116.

M.M. Kimball (1981) 'Women and science: a critique of biological theories', *International Journal of Women's Studies* 4:318–38.

L. Leibowitz (1978) *Females, Males, Families: a Biosocial Approach*, Cambridge, Mass: Duxbury.

H. Longino and R. Doell (1983) 'Body, bias, and behaviour: a comparative analysis of reasoning in two areas of biological science', *Signs* 9:206–27.

M. Lowe (1983) 'The dialectic of biology and culture', in M. Lowe and R. Hubbard, eds *Woman's Nature: Rationalisations of Inequality*, Oxford: Pergamon, pp. 39–62.

C.P. MacCormack (1977) 'Biological events and cultural control', *Signs* 3:93–100.

K. Messing (1983) 'The scientific mystique: can a white lab coat guarantee purity in the search for knowledge about the nature of women?' in M. Lowe and R. Hubbard, eds *Woman's Nature: Rationalizations of Inequality*, Oxford: Pergamon, pp. 75–88.

A. Oakley (1976) *Sex, Gender and Society*, Temple Smith.

M. Ruse (1981) *Is Science Sexist? And Other Problems in the Biomedical Sciences*, Dordrecht: Reidel.

V. Sapiro, ed. (1985) *Women, Biology and Public Policy*, Beverly Hills: Sage.

J. Sayers (1982) *Biological Politics: Feminist and Anti-Feminist Perspectives*, Tavistock.

S. Sheilds (1978) 'Sex and the biased scientist', *New Scientist* 1132:752–4.

C. Smith-Rosenberg and C. Rosenberg (1973) 'The female animal: medical and biological views of woman and her role in nineteenth-century America', *Journal of American History* 60:332–56.

E. Tobach and B. Rosoff, eds (1978) *Genes and Gender*, New York: Gordian.

M.W. Watts (1984) *Biopolitics and Gender*, New York: Haworth. Also published as *Women & Politics* 3, 2/3 (1983).

DEVELOPMENT, THE 'THIRD WORLD' AND TECHNOLOGY

The terms 'development' and 'third world' are very problematic. I have used them merely to designate studies of technology and gender relations outside the industrialised west. The following list offers only some starting points and some interesting investigations in this field. These items are helpful reminders of the need for conceptualising the sexual division of labour internationally.

L. Arizpe and J. Aranda (1981) 'The "comparative advantages" of women's disadvantages: women workers in the strawberry export agribusiness in Mexico', *Signs* 7.

L. Beneria and G. Sen (1981) 'Accumulation, reproduction, and women's role in economic development: Boserup revisited,' *Signs* 7:279–98.

—(1982) 'Class and gender inequalities and women's role in economic development – theoretical and practical implications', *Feminist Studies* 8,1.

E. Boserup (1970) *Women's Role in Economic Development*, New York: St. Martin's.

E. Boulding (1981) 'Integration into what? Reflections on development planning for women', in R. Dauber and M.L. Cain, eds *Women and Technological Change in Developing Countries*, Boulder: Westview, pp. 9–30.

Changing Role of SE Asian Women, special joint issue of *Pacific Research*, July/Oct, *9*, 5–6 (1978) and *Southeast Asia Chronicle* Jan/Feb, 66 (1979).

W. Chapkis and C. Enloe (1983) *Of Common Cloth: Women in the Global Textile Industry*, Amsterdam, and Washington DC: Transnational Institute.

P. D'Onofrio-Flores (1982) 'Technology, economic development and the division of labor by sex', in P.M. D'Onofrio-Flores and S.M. Pfafflin, eds *Scientific-Technological Change and the Role of Women in Development*, Boulder: Westview, pp. 13–28.

P. D'Onofrio-Flores and S.M. Pfafflin, eds (1982) *Scientific-Technological Change and the Role of Women in Development*, Boulder: Westview.

D. Elson and R. Pearson (1981) ' "Nimble fingers make cheap workers": an analysis of women's employment in third world export manufacturing', *Feminist Review* 7:87–107.

M.P. Fernandez-Kelly (1983) 'Gender and industry on Mexico's new frontier', in J. Zimmerman, ed. *The Technological Woman: Interfacing with Tomorrow*, New York: Praeger, pp. 18–29.

A. Fuentes and B. Ehrenreich (1983) *Women in the Global Factory*, Boston: South End.

R. Grossman (1986) 'Women's place in the integrated circuit', *Radical America* 14,1:29–50.

L.Y.C. Lim (1981) 'Women's work in multinational electronics factories', in R. Dauber and M.L. Cain, eds *Women and Technological Change in Developing Countries*, Boulder: Westview, pp. 181–92.

S. Mitter (1986) *Common Fate, Common Bond*, Pluto.

ILO Office for Women, 'Women, technology and the development process', in R. Dauber and M.L. Cain eds (1981) *Women and Technological Change in Developing Countries*, Boulder: Westview, pp. 33–47.

B. Rogers (1981) *The Domestication of Women: Discrimination in Developing Societies*, New York: St. Martin's.

M. Srinivasan (1982) 'The impact of science and technology and the role of women in science in Mexico', in P.M. D'Onofrio-Flores and S.M. Pfafflin, eds (1982), pp. 113–48.

A. Tadesse (1982) 'Women and technology in peripheral countries: an overview', in P.M. D'Onofrio-Flores and S.M. Pfafflin, eds (1982), pp. 77–111.

I. Tinker (1981) 'New technologies for food-related activities: an equity strategy', in R. Dauber and M.L. Cain eds (1981), pp. 51–88.

A. Whitehead (1985) 'The Green Revolution and women's work in the third world', in W. Faulkner and E. Arnold, eds *Smothered by Invention: Technology in Women's Lives*, Pluto, pp. 182–99.

DOMESTIC SCIENCE AND TECHNOLOGY

The works of Cowan, Hayden and Ravetz are prime sources for a feminist perspective on the history of domestic technology. (See Ravetz's review of R. S. Cowan's *More Work for Mother* in this collection.) By contrast, C. Davidson's *A Woman's Work is Never Done*, although containing some useful information, is almost a coffee-table book, with little analysis. B. Ehrenreich and D. English's *For Her Own Good* examines the emergence of domestic science.

It seemed important to canvass more widely and include studies of domestic labour with a less specific focus on technology. Oakley's studies are crucial in providing close-up examinations of contemporary housewives in Britain. E. Malos's *The Politics of Housework* is an extremely valuable collection, containing a number of articles analysing housework and tracing its history. It also includes reprints of the articles from the 'domestic labour – wages for housework' debate.

P. Bereano, C. Bose and E. Arnold (1985) 'Kitchen technology and the liberation of women from housework', in W. Faulkner and E. Arnold, eds *Smothered by Invention: Technology in Women's Lives*, Pluto, pp. 162–81.

C. Bose and P. Bereano (1983) 'Household technologies: Burden or Blessing?', in J. Zimmerman, ed. *The Technological Woman: Interfacing with Tomorrow*, Praeger.

C. Bose, P. Bereano and M. Malloy (1984) 'Household technology and the social construction of housework', *Technology and Culture* 25:53–82.

L. Burr (1985) 'Housework and the appliance of science', in W. Faulkner and E. Arnold, eds *Smothered by Invention: Technology in Women's Lives*, Pluto, pp. 144–61.

R.S. Cowan (1974) 'A case study of technological and social change: the washing machine and the working life', in M.S. Hartman and L. Banner, eds *Clio's Consciousness Raised*, New York: Harper Row, pp. 245–53.

—(1976) 'The "Industrial Revolution" in the home: household technology and social change in the twentieth century', *Technology and Culture* 17:1–23. Reprinted as 'The Industrial Revolution in the home', in D. MacKenzie and J. Wacjman, eds (1985) *The Social Shaping of Technology*, Milton Keynes: Open University, pp. 181–201.

—(1979) 'From Virginia Dare to Virginia Slims: women and technology in American life', *Technology and Culture* 20:51–63.

—(1983) *More Work for Mother: The Ironies of Household Technology from the Open Hearth to the Microwave*, New York: Basic.

C. Davidson (1982) *A Woman's Work is Never Done: A History of Housework in the British Isles 1650–1950*, Chatto & Windus.

M. Doorly (1983) 'A woman's place: Dolores Hayden on the "grand domestic revolution" ', reprinted from *The Guardian* (1983) in D. MacKenzie and J. Wacjman, eds (1985) *The Social Shaping of Technology*, Milton Keynes: Open University, pp. 219–22.

B. Ehrenreich and D. English (1975) 'The manufacture of housework', *Socialist Revolution* 26:5–40.

—(1979) *For Her Own Good: 150 Years of the Experts' Advice to Women*, Pluto.

C. Hall (1979) 'The early formation of Victorian domestic ideology', in S. Burman, ed. *Fit Work for Women*, Croom Helm, pp. 15–33.

D. Hayden (1981) *The Grand Domestic Revolution: A History of Feminist Design for American Homes, Neighbourhoods and Cities*, Cambridge, Mass: MIT Press.

—(1985) *Redesigning the American Dream*, New York: Norton.

E. Kaluzynska (1980) 'Wiping the floor with theory – a survey of writings on housework', *Feminist Review* 6:27–54.

M.M. Mackintosh (1979) 'Domestic labour and the household', in S. Burman, ed. *Fit Work for Women*, Croom Helm, pp. 173–91.

E. Malos, ed. (1980) *The Politics of Housework*, Allison & Busby.

Matrix eds (1984) *Making Space: Women and the Man-Made Environment*, Pluto.

A. Oakley (1974) *Housewife*, Allen Lane.

— (1974) *The Sociology of Housework*, Oxford: Martin Robertson.

A. Ravetz (1965) 'Modern technology and an ancient occupation: housework in present-day society', *Technology and Culture* 6:256–60.

S. Strasser (1982) *Never Done: A History of American Housework*, New York: Pantheon.

J. Vanek (1974) 'Time spent on housework', *Scientific American* 231,5:116–20.

EDUCATION AND TRAINING

This is such a broad topic that it requires a separate bibliography. Although somewhat eclectic, the list below includes some of the more interesting feminist analyses of power relations within education. It is divided into two sections, the first on general perspectives on education and the second on science education.

Education and Training: General

S. Acker and D.W. Piper, eds (1984) *Is Higher Education Fair to Women?*, Guildford: SRHE and NFER Nelson.

M. Arnot (1986) 'State education policy and girls' educational experiences', in V. Beechey and E. Whitelegg' eds *Women in Britain Today*, Milton Keynes: Open University, pp. 132–72.

M. Arnot ed. (1985) *Race and Gender: Equal Opportunities Policies in Education*, Oxford: Pergamon.

T. Blackstone (1976) 'The education of girls today', in J. Mitchell and A. Oakley, eds *The Rights and Wrongs of Women*, Harmondsworth: Penguin, pp. 199–216.

J. Burnstyn (1977) 'Women's education in England during the nineteenth century: a review of the literature, 1970–76', *History of Education* 6,1.

—(1980) *Victorian Education and the Ideal of Womanhood*, Croom Helm.

M. Byrant (1979) *The Unexpected Revolution: a Study in the History of the Education of Women and Girls in the Nineteenth Century*, Windsor: NFER.

E. Byrne (1978) *Women and Education*, Tavistock.

M. Culley and C. Portuguese, eds (1985) *Gendered Subjects: The Dynamics of Feminist Teaching*, Routledge & Kegan Paul.

M. David (1980) *The State, the Family and Education*, Routledge & Kegan Paul.

A. Davin (1979) ' "Mind that you do as you are told": reading books for board school girls, 1870–1902', *Feminist Review* 3:89–98.

R. Deem (1978) *Women and Schooling*, Routledge & Kegan Paul.

—(1984) *Co-Education Reconsidered*, Milton Keynes: Open University.

—(1986) *Schooling for Women's Work*, Routledge & Kegan Paul.

C. Dyhouse (1981) *Girls Growing Up in Late Victorian and Edwardian England*, Routledge & Kegan Paul.

M. Hughes and M. Kennedy, eds (1985) *New Futures: Changing Women's Education*, Routledge & Kegan Paul.

J. Kamm (1965) *Hope Deferred: Girls' Education in English History*, Methuen.

P. Marks (1976) 'Femininity in the classroom: an account of changing attitudes', in J. Mitchell and A. Oakley, eds *The Rights and Wrongs of Women*, Harmondsworth: Penguin, pp. 176–198.

S. Sharpe (1976) *Just Like a Girl: How Girls Learn to Be Women*, Harmondsworth: Penguin.

D. Spender and E. Sarah, eds (1980) *Learning to Lose: Sexism and Education*, Women's Press.

M. Stanworth (1983) *Gender and Schooling: A Study of Sexual Divisions in the Classroom*, Hutchinson.

P. Stock (1978) *Better than Rubies: A History of Women's Education*, New York: Capricorn.

R.M. Tullberg (1980) 'Women and degrees at Cambridge University 1826–1897', in M. Vicinus, ed. *A Widening Sphere: Changing Roles of Victorian Women*, Methuen, pp. 117–45.

B. Turner (1974) *Equality for Some: The Story of Girls' Education*, Ward Lock.

V. Walkerdine (1981) 'Sex, power and pedagogy', *Screen Education* 38:14–25.

G. Weiner, ed. (1985) *Just a Bunch of Girls: Feminist Approaches to Schooling*, Milton Keynes: Open University.

A. Wickham (1982) 'The state and training programmes for women', in E. White-

legg *et al.*, eds *The Changing Experience of Women*, Oxford: Martin Robertson, pp. 147–63.
—(1985) *Women and Training*, Milton Keynes: Open University.
—(1985) 'Gender divisions, training and the state', in R. Dale, ed. *Education, Training and Employment: Towards a New Vocationalism?*, Oxford: Pergamon.
F. Widdowson (1980) *Going Up into the Next Class: Women and Elementary Education*, WRRC.
A.M. Wolpe (1974) 'The official ideology of education for girls', in M. Flude and J. Ahier, eds *Educability, Schools and Ideology*, Croom Helm.

Science Education

L. Curran (1980) 'Science education: did she drop out or was she pushed?', in Brighton Women and Science Group, *Alice Through the Microscope: The Power of Science Over Women's Lives*, Virago, pp. 22–41.
J. Harding (1980) 'Sex differences in performance in science examinations', in R. Deem *Schooling for Women's Work*, Routlege & Kegan Paul, pp. 87–97.
A. Kelly, ed. (1981) *The Missing Half: Girls and Science Education*, Manchester: Manchester University.
S.V. Rosser (1985) 'Integrating the feminist perspective into courses in introductory biology', in M.R. Schuster and S.R. Van Dyne, eds *Women's Place in the Academy: Transforming the Liberal Arts Curriculum*, Totowa, NJ: Rowman & Allanheld, pp. 258–76.
—(1986) *Teaching Science and Health from a Feminist Perspective*, Oxford: Pergamon.
Science for People, 'Women teaching science: discussion, *Science for People* 58:12–14.
M.H. Whatley (1986) 'Taking feminist science to the classroom: where do we go from here?', in R. Bleier, ed. *Feminist Approaches to Science*, Oxford: Pergamon, pp. 181–90.
J. Whytt (1986) *Girls into Science and Technology: The Story of a Project*, Routlege & Kegan Paul.

FRAMEWORKS: CONCEPTUALISING GENDER RELATIONS AND EXPERTISE

This is something of a catch-all category. It includes examinations of gender dimensions of professionalism (for example Apter's *Why Women Don't Have Wives*, Marshall's *Managers*, Tolson's *The Limits of Masculinity*, Hales' *Living Thinkwork*). It also includes studies of those in unusual locations (in gender terms) within the workforce (see Schreiber and Walshok). In addition, this category incorporates analyses of how the sexual division of labour shapes expertise (Virginia Woolf, of course, had much to say on this topic) and broad explanations of gender relations and expertise, particularly scientific expertise (see Daly, Easlea, Fee, Harding, Keller, Rose references). I have also listed a few 'women's studies' primers (The Bristol Women's Studies Group reader, *Half the Sky*, some of Dale Spender's studies of male control of intellectual production and Bowles and Klein's *Theories of Women's Studies*); these suggest innovations in education and other sites of intellectual work. Alison Jagger compares liberal feminist, traditional marxist, radical feminist and socialist feminist theories of human nature. Fritoj Capra (*The Turning Point*) and C. Spretnak and F. Capra (*Green Politics*) see feminism, the Green movement and other social movements organically coming together in a new social philosophy. Nancy Chodorow's *Reproduction of Motherhood* is included because it has been used extensively (see Easlea and Keller) to explain the psycho-social roots of masculinist science.

Also consult references under: *Philosophy and Epistemology*.

T. Apter (1985) *Why Women Don't Have Wives: Professional Success and Motherhood*, Macmillan.

R. Arditti (1979) 'Feminism and science', in R. Arditti, P. Brennam and S. Cavrak, eds *Science and Liberation*, Boston: South End. Reprinted in E. Whitelegg *et al.*, eds (1982) *The Changing Experience of Women*, Oxford: Martin Robertson, pp. 136–46.

E. Arnold and W. Faulkner (1985) 'Smothered by invention: the masculinity of technology', in W. Faulkner and E. Arnold, eds *Smothered by Invention: Technology in Women's Lives*, Pluto, pp. 18–50.

S. de Beauvoir (1949) *The Second Sex*, H.M. Parshley, trans. and ed., Harmondsworth: Penguin, 1983.

Ruth Bleier, ed. (1986) *Feminist Approaches to Science*, Oxford: Pergamon.

G. Bowles and R.D. Klein (1983) *Theories of Women's Studies*, Routledge & Kegan Paul.

Brighton Women and Science Group (1980) *Alice Through the Microscope: The Power of Science Over Women's Lives*, Virago.

Bristol Women's Studies Group, ed. (1979) *Half the Sky: An Introduction to Women's Studies*, Virago.

H. Burrage (1985) 'In men's hands', *Science for People* 58:16–17.

E. Cadman, G. Chester and A. Pivot (1981) *Rolling Our Own: Women as Printers, Publishers and Distributors*, Minority Press Group.

F. Capra (1982) *The Turning Point: Science, Society, and the Rising Culture*, Flamingo.

S.C. Carothers and P. Krull (1984) 'Contrasting sexual harassment in female and male-dominated occupations', in K.B. Sacks and D. Remy, eds *My Troubles*

are Going to Have Troubles with Me: Everyday Trials and Triumphs of Women Workers, Rutgers, N.J: Rutgers University.
N. Chodorow (1978) *The Reproduction of Mothering: Psychoanalysis and the Sociology of Gender*, London: University of California.
C. Cockburn (1981) 'The material of male power', *Feminist Review* 9:41–58.
M. Daly (1979) *Gyn/Ecology: The Metaethics of Radical Feminism*, Women's Press.
B. Easlea (1981) *Science and Sexual Oppression: Patriarchy's Confrontation with Woman and Nature*, Weidenfeld & Nicolson.
—(1985) 'Exploding masculinity', *Science for People* 59:17–18.
B. Ehrenreich and D. English (1979) *For Her Own Good: 150 Years of the Experts' Advice to Women*, Pluto.
A. Fausto-Sterling (1981) 'Women and science', *Women's Studies International Quarterly* 4:41–50.
S.M. Gearhart (1983) 'An end to technology: a modest proposal', in J. Rothschild, ed. *Machina Ex Dea*: *Feminist Perspectives on Technology*, Pergamon, pp. 171–82.
D. Griffiths (1985) 'The exclusion of women from technology', in W. Faulkner and E. Arnold, eds *Smothered by Invention: Technology in Women's Lives*, Pluto, pp. 51–71.
M. Hales (1980) *Living Thinkwork: Where Do Labour Processes Come From?*, CSE Books.
S. Harding (1986) *The Science Question in Feminism*, Milton Keynes: Open University.
M. Howell (1979) 'Can we be both feminists and professionals?', *Women's Studies International Quarterly* 2,1:1–7.
L. Irigaray (1985) 'Is the subject of science sexed?', *Cultural Critique* 1:73–89.
A.M. Jagger (1983) *Feminist Politics and Human Nature*, Brighton: Harvester.
L. Jordanova (1982) 'Conceptualising power over women', *Radical Science Journal* 12:124–28. Review of B. Ehrenreich and D. English, *For Her Own Good: 150 Years of the Experts' Advice to Women*.
E.F. Keller (1980) 'Feminist critique of Science: a forward or backward move?', *Fundamenta Scientiae* 1:341–9.
—(1982) 'Feminism and science', *Signs* 7:589–602. Reprinted in N.O. Keohane, M.Z. Rosaldo and B.C. Gelpi, eds (1982) *Feminist Theory: A Critique of Ideology*, Brighton: Harvester.
—(1983) 'Feminism as an analytic tool for the study of science', *Academe* 69;15–21.
—(1985) *Reflections on Gender and Science*, Yale University.
—(1985) 'How gender matters, of why it's so hard for us to count past two'. Speech to the British Association for the Advancement of Science, Conference.
J. Marshall (1984) *Managers: Travellers in a Male World*, Chichester: John Wiley & Sons.
M. Namenwirth (1986) 'Science seen through a feminist prism', in R. Bleier, ed. *Feminist Approaches to Science*, Oxford: Pergamon, pp. 18–41.
B. Richards (1985) 'The bomb: men or the state', *Science for the People* 57:12–15.

Review of B. Easlea *Fathering the Unthinkable* and R. Aronson, *The Dialectics of Disaster*.
H. Rose (1982) 'Making science feminist', in E. Whitelegg *et al.*, eds *The Changing Experience of Women*, Oxford: Martin Robertson, pp. 352–72.
J. Russ (1984) *How to Suppress Women's Writing*, Women's Press.
C.T. Schreiber (1979) *Changing Places: Men and Women in Transitional Occupations*, Cambridge, Mass: MIT Press.
D. Spender (1980) *Man Made Language*, Routledge & Kegan Paul.
—(1981) 'The Gatekeepers: A feminist critique of academic publishing', in H. Roberts, ed. *Doing Feminist Research*, Routledge & Kegan Paul, pp. 186–202.
—(1981) *Men's Studies Modified: The Impact of Feminism on the Academic Disciplines*, Oxford: Pergamon.
—(1983) *Women of Ideas: (And What Men Have Done to Them)*, Routledge & Kegan Paul.
C. Spretnak and F. Capra (1984) *Green Politics*, Paladin.
L. Stehelin (1976) 'Science, women and ideology', in H. Rose and S. Rose, eds *The Radicalisation of Science: Ideology of/in the Natural Sciences*, Macmillan, pp. 76–89.
A. Tolson (1977) *The Limits of Masculinity*, Tavistock.
M.L. Walshok (1981) *Blue Collar Women: Pioneers on the Male Frontier*, New York: Anchor.
C. Wolf (1984) *Cassandra: A Novel and Four Essays*, J. Van Heurck, trans., Virago.
V. Woolf (1928) *A Room of One's Own*, Collins, 1985.
—(1938) *Three Guineas*, Harmondsworth: Penguin, 1977.
—(1979) *Virginia Woolf: Women and Writing*, M. Barrett, ed., Women's Press.

HISTORIES OF SCIENCE AND TECHNOLOGY

This category includes the studies of the Scientific Revolution which pioneered the investigation of the gender dynamics within modern science: Brian Easlea's *Witch-hunting, Magic and the New Philosophy* and C. Merchant's *The Death of Nature*. Easlea's *Science and Sexual Oppression* is a broader survey of the history of science and its gender relations. Evelyn Fox Keller has chapters on Bacon's philosophy and other moments in the history of science in her book.

The Watson and Sayre books provide very different perspectives on one episode in the history of science – the discovery of DNA – and very different slants on the sexual politics of the scientists involved. This should remind us that many of the biographies and autobiographies of women working in science and technologies are rich sources of an often-hidden gender dimension to the histories of science and technology. Autumn Stanley has set her project as the recovery of women's hidden contribution to the history of technology.

This list also includes Louise M. Newman's compilation from the periodical *Popular Science*, which was a forum for scientific debate about women's role in American society at the turn of the century. Likewise, Judith Walkowitz's study of the Men and Women's Club, in which Karl Pearson was a leading figure, provides some insight about eugenicist and general scientific thought in intellectual circles of late nineteenth-century London.

Also consult references under: *Scientific and High-Technology Workers.*

E. Easlea (1980) *Witch-hunting, Magic and the New Philosophy, an Introduction to Debates of the Scientific Revolution, 1450–1750*, Brighton: Harvester.

—(1981) *Science and Sexual Oppression: Patriarchy's Confrontation with Woman and Nature*, Weidenfeld & Nicolson.

E.F. Keller (1985) *Reflections on Gender and Science*, Yale University.

C. Merchant (1980) *The Death of Nature: Women, Ecology, and the Scientific Revolution*, Harper & Row.

L.M. Newman, ed. (1984) *Men's Ideas/Women's Realities: Popular Science, 1870–1915*, Oxford: Pergamon.

A. Sayre (1975) *Rosalind Franklin and DNA*, New York: Norton.

A. Stanley (1981) 'Daughter of Isis, daughter of Demeter: when women reaped and sowed', *Women's Studies International Quarterly* 4,3.

—(1983) 'Women hold up two thirds of the sky: notes for a revised history of technology', in J. Rothschild, ed. *Machina Ex Dea: Feminist Perspectives on Technology*, Oxford: Pergamon, pp. 3–22.

M.M. Trescott, ed. (1979) *Dynamos and Virgins Revisited: Women and Technological Change in History*, Scarecrow.

J.R. Walkowitz (1986) 'Science, feminism and romance: the Men and Women's Club 1885–1889', *History Workshop Journal* 21:36–59.

J. Watson (1969) *The Double Helix*, New York: New American Library.

MATHEMATICS

M. Campbell (1974) *Why Would a Girl Go Into Mathematics?*, Westbury, N.Y: Feminist Press.

L.H. Fox, *et al.* (1980) *Women and the Mathematical Mystique*, Baltimore, MD: Johns Hopkins University.

L.M. Osen (1974) *Women in Mathematics*, Cambridge, Mass: M.I.T.

S. Smith (1986) *Separate Tables: An Investigation into Single-Sex Setting in Mathematics*, Manchester Equal Opportunities Commission.

R. Walden and V. Walkerdine (1985) *Girls and Mathematics: From Primary to Secondary Schooling*, Bedford Way Paper 24, University of London Institute of Education.

G. Weiner (1980) 'Sex differences in mathematical performance: a review of research and possible action', in R. Deem, ed. *Schooling for Women's Work*, Routledge & Kegan Paul, pp. 76–86.

MEDICINE

Some of the items in this list are from the history of medicine (for example Figlio, Smith-Rosenberg, Harrison). Many of them look at the history of professionalisation within medicine (Ehrenreich) and English's *Witches, Midwives and Nurses* and *For Her Own Good*; Donnison's *Midwives and Medical Men*). Others are more concerned with the treatment of women as patients.

Also consult references under: *Biology*; *Reproductive Medicine and Technology*; *Women's Health Movement*.

Z. Alexander and A. Dewjee, eds (1984) *Wonderful Adventures of Mrs Seacole in Many Lands*, Bristol: Falling Wall.

W.R. Arney (1982) *Power and the Profession of Obstetrics*, University of Chicago.

E.L. Bassuk (1986) 'The rest cure: repetition or resolution of Victorian women's conflicts', in S. Rubin Suleiman, ed. *The Female Body in Western Culture; Contemporary Perspectives*, Harvard University, pp. 139–51.

L. Bland (1982) ' "Guardians of the race" or "vampires upon the nation's health"? Female sexuality and its regulation in early twentieth-century Britain', in E. Whitelegg *et al.*, eds *The Changing Experience of Women*, Oxford: Martin Robertson, pp. 373–88.

Boston Nurses Group (1978) 'The false promise: professionalism in nursing', *Science for the People* 10,3:20–34.

C. Brown (1975) 'Women workers in the Health Service Industry', *International Journal of Health Services* 5:173–84.

L. Comer (1974) 'Medical mystifications', in S. Allen, L. Sanders and J. Wallis, eds *Conditions of Illusion: Papers from the Women's Movement*, Leeds: Feminist Books, pp. 45–50.

C. Davies ed. (1983) *Rewriting Nursing History*, Croom Helm.

M.A. Doane (1986) 'The clinical eye: medical discourses in the "Woman's Film" of the 1940s', in S. Rubin Suleiman, ed. *The Female Body in Western Culture: Contemporary Perspectives*, Harvard University, pp. 152–74.

J. Donnison (1977) *Midwives and Medical Men: A History of Inter-Professional Rivalries and Women's Rights*, New York: Schocken Books.

L. Doyal and M.A. Elston (1986) 'Women, health and medicine', in V. Beechey and E. Whitelegg, eds *Women in Britain Today*, Milton Keynes: Open University, pp. 173–208.

L. Doyal and I. Pennell (1979) *The Political Economy of Health*, Pluto.

L. Duffin (1978) 'The conspicuous consumptive: woman as invalid', in S. Delamont and L. Duffin, eds *The Nineteenth Century Woman*, Croom Helm.

A. Eccles (1982) *Obstetrics and Gynaecology in Tudor and Stuart England*, Croom Helm.

B. Ehrenreich and D. English (1976) *Complaints and Disorders: The Sexual Politics of Sickness*, Writers and Readers.

—(1976a) *Witches, Midwives and Nurses: A History of Women Healers*, Writers and Readers.

—(1979) *For Her Own Good: 150 Years of the Experts' Advice to Women*, Pluto.

M.A. Elston (1977) 'Women doctors: whose problem?' in M. Stacey, M. Reid, C. Heath and R. Dingwall, eds *Health Care and Health Knowledge*, Croom Helm, pp. 115–38.

—(1980) 'Half our future doctors?', in R. Silverstone and A.M. Ward, eds *The Careers of Professional Women*, Croom Helm, pp. 99–137.

—(1981) 'Medicine as "old husbands' tales": the impact of feminism', in D. Spender, ed. *Men's Studies Modified: The Impact of Feminism on the Academic Disciplines*, Oxford: Pergamon, pp. 189–211.

W. Faulkner (1985) 'Medical technology and the right to heal', in W. Faulkner and E. Arnold, eds *Smothered by Invention: Technology in Women's Lives*, Pluto, pp. 87–108.

K. Figlio (1978) 'Chlorosis and chronic disease in nineteenth century England: the social construction of somatic disease in capitalist society', *Social History* 3:167–97. Revised version (1979) *International Health Services* 8: 589–617.

D. Gorham (1982) *The Victorian Girl and the Feminine Ideal*, Croom Helm.

B. Harrison (1978) 'Women's health and the women's movement in Britain: 1840–1940', in *The Proceedings of the Roots of Sociobiology Conference* sponsored by 'Past and Present' in conjunction with the British Society for History of Science.

J. Leeson and J. Gray (1979) *Women and Medicine*, Tavistock.

J. Lober (1984) *Women Physicians: Careers, Status and Power*, Tavistock.

D.R. Mandelbaum (1978) 'Women in medicine', *Signs* 4,1:136–45.

H. Roberts (1981) 'Women and their doctors: power and powerlessness in the research process', in H. Roberts, ed. *Doing Feminist Research*, Routledge & Kegan Paul, pp. 7–29.

B. Rowland (1981) *Medieval Women's Guide to Health: The First English Gynaecological Handbook*, Croom Helm.

J. Salvage (1985) *The Politics of Nursing*, Heinemann.

D. Scully and P. Bart (1973) 'A funny thing happened on my way to the orifice: woman in gynaecology textbooks', *American Journal of Sociology* 78:1045–50.

E. Shorter (1983) *A History of Women's Bodies*, Allen Lane.

E.M. Sigsworth and T.J. Wyke (1972) 'A study of Victorian prostitution and venereal disease', in M. Vicinus, ed. *Suffer and Be Still: Women in the Victorian Age*, Indiana University, pp. 77–99.

C. Smith-Rosenberg (1972) 'The hysterical woman: sex roles and role conflict in nineteenth-century America', *Social Research* 39:652–78.

H. Standing (1980) ' "Sickness is a woman's business?", reflections on the attri-

bution of illness', in Brighton Women and Science Group *Alice Through the Microscope: The Power of Science over Women's Lives*, Virago, pp. 124–38.
J. Towler and J. Bramall (1986) *Midwives in History and Society*, Croom Helm.
M.R. Walsh (1977) *'Doctors Wanted: No Women Need Apply'. Sexual Barriers in the Medical Profession*, 1835–1975, Yale University.

NATURE/CULTURE/GENDER

This list covers some of the many contributions to debates about how gender divisions relate to the nature/culture dichotomy. This has been an important debate, particularly within anthropology. De Beauvoir's *Second Sex* was an influential formulation for feminism, positing that women were enslaved to nature, while men 'transcended' nature and entered the realm of culture. Ortner reformulates De Beauvoir's argument, claiming that women are devalued in all societies because they are seen to be occupying a transitional role between nature and culture. Penelope Brown and Ludi Jordanova, together with the contributors to the MacCormack and Strathern collection (*Nature, Culture and Gender*), take issue with these conceptualisations of the nature/culture and male/female dichotomies. Susan Griffin, representing a new strand of feminism, offers a poetic celebration of the women-nature bond.

Also consult references under: *Specific Fields – Anthropology*; *Women's Peace Movement.*

E. Ardener (1972) 'Belief and the problem of women', in J.S. La Fontaine, ed. *The Interpretation of Ritual*, Tavistock. Reprinted in S. Ardener (1975) *Perceiving Women*, Malaby.
J.A. Barnes (1973) 'Genetrix: genitor: nature: culture', in J. Goody, ed. *The Character of Kinship*, Cambridge University.
S. de Beavoir (1949) *The Second Sex*, H.M. Parshy, trans., Harmondsworth: Penguin, 1973.
M. Block and J. Block (1980) 'Women and the dialectics of nature in eighteenth century French thought', in C. MacCormack and M. Strathern, eds. *Nature, Culture and Gender*, Cambridge: Cambridge University, pp. 25–41.
P. Brown and L.J. Jordanova (1981) 'Oppressive dichotomies: the nature/culture debate', in Cambridge Women's Studies Group, ed. *Women in Society: Interdisciplinary Essays*, Virago, pp. 224–41. This article is also reprinted in E. Whitelegg *et al.* (1982) *The Changing Experience of Women*, Oxford: Martin Robertson, pp. 389–99.
J.C. Goodale (1980) 'Gender, sexuality and marriage: a Kaulong model of nature and culture', in C. MacCormack and M. Strathern, eds *Nature, Culture and Gender*, Cambridge: Cambridge University, pp. 119–42.

S. Griffin (1984) *Woman and Nature: The Roaring Inside Her*, Women's Press.

O. Harris (1980) 'The power of signs: gender, culture and the wild in the Bolivian Andes', in C. MacCormack and M. Strathern, eds *Nature, Culture and Gender*, Cambridge: Cambridge University, pp. 70–94.

L.J. Jordanova (1980) 'Natural facts: a historical perspective on science and sexuality', in C. MacCormack and M. Strathern, eds *Nature, Culture and Gender*, Cambridge: Cambridge University, pp. 42–69.

C. Lévi-Strauss (1949) *The Elementary Structures of Kinship*, Eyre & Spottiswood, 1969.

C. MacCormack (1980) 'Nature, culture and gender: a critique', in C. MacCormack and M. Strathern, eds *Nature, Culture and Gender*, Cambridge: Cambridge University, pp. 1–24.

N.C. Mathieu (1978) 'Man-culture and woman-nature', *Women's Studies International Quarterly* 1:55–65.

S. Ortner (1974) 'Is female to male as nature is to culture?', in M.Z. Rosaldo and L. Lamphere, eds *Women, Culture and Society*, Stanford, Calif: Stanford University, pp. 64–87.

M. Strathern (1980) 'No nature, no culture: the Hagen case', in C. MacCormack and M. Strathern, eds *Nature, Culture and Gender*, Cambridge: Cambridge University, pp. 174–222.

PHILOSOPHY AND EPISTEMOLOGY

One of the most interesting features of the recent women's movement has been the investigation of epistemological issues – transformed definitions of knowledge and gender relations within knowledge production. Most of this list represents new feminist explorations in this area. However, Janet Radcliffe Richards remains a *Sceptical Feminist*. Carol McMillan supports a return to traditional female roles by arguing that feminism is philosophically inadequate and constitutes a 'revolt against nature'.

Also consult references under: *Frameworks: Conceptualising Gender Relations and Expertise*.

M. Daly (1979) *Gyn/Ecology: The Metaethics of Radical Feminism*, Women's Press.

E. Fee (1981) 'Is feminism a threat to scientific objectivity?', *International Journal of Women's Studies* 4:378–92.

—(1982) 'A feminist critique of scientific objectivity', *Science for the People* 14: 5–8, 3–33.

—(1986) 'Critiques of modern science: the relationship of feminism to other radical epistemologies', in R. Bleier, ed. *Feminist Approaches to Science*, Oxford: Pergamon, pp. 42–56.

J. Flax (1983) 'Political philosophy and the patriarchal unconscious: a psychoanalytic perspective on epistemology and metaphysics', in S. Harding and M.

Hintikka, eds *Discovering Reality: Feminist Perspectives on Epistemology, Metaphysics, Methodology and Philosophy of Science*, Dordrecht: Reidel.

Lynda M. Glennon (1979) *Women and Dualism: A Sociology of Knowledge Analysis*, New York: Longman.

C. Gould, ed. (1983) *Beyond Domination: New Perspectives in Women and Philosophy*, Totowa, N.J.: Rowan & Allenheld.

C. Gould and M. Wartofsky, eds (1976) *Women and Philosophy: Towards a Philosophy of Liberation*, New York: Putnam.

J. Grimshaw (1982) 'Feminism: history and morality', *Radical Philosophy* 30: 1–6.

—(1983) 'Review of C. McMillan, *Women, Reason and Nature*', *Radical Philosophy* 34: 33–45.

—(1986) *Feminist Philosophers*, Brighton: Harvester.

D. Haraway (1984) 'Class, race, sex, scientific objects of knowledge: a socialist-feminist perspective on the social construction of productive knowledge and some political consequences', in V. Haas and C. Perucci, eds *Women in Scientific and Engineering Professions*, Ann Arbor: University of Michigan, pp. 212–29.

A. Hardie (1983) Review of C. McMillan, *Women, Reason and Nature*, *Radical Philosophy* 34.

S. Harding (1982) 'Is gender a variable in conceptions of rationality? A survey of issues', *Dialecta* 36:2–3. Reprinted in C. Gould, ed. (1983) *Beyond Domination: New Perspectives on Women and Philosophy*, Totowa, NJ: Rowan & Allenheld.

S. Harding and M.B. Hintikka, eds (1983) *Discovering Reality: Feminist Perspectives on Epistemology, Metaphysics, Methodology and Philosophy of Science*, Dordrecht: Reidel.

N. Harstock (1983) 'The feminist standpoint: developing the ground for a specifically feminist historical materialism', in S. Harding and M. Hintikka, eds *Discovering Reality: Feminist Perspectives on Epistemology, Metaphysics, Methodology and Philosophy of Science*, Dordrecht: Reidel.

G. Lloyd (1984) *The Man of Reason: 'Male' and 'Female' in Western Philosophy*, Methuen.

C. McMillan (1982) *Women, Reason and Nature: Some Philosophical Problems with Feminism*, Blackwell.

J. Moulton (1983) 'A paradigm of philosophy: the adversary method', in S. Harding and M. Hintikka, eds *Discovering Reality: Feminist Perspectives on Epistemology, Metaphysics, Methodology and Philosophy*, Dordrecht: Reidel.

J. Radcliffe Richards (1980) *The Sceptical Feminist: A Philosophical Enquiry*, Harmondsworth: Penguin.

H. Rose (1982) 'Making science feminist', in E. Whitelegg *et al.*, eds *The Changing Experience of Women*, Oxford: Martin Robertson, pp. 352–72.

—(1983) 'Hand, brain and heart: a feminist epistemology for the natural sciences', *Signs* 9:73–90.

—(1986) 'Beyond masculinist realities: a feminist epistemology', in R. Bleier, ed. *Feminist Approaches to Science*, Oxford: Pergamon, pp. 57–76.

S.V. Rosser (1984) 'A call for feminist science', *International Journal of Women's Studies* 7:3–9.

S. Ruddick (1980) 'Maternal thinking', *Feminist Studies* 6,2.

M. Vetterling-Braggin F.A. Elliston and J. English, eds, (1977) *Feminism and Philosophy*, Totowa, N.J: Rowan & Allenheld.

C. Wolf (1984) *Cassandra: A Novel and Four Essays*, J. Van Heurck, trans., Virago.

POST-INDUSTRIALISM AND POST-MODERNISM

These articles look at how gender fits into these broad theories of contemporary social development. Dolkhart and Harstock are concerned that theories of post-industrialism seem to neglect women. Haraway and Owens look at post-modernism. Haraway's is the most interesting, challenging, controversial and outrageous consideration of feminism and post-modernism that I have encountered.

J. Dolkhart and N. Harstock (1975) 'Feminist visions of the future', *Quest: a Feminist Quarterly* 2,1:2–6.

D. Haraway (1985) 'A manifesto for Cyborgs: science, technology and socialist feminism in the 1980s', *Socialist Review* 80:65–107.

S. Harding (1986) *The Science Question in Feminism*, Milton Keynes: Open University Press.

C. Owens (1985) 'The discourse of others: feminists and postmodernism' in H. Foster, ed. *Postmodern Culture*, Pluto, pp. 57–82.

PRIMATOLOGY, EVOLUTIONARY THEORY AND SOCIOBIOLOGY

This selection of items should be cross-referenced with the entries under *Biology*.

L. Bland (1981) ' "It's only human nature?": sociobiology and sex differences', *Schooling and Culture* 10:6–14.

R. Bleier (1984) 'Social and political bias in Science: an examination of animal studies and their generalization to human behaviour and evolution', in E. Tobach and B. Rosoff, eds *Genes and Gender II*, New York: Gordian, pp. 49–69.

M.D. Caulfield (1985) 'Sexuality in human evolution: what is "natural" in sex?', *Feminist Studies* 11, 2.

J. Conway (1972) 'Stereotypes of femininity in a theory of sexual evolution', in M. Vicinus, ed. *Suffer and Be Still: Women in the Victorian Age*, Indiana University, pp. 140–54.

L. Duffin (1978) 'Prisoners of progress women and evolution' in S. Delamont and L. Duffin, eds *The Nineteenth-Century Woman: Her Cultural and Physical World*, Croom Helm, pp. 57–91.

M. Gross, and M.B. Averill (1983), 'Evolution and patriarchal myths of scarcity and competition', in S. Harding and M. Hintikka, eds *Discovering Reality: Feminist Perspectives on Epistemology, Metaphysics, Methodology and Philosophy of Science*, Dordrecht: Reidel.

D. Haraway (1978) 'Animal sociology and a natural economy of the body politic, part I: a political physiology of dominance', *Signs* 4:21–36.

—(1978a) 'Animal sociology and a natural economy of the body politic, part II: the past is the contested zone: human nature and theories of production and reproduction in primate behavior studies', *Signs* 4:37–60.

—(1979) 'Sex, mind and profit: from human engineering to sociobiology', *Radical History Review* 20:206–37.

—(1983) 'Signs of dominance: from a physiology to a cybernetics of primate society', *Studies in the History of Biology* 6:129–219.

—(1983a) 'The contest for primate nature: daughters of man the hunter in the field, 1960–80', in M. Kann, ed. *The Future of American Democracy*, Philadelphia: Temple University, pp. 175–208.

—(1986) 'Primatology is politics by other means', in R. Bleier, ed. *Feminist Approaches to Science*, Oxford: Pergamon, pp. 77–118.

S.B. Hardy (1981) *The Woman that Never Evolved*, Cambridge, Mass: Harvard University.

B. Harrison (1978) 'Women's health and the women's movement in Britain: 1840–1940', in *The Proceedings of the Roots of Sociobiology Conference* sponsored by 'Past and Present' in conjunction with British Society for History of Science.

—(1986) 'Empathy, polyandry, and the myth of the coy female', in R. Bleier, ed. *Feminist Approaches to Science*, Oxford: Pergamon, pp. 119–47.

R. Hubbard (1979) 'Have only men evolved?', in R. Hubbard, M. Henifin and B. Fried, eds *Biological Woman: The Convenient Myth*, Cambridge, Mass: Schenkman.

D. Janson-Smith (1980) 'Sociobiology: so what?', in Brighton Women and Science Group *Alice Through the Microscope: the Power of Science over Women's Lives'*, Virago, pp. 62–86.

M. Lowe (1978) 'Sociobiology and sex differences', *Signs* 4,1.

E. Reed (1978) *Sexism and Science*, New York: Pathfinder.

S.V. Rosser (1982) 'Androgyny and sociobiology', *International Journal of Women's Studies* 5:435–44.

S.A. Shields (1975) 'Functionalism, Darwinism and the psychology of women: a study in social myth', *American Psychology* July:739–54.

N. Tanner and A. Zihlman (1976) 'Women in evolution, part 1: innovation and selection in human origins', *Signs: Journal of Women in Culture and Society* 1,3.

A. Zihlman (1978) 'Women in evolution, part 2: subsistence and social organization among early hominids', *Signs: Journal of Women in Culture and Society* 4,1.

REPRODUCTIVE MEDICINE, TECHNOLOGY AND POLITICS

Listed here are some of the analyses of new reproductive technologies. The feminist collection edited by R. Arditti *et al.*, *Test-Tube Women*, is a particularly interesting one. This selection covers the related areas of abortion, contraception, and childbirth, as well as histories of birth control and motherhood.

R. Arditti, R. Duelli Klein and S. Minden, eds. (1984) *Test-Tube Women: What Future for Motherhood?*, Pandora.

M. Atwood (1985) *The Handmaiden's Tale*, Toronto.

J.A. Banks, and O. Banks (1964) *Feminism and Family Planning in Victorian England*, Liverpool University.

—(1971) *Prosperity and Parenthood*, Routledge & Kegan Paul.

M. Berer (1985) 'Infertility – a suitable case for treatment', *Marxism Today* 29,6:29–31.

—(1986) 'Breeding conspiracies: feminism and the new reproductive technologies', *Trouble and Strife* 9:29–35.

G. Bloch (1983) 'Racism and sexism in Nazi Germany: motherhood, compulsory sterilization and the state', *Signs: Journal of Women in Culture and Society* 8,3.

D. Breen (1978) 'An unfortunate fit between the woman's internal world and some hospital practices', in S. Lipshitz, ed. *Tearing the Veil*, Routledge & Kegan Paul, pp. 15–35.

R. Bridenthal, A. Grossmann and M. Kaplan, eds (1984) *When Biology Became Destiny: Women in Weimar and Nazi Germany*, New York: Monthly Review Press.

The Brighton Women and Science Group (1980) 'Technology in the lying-in-room', in Brighton Women and Science Group, ed. *Alice Through the Microscope: The Power of Science Over Women's Lives*, Virago, pp. 165–181.

B. Brookes (1986) 'Women and reproduction *c.* 1860–1919', in J. Lewis, ed. *Women's Experience of Home and Family 1850–1940*, Oxford: Blackwell, pp. 149–171.

L. Caldwell (1981) 'Abortion in Italy', *Feminist Review* 7:49–63.

I. Chalmers, A. Oakley and A. MacFarlane (1980) 'Perinatal health services: an immodest proposal', *British Medical Journal* 1:842–5.

G. Corea (1985) *The Mother Machine*, Harper & Row.

A. Davin (1978) 'Imperialism and motherhood', *History Workshop Journal* 5:9–66.

S. Day (1982) 'Is obstetric technology depressing?', *Radical Science Journal* 12:17–45.

A. Donchin (1986) 'The future of mothering: reproductive technology and feminist theory', *Hypatia: a Journal of Feminist Philosophy* 1,2:121–39.

B. Ehrenreich and D. English (1976) *Witches, Midwives and Nurses: A History of Women Healers*, Writers & Readers.

—(1979) *For Her Own Good: 150 Years of the Experts' Advice to Women*, Pluto.

J. Elkington (1985) *The Poisoned Womb: Human Reproduction in a Polluted World*, Harmondsworth: Penguin.

F. Evans (1985) 'Managers and labourers: women's attitudes to reproductive technology', in W. Faulkner and E. Arnold, eds *Smothered by Invention: Technology in Women's Lives*, Pluto, pp. 109–27.

Z. Fairbairns (1982) *Benefits*, Virago.

Finnret (1984) *Reproductive Wrongs: Male Power and the New Reproductive Technologies*, Manchester: Amazon.

S. Firestone (1970) *The Dialectic of Sex: The Case for Feminist Revolution*, R. Delmar, intro., Women's Press 1979.

P. Fryer (1967) *The Birth Controllers*, Corgi.

L. Gordon (1977) *Woman's Body, Women's Right: A Social History of Birth Control in America*, Harmdondsworth: Penguin.

—(1977a) 'Birth control: an historical study', *Science for the People* Jan/Feb:11–16.

—(1977b) 'Birth control and the eugenicists', *Science for the People* Mar/Apr:8–15.

H. Graham, and A. Oakley (1982) 'Competing ideologies of reproduction: medical and maternal perspectives on pregnancy', in E. Whitelegg *et. al.*, eds *The Changing Experience of Women*, Oxford: Martin Robertson, pp. 309–26.

K. Greenwood, and L. King (1981) 'Contraception and abortion', in Cambridge Women's Studies Group *Women in Society*, Virago, pp. 168–84.

V. Greenwood, and J. Young (1976) *Abortion in Demand*, Pluto.

J. Hanmer (1983) 'Reproductive technology: the future for women', in J. Rothschild, ed. *Machina Ex Dea: Feminist Perspectives on Technology*, Oxford: Pergamon, pp. 183–97.

J. Hanmer and P. Allen (1980) 'Reproductive engineering: the final solution?', in Brighton Women and Science Group *Alice Through the Microscope: The Power of Science Over Women's Lives*, Virago, pp. 208–27.

S. Himmelweit (1980) 'Abortion: individual choice and social control', *Feminist Review* 5:65–8.

W. Hollway (1979) 'Ideology and medical abortion', *Radical Science Journal* 8:39–59.

H. Homans, ed. (1985) *The Sexual Politics of Reproduction*, Aldershot: Gower.

J. Jaquette, and K. Staudt (1985) 'Women "at risk" reproducers: biology, science, and population in US foreign policy', in V. Sapiro, ed. *Women, Biology and Public Policy*, Beverly Hills: Sage.

J. Jennings (1982) 'Who controls childbirth?', *Radical Science Journal* 12:9–16.

P. Knight (1977) 'Women and abortion in Victorian and Edwardian England', *History Workshop* 4.

S. Laws (1985) 'A truly international conference: a report on the women's international tribunal and meeting on reproductive rights in Amsterdam, July 1984', *Trouble and Strife* 5:34–42.

A. Leathard (1980) *The Fight for Family Planning*, Macmillan.

J. Lewis (1979) 'The ideology and politics of birth control in inter-war England', *Women's Studies International Quarterly* 2,1:33–48.

K. Lukes (1984) *Abortion and the Politics of Motherhood*, Berkeley: Univ. of California.

A. McLaren (1977) 'Abortion in England 1900–1914', *Victorian Studies* 20,4.

—(1977a) 'Women's work and the regulation of family size: the question of abortion in nineteenth century England', *History Workshop* 4.

—(1984) *Reproductive Rituals*, Methuen.

E. Newman (1985) 'Who controls birth control?', in W. Faulkner and E. Arnold, eds *Smothered by Invention: Technology in Women's Lives*, Pluto, pp. 128–43.

A. Oakley (1976) 'Wisewoman and medicine man: changes in the management of childbirth', in J. Mitchell and A. Oakley, eds *The Rights and Wrongs of Women*, Harmondsworth: Penguin, pp. 17–58.

—(1979) *Becoming a Mother*, Oxford: Martin Robertson.

—(1980) *Women Confined: Towards a Sociology of Childbirth*, Oxford: Martin Robertson.

—(1981) *From Here to Maternity*, Harmondsworth: Pelican.

—(1985) *The Captured Womb: History of the Medical Care of Pregnant Women*, Oxford: Blackwell.

M. O'Brien (1981) *The Politics of Reproduction*, Routledge & Kegan Paul.

N. Pfeffer (1985) 'Not so new technology: infertility and feminism', *Trouble and Strife* 5:46–50.

N. Pfeffer and A. Woollett (1983) *The Experience of Infertility*, Virago.

Radical Science Journal (1982) 'Introduction: unnatural childbirth?', *Radical Science Journal* 12:2–8.

J. Rakusen and N. Davidson (1982) *Out of Our Hands: What Technology Does to Pregnancy*, Pan.

J. Reed (1978) *From Private Vice to Public Virtue: the Birth Control Movement and American Society since 1830,* New York: Basic.

A. Rich (1977) *Of Women Born: Motherhood as an Experience and Institution*, Virago.

D. Riley (1981) 'Feminist thought and reproductive control: the state and "the right to choose" ', in Cambridge Women's Studies Group *Women in Society: Interdisciplinary Essays*, Virago, pp. 185–99.

H. Roberts, ed. (1981) *Women, Health and Reproduction*, Routledge & Kegan Paul.

H. Rose and J. Hanmer (1976) 'Women's liberation: reproduction and the technological fix', in H. Rose and S. Rose, eds *The Political Economy of Science: Ideology of/in the Natural Sciences*, Macmillan, pp. 96–111.

P. Singer and D. Wells (1984) *The Reproductive Revolution*, Oxford University.

V. Walsh (1980) 'Contraception: the growth of a technology', in Brighton Women and Science Group *Alice Through the Microscope: The Power of Science Over Women's Lives*, Virago, pp. 182–207.

W. Walters and P. Singer, eds (1982) *Test-tube Babies: a Guide Moral Questions, Present Techniques and Future Possibilities*, Oxford University.

M. Warnock, *et al.* (1985) *A Question of Life: the Warnock Report on Human Fertilisation and Embryology*, Oxford: Blackwell.

W. Wood and A. Westmore (1983) *Test-tube Conception*, George Allen & Unwin.
S. Young (1975) 'The politics of abortion: women and the crisis in the National Health Service', *Radical Science* 2/3:51–64.
E. Yoxen (1985) 'Licensing reproductive technologies?', *Radical Science* 17:138–48.

SCIENCE FICTION AND FANTASY

Recent feminism has been noted for its explorations in and transformations of the genre of science fiction. Within these modes there have been imaginative deconstructions of gender divisions and fresh investigations of new utopias. The list below just provides a taste of what is available. Pamela Sargent's *Women of Wonder*, an anthology, is a good sampler for the uninitiated. I have not included Doris Lessing's *Canopus in Argos* series because she would reject the label 'feminist', but some would also link these to the new genre. I have taken the liberty of including Mary Shelley's *Frankenstein* and Charlotte Perkins Gilman's *Herland* as precursors of the current flowering. Two entries in this category (the Barr and Eichler) are reviews of the genre.

M. Atwood (1985) *The Handmaid's Tale*, Toronto: McClellan & Stewart.
M.S. Barr, ed. (1984) 'Oh well, Orwell – Big Sister is watching herself: feminist science fiction in 1984', *Women's Studies International Forum* 7,2 (special issue).
M. Eichler (1981) 'Science fiction as desirable feminist scenarios', *Women's Studies International Quarterly* 4,1:51–64.
Z. Fairbairns (1982) *Benefits*, Virago.
S.M. Gearhart (1985) *The Wanderground*, Women's Press.
C.P. Gilman (1915) *Herland*, Women's Press, 1979.
A. La Tourette (1985) *Cry Wolf*, Virago.
U. Le Guin (1969) *The Left Hand of Darkness*, New York: Ace.
—(1976) *The Disposessed*, New York: Panther.
V. McIntyre (1978) *Dreamsnake*, Pan.
P. Sargent, ed. (1982) *Women of Wonder*, Harmondsworth: Penguin.
M. Shelley (1831) *Frankenstein: or the Modern Prometheus*, Oxford University, 1969.
J. Palmer (1985) *The Planet Dweller*, Women's Press.
M. Piercy (1976) *Woman on the Edge of Time*, New York. Fawcett Crest.
J. Russ (1975) *The Female Man*, Women's Press, 1985.
—(1985) *Extra(ordinary) People*, Women's Press.

SCIENTIFIC AND HIGH-TECHNOLOGY WORKERS

The title of this section is an attempt to avoid the category 'Women as Scientists and Engineers'. However, most of the literature and most of the references here do fall into this slot: biographies, autobiographies and general accounts of women working in the male-dominated domains of scientific research, engineering, and 'high' technology. I have also included Tracy Kidder's *Soul of the New Machine* as a rather unanalysed presentation of gender relations at the leading edge of the computing industry and James Watson's *Double Helix* as a similar example from the leading edge of scientific research (contrast with Anne Sayre's *Rosalind Franklin and DNA*). It should be noted that materials on those working in medicine have been classified under that category.

M.L. Aldrich (1978) 'Review essay: women in science', *Signs* 4:126–35.

M. Alic (1986) *Hypatia's Heritage: A History of Women in Science from Antiquity to the Late Nineteenth Century*, Women's Press.

L.B. Arnold (1984) *Four Lives in Science: Women's Education in the Nineteenth Century*, New York: Schocken.

E.T. Baker (1964) *Technology and Women's Work*, New York: Colombia University.

R.S. Baldwin (1981) *The Fungus Fighters: Two Women Scientists and Their Discovery*, Ithaca, NY: Cornell University.

L. Birke (1985) 'Citizenship of science' *New Scientist* 28 Nov:57–8. Review of J. Butler Kahle, ed. *Women in Science: A Report from the Field.*

G.M. Breakwell and B. Weinberger (1983) *The Right Woman for the Job: Recruiting Women Engineering Technician Trainees*, Manpower Services Commission.

C. Cockburn (1983) 'Caught in the wheels', *Marxism Today* 27:16–20. Reprinted as 'Caught in the wheels; the high cost of being a female cog in the male machinery of engineering', in D. MacKenzie and Judy Wajcman, eds (1985) *The Social Shaping of Technology*, Milton Keynes: Open University, pp. 55–62.

—(1985) *Machinery of Dominance: Women, Men and Technical Know-How*, Pluto.

M. Couture-Cherki (1976) 'Women in physics', in E. Rose and S. Rose, eds *The Radicalisation of Science: The Ideology of/in the Natural Sciences*, Macmillan, pp. 76–89.

B. Drake (1918) *Women in the Engineering Trade*, Labour Research Dept.

J. Goodfield (1982) *An Imagined World: A Story of Scientific Discovery*, Harmondsworth: Penguin.

V. Gornick (1983) *Women in Science: Portraits from a World in Transition*, New York: Simon & Schuster.

V.B. Haas and C.C. Perrucci, eds (1984) *Women in Scientific and Engineering Professions*, Ann Arbor: University of Michigan.

S. Hacker (1981) 'The culture of engineering: woman, workplace and machine', *Women's Studies International Quarterly* 4,3.

H. Hein (1981) 'Women and science: fitting men to think about nature', *International Journal of Women's Studies* 4:369–77.

L.S. Hornig (1979) *Climbing the Academic Ladder: Doctoral Women Scientists in Academe*, Washington: National Academy of Sciences.

J. Kahle, ed. (1985) *Women in Science: A Report from the Field*, Aldershot: Falmer.

E.F. Keller (1977) 'The anomaly of a woman in physics', in S. Ruddick and P. Daniels, eds *Working it Out*, New York: Pantheon.

—(1983) *A Feeling for the Organism: the Life and Work of Barbara McClintock*, New York: W.H. Freeman.

T. Kidder (1982) *The Soul of a New Machine*, Allen Lane.

P. Kraft (1977) *Programmers and Managers: The Routinisation of Computer Programming in the United States*, New York: Springer Verlag.

A. Lloyd and L. Newell (1985) 'Women and computers', in W. Faulkner and E. Arnold, eds *Smothered by Invention: Technology in Women's Lives*, Pluto, pp. 238–51.

P. Newton and J. Brocklesby (1983) *Getting on in Engineering: Becoming a Woman Technician*. Report to the Engineering Industry Training Board, the Equal Opportunities Commission and the Social Science Research Council, Huddersfield Polytechnic.

K. Overfield (1981) 'Dirty fingers, grime and slag heaps: purity and the scientific ethic', in D. Spender, ed. *Men's Studies Modified*, Oxford: Pergamon, pp. 237–48.

D. Richer (1982) *Women Scientists: The Road to Liberation*, Macmillan.

S.V. Rosser (1986) 'The relationship between women's studies and women in science', in R. Bleier, ed. *Feminist Approaches to Science*, Oxford: Pergamon, pp. 165–80.

M.W. Rossiter (1982) *Women Scientists in America: Struggles and Strategies to 1940,* Baltimore MD: Johns Hopkins University.

A. Sayre (1975) *Rosalind Franklin and DNA*, New York: Norton.

G.L. Simmons (1981) *Women in Computing*, Manchester: The National Computing Centre.

L. Standish (1982) 'Women, work, and the scientific enterprise', *Science for the People* 14,5:12–19.

B.D. Stanford (1986) 'Women and science: re-naming and re-searching reality', *Science for the People* 18,1:5–9, 27.

N. Swords-Isherwood (1985) 'Women in British engineering', in W. Faulkner and E. Arnold, eds *Smothered by Invention: Technology in Women's Lives*, Pluto, pp. 72–86.

D. Warner (1979) *Graceanna Lewis, Scientist and Humanitarian*, Washington: Smithsonian Institute.

J. Watson (1969) *The Double Helix*, New York: New American Library.
N. Weisstein (1977) 'Adventures of a woman in science', in S. Ruddick and P. Daniels *Working It Out*, New York: Pantheon, pp. 241–50.

SPECIFIC AREAS OF EXPERTISE

In this rag-bag category, I list some interesting critical perspectives on gender relations in various disciplines and professional practices.

Anthropology

R. Coward (1983) *Patriarchal Precedents: Sexuality and Social Relations*, Routledge & Kegan Paul.
E. Fee (1973) 'The sexual politics of Victorian social anthropology', *Feminist Studies* 1:23–9.
S. Ortner and H. Whitehead (1981) *Sexual Meanings: the Cultural Construction of Gender and Sexuality*, Cambridge University.
E. Reed (1975) *Woman's Evolution. From Matriarchal Clan to Patriarchal Family*, New York: Pathfinder.
R. Reiter, ed. (1975) *Toward an Anthropology of Women*, Monthly Review Press.
A. Zihlman (1981) 'Women as shapers of the human adaptation', in F. Dahlberg, ed. *Woman the Gatherer*, Yale University.

Design

I. Anscombe (1984) *A Woman's Touch: Women in Design from 1860 to the Present Day*, Virago.
D. Hayden (1985) *Redesigning the American Dream*, Norton.
Matrix, eds. (1984) *Making Space: Women and the Man-Made Environment*, Pluto.

History

D. Beddoe (1983) *Discovering Women's History: A Practical Manual*, Pandora.
Anna Davin (1985) 'What is women's history?', *History Today* 35.

Psychiatry, Psychology and Psychoanalysis

I.K. Broverman, D.M. Broverman, F.E. Clarkson, P.S. Rosencrantz and S.R. Vogel (1970) 'Sex role stereotyping and clinical judgements of mental health', *Journal of Consulting Psychology* 34,1:1–7.
P. Chesler (1973) *Women and Madness*, New York: Avon.
R. Coward (1983) *Patriarchal Precedents: Sexuality and Social Relations*, Routledge & Kegan Paul.
J. Flax (1983), 'Political philosophy and the patriarchal unconscious: a psychoana-

lytic perspective on epistemology and metaphysics', in S.Harding and M.Hintikka, eds *Discovering Reality: Feminist Perspectives on Epistemology, Metaphysics, Methodology and Philosophy of Science*, Dordrecht: Reidel.

J. Gallop (1982) *Feminism and Psychoanalysis: The Daughter's Seduction*, Macmillan.

G. Gilligan (1982) *In a Different Voice: Psychological Theory and Women's Development*, Harvard University.

L. Jordanova (1981) 'Mental illness, mental health: changing norms and expectations', in Cambridge Women's Studies Group, eds *Women in Society: Interdisciplinary Essays*, Virago, pp. 95–114.

J. Lennane and J. Lennane (1982) 'Alleged psychogenic disorders in women – a possible manifestation of sexual prejudice', in E. Whitelegg *et al.*, eds *The Changing Experience of Women*, Oxford: Martin Robertson, pp. 297–308.

J.B. Miller (1976) *Towards a New Psychology of Women*, Harmondsworth: Penguin.

J. Mitchell (1971) *Woman's Estate*, Harmondsworth: Penguin.

—(1974) *Psychoanalysis and Feminism*, Harmondsworth: Penguin.

J. Mitchell and J. Rose (1982) intros. to J. Mitchell and J. Rose, eds *Feminine Sexuality: Jacques Lacan and the Ecole Freudienne*, J. Rose, trans., Macmillan.

S.P. Penfold and G.A. Walker (1984) *Women and the Psychiatric Paradox*, Milton Keynes: Open University.

J. Sayers (1986) *Sexual Contradictions: Psychology, Psychoanalysis and Feminism*, Tavistock.

D.E. Smith and S.J. David (1975) *Women Look at Psychiatry*, Vancouver: Press Gang.

E. Wilson (1981) 'Psychoanalysis: psychic law and order', *Feminist Review* 8:63–78.

Sociology and Politics

L.M.G. Clark and L. Lange, eds. (1979) *The Sexism of Social and Political Theory: Women and Reproduction from Plato to Nietsche*, University of Toronto.

J.B. Elshtain (1981) *Public Man, Private Woman: Women in Social and Political Thought*, Oxford University.

J. Evans, *et al.* (1986) *Feminism and Political Theory*, Sage.

A. Kelly (1978) 'Feminism and research', *Women's Studies International Quarterly* 1,2:225–32.

M. Millman and R.M. Kanter, eds (1975) *Another Voice: Feminist Perspectives on Social Life and Social Science*, New York: Anchor.

H. Roberts, ed. (1981) *Doing Feminist Research*, Routlege & Kegan Paul.

J. Siltanen and M. Stanworth, eds (1984) *Women and the Public Sphere: A Critique of Sociology and Politics*, Hutchinson.

D. Smith (1974) 'Women's perspective as a radical critique of sociology', *Sociological Inquiry* 44.

—(1977) 'Some implications of a sociology for women', in N. Glazer and H. Waehrer, eds *Woman in a Man-Made World: A Socioeconomic Handbook*, Chicago: Rand-McNally.

—(1979) 'A sociology for women', in J. Sherman and E.T. Beck, *The Prism of Sex: Essays in the Sociology of Knowledge*, Madison: University of Wisconsin.

M. Stacey and M. Price (1981) *Women, Power and Politics*, Tavistock.

L. Stanley and S. Wise (1983) *Breaking Out: Feminist Consciousness and Feminist Research*, Routledge & Kegan Paul.

M. Westkott (1979) 'Feminist criticism of the social sciences', *Harvard Educational Review* 49.

TECHNOLOGY AND PAID EMPLOYMENT

This category is divided into two sections. The first section includes references which examine general issues about gender relations and technology in paid work. The second section looks at particular kinds of paid employment. Of course, it is also important to consider the relationships between women's paid and unpaid (domestic) labour; see section on *Domestic Science and Technology*.

General

E. Baxandall, E. Ewen and L. Gordon (1976) 'The working class has two sexes', *Monthly Review* 28:1–9.

P. Bereano and C. Bose (1983) 'Women and technology: a university course and annotated bibliography', *Science for the People* 15,3:31–4.

M. Bergom-Larsson (1982) 'Women and technology in the industrialized countries', in P.M. D'Onofrio-Flores and S.M. Pfafflin, eds *Scientific-Technological Change and the Role of Women in Development*, Boulder: Westview, pp. 29–75.

E. Boulding (1976) 'Familial constraints in women's work roles', in M. Blaxall and B. Reagan, eds *Women and the Workplace*, University of Chicago, pp. 95–117.

H. Braverman (1974) *Labor and Monopoly Capital: The Degradation of Work in the Twentieth Century*, Monthly Review Press.

M.L. Cain (1981) 'Overview: women and technology – resources for our future', in R. Dauber and M.L. Cain, eds *Women and Technological Change in Developing Countries*, Boulder: Westview, pp. 3–8.

M. Carr (1981) 'Technologies appropriate for women: theory, practice and policy', in R. Dauber and M.L. Cain eds *Women and Technological Change in Developing Countries*, Boulder: Westview, pp. 193–203.

C. Cockburn (1981) 'The material of male power', *Feminist Review* 9:41–58.

R. Elliot (1978) 'Bringing it all back home', *Undercurrents* 29:17–19.

W. Faulkner and E. Arnold (1985) *Smothered by Invention: Technology in Women's Lives*, Pluto.

A. Game and R. Pringle (1983) *Gender at Work*, Pluto.

A. Phillips and B. Taylor (1980) 'Sex and skill: notes towards a feminist economics', *Feminist Review* 6:79–88.

J. Rothschild, ed. (1983) *Machina Ex Dea: Feminist Perspectives on Technology*, Oxford: Pergamon.

J. Scott (1982) 'The mechanization of women's work', *Scientific American* July.

The Tech and Tools Book, Intermediate Technology Publications, 1986.

J. Zimmerman (1982) 'Technology and the future of women: haven't we met somewhere before?', in J. Rothschild, ed. *Women, Technology and Innovation*, Pergamon, pp. 355–67.

—ed. *The Technological Woman: Interfacing with Tomorrow*, New York: Praegar.

Specific Kinds of Paid Employment

E. Arnold, L. Birke and W. Faulkner (1982) 'Women and microelectronics: the case of word processors', in J. Rothschild, ed. *Women, Technology and Innovation*, Oxford: Pergamon, pp. 321–40.

M. Attwood and F. Hatton (1983) 'Getting on: gender differences in career development, a case study in the hairdressing industry', in E. Garmarnikow *et al.*, eds *Gender, Class and Work*, Heinemann.

J. Barker and H. Downing (1980) 'Word processing and the transformation of patriarchal relations of control in the office', *Capital and Class* 10:64–99. Reprinted in D. MacKenzie and J. Wajcman, eds (1985) *The Social Shaping of Technology*, Milton Keynes: Open University, pp. 147–64.

M.L. Benston (1983) 'For women the chips are down', in J. Zimmerman, ed. *The Technological Woman: Interfacing with Tomorrow*, New York: Praeger, pp. 44–54.

C. Cockburn (1983) *Brothers: Male Dominance and Technological Change*, Pluto.

M. Davies (1974) 'Woman's place is at the typewriter: the feminization of the clerical workforce', *Radical America* 8,4.

R. Deakin (1984) *Women and Computing: The Golden Opportunity*, Papermac.

C. Enloe (1983) *Does Khaki Become You?*, Pluto.

R.L. Feldberg and E.N. Glenn (1983) 'Technology and work degradation: effects of office automation on women clerical workers', in J. Rothschild, ed. *Machina Ex Dea: Feminist Perspectives on Technology*, Oxford: Pergamon, pp. 59–78.

R. Gordon (1985) 'The computerization of daily life, the sexual division of labor, and the homework economy', in R. Gordon, ed. *Microelectronics in Transition*, Norwood: Ablex.

J. Greenbaum (1976) 'Division of labor in the computer field', *Monthly Review* 28,3:40–55.

B.A. Gutek (1983) 'Women's work in the office of the future', in J. Zimmerman, ed. *The Technological Woman: Interfacing with Tomorrow*, New York: Praeger, pp. 159–68.

S. Harlan (1982) 'Craftworkers and clerks: the effect of male co-worker hostility on women's satisfaction with non-traditional jobs', *Social Problems* 29,3.

F. Hunt (1986) 'Opportunities lost and gained: mechanization and women's work in the London bookbinding and printing trades', in A.V. John, ed. *Unequal Opportunities: Women's Employment in England 1800–1918*, Oxford: Blackwell.

U. Huws (1984) *The New Homeworkers: New Technology and the Changing Location of White-Collar Workers*, Low Pay Unit Pamphlet No. 28.

E. Langer (1970) *The Women of the Telephone Company*, Somerville: New England Free Press.

R. Milkman (1982) 'Redefining "women's work": the sexual division of labour in the auto industry during World War II', *Feminist Studies* 8,2.

J. Morgall (1981) 'Typing our way to freedom: is it true that new office technology can liberate women?', *Feminist Review* 9:87–103.

Science Policy Research Unit (1982) *Microelectronics and Women's Employment in Britain*, University of Sussex.

E. Softley (1985) 'Word processing: new opportunities for women office workers?', in W. Faulkner and E. Arnold, eds *Smothered by Invention: Technology in Women's Lives*, Pluto, pp. 222–37.

SPRU Women and Technology Studies (1985) 'Microelectronics and the jobs women do', in W. Faulkner and E. Arnold, eds *Smothered by Invention: Technology in Women's Lives*, Pluto, pp. 200–21.

P. Summerfield (1977) 'Women workers in the Second World War', *Capital and Class* 1:27–42.

D. Wernek (1985) *Microelectronics and office jobs: the impact of the chip on women's employment*, Geneva: International Labour Office.

J. West (1982) 'New technology and office work', in J. West, ed. *Work, Women and the Labour Market*, Routledge & Kegan Paul, pp. 61–79.

THE WOMEN'S HEALTH MOVEMENT

This selection includes documentation and evaluations of the recent women's health movement. I have also supplemented these with references to some feminist analyses of some of the contemporary ailments suffered by women in the west (e.g. anorexia nervosa).

Boston Women's Health Collective (1978) *Our Bodies Ourselves: A Health Book By and For Women*, British Edition, eds, A. Phillips and J. Rakusen, Harmondsworth: Penguin.

Brent Women's Centre, 'How to run a health course', *Spare Rib* 94. Reprinted in M. Rowe, ed. (1982) *Spare Rib Reader*, Harmondsworth: Penguin, pp. 416–20.

N. Caskey (1986) 'Interpreting anorexia nervosa', in S. Rubin Suleiman, ed. *The Female Body in Western Culture: Contemporary Perspectives*, Harvard University, pp. 139–51.

C. Dreifus, ed. (1977) *Seizing Our Bodies: The Politics of Women's Health*, New York: Random House.

M.A. Elston (1979) 'Reclaiming our bodies: health handbooks by and for women', *Women's Studies International Quarterly* 2,1:117–25.

E. Fee (1975) 'Women and health care: A comparison of theories', *International Journal of Health Services* 5,3:397–425.

E. Fee, ed. (1982) *Women and Health: The Politics of Sex in Medicine*, Farmingdale, NY: Baywood.

N. Fett (1978) 'Women's occupational health and the women's health movement', *Preventive Medicine* 7:366–71.

C. Kenner (1985) *No Time for Women: Exploring Women's Health in the 1930s and Today*, Pandora.

H. Marieskind (1975) 'The women's health movement', *International Journal of Health Services* 5,2.

M. O'Donnell (1978) 'Lesbian health care: issues and literature', *Science for the People* 10,3:8–19.

S. Orbach (1978) *Fat is a feminist issue,* Paddington.

H. Roberts, ed. (1981) *Women, Health and Reproduction*, Routledge & Kegan Paul.

Sue V. Rosser (1986) *Teaching Science and Health from a Feminist Perspective*, Oxford: Pergamon.

S.B. Ruzer (1978) *The Women's Health Movement*, New York: Praeger.

C. Ryan (1975) 'Our bodies, ourselves: the fallacy of seeking individual solutions for societal contradictions', *International Journal of Health Services* 5,2:335–8.

L. Saffron (1985) 'Clinical smears: problems with well women clinics', *Trouble and Strife* 5:13–6.

J.M. Stellman (1977) *Women's Work, Women's Health: Myths and Realities*, New York: Pantheon.

M. Turshen (1976) 'Women and health: a review of the literature', *Science for the People* 5,8:17–8, 31.

THE WOMEN'S PEACE MOVEMENT AND ANTI-NUCLEAR PROTESTS

This section lists some writings from within the women's peace movement (for example, Caldicott's and Leland's *Reclaim the Earth* and Thompson's *Over Our Dead Bodies*). Many of the other references are to considerations of the peace movement from within feminism. Blackwood's *On the Perimeter* is an exception, being an outsider's (in the end, positive) view of the Greenham Common protest. Rosalie Bertell's *No Immediate Danger* attempts to provide a feminist perspective on the wider issue of nuclear energy.

R. Bertell (1985) *No Immediate Danger: Prognosis for a Radioactive Earth*, Women's Press.

C. Blackwood (1984) *On the Perimeter*, Heinemann.

E. Boulding (1981) 'Perspectives of women researchers on disarmament, national security and world order', *Women's Studies International Quarterly* 5,1.

W. Brown (1984) *Black Women and the Peace Movement*, Bristol: Falling Wall.

L. Caldicott and S. Leland, eds (1983) *Reclaim the Earth, Women Speak Out for Life and Earth*, Women's Press.

B. Easlea (1983) *Fathering the Unthinkable: Masculinity, Scientists and the Nuclear Arms Race*, Pluto.

Feminism and Non-Violence Group (1979) *Breaching the Peace: Feminism and Non-Violence*, Onlywomen.

S; Finch, *et al.* (1986) from Hackney Greenham Groups, 'Socialist-feminists and Greenham', *Feminist Review* 23:93–100.

B. Harford and S. Hopkins, eds (1984) *Greenham Common: Women at the Wire*, Women's Press.

L. Jones, ed. (1983) *Keeping the Peace: A Women's Peace Handbook*, Women's Press.

K. Soper and A. Assiter (1983) 'Greenham Common: an exchange', *Radical Philosophy* 3:21–4.

D. Thompson, ed. (1983) *Over Our Dead Bodies: Women Against the Bomb*, Virago.

A. La Tourette (1985) *Cry Wolf*, Virago.

R. Wallsgrove (1983) 'Greenham Common – so why am I still so ambivalent?', *Trouble and Strife* 1:4–6.

A. Wiltsher (1985) *Most Dangerous Women*: *Feminist Peace Campaigners of the Great War*, Pandora.

C. Wolf (1984) *Cassandra: A Novel and Four essays*, J. Van Heurck, trans. Virago.

SPECIAL ISSUES OF JOURNALS

'Oh well, Orwell—Big Sister is watching herself: feminist science fiction in 1984', *Women's Studies International Forum* 7, 2, ed. M. S. Barr.

'Women and Science', *Science for People* 29 (1978).

'Women and Science', *International Journal of Women's Studies* 4 (Sept/Oct 1981).

'Women, Gender and Philosophy', *Radical Philosophy* 34 (summer 1983).

'Women in Science: a man's world', *Impact of Science on Society* 25 (1975).

'Women, Science and Society', *Signs* 4 (1981).

'Women, Technology and Innovation', *Women's Studies International Quarterly* 4 (1981).

'Women's Issue', *Undercurrents* 29 (Aug/Sept 1978).

CONNECTIONS

COMRADELY PUBLICATIONS AND GROUPS

ALTERNATIVE PRESS INDEX
Alternative Press Centre, PO Box 33109, Baltimore, MD 21218, USA.

ALTERNATIVES – Perspectives on Society, Technology and Environment
Faculty of Environmental Studies, University of Waterloo, Ontario, N2L 3GA, Canada.

AMPO – Japan-Asia Quarterly Review
PO Box 5250, Tokyo International, Japan.

ANTIPODE – A Radical Journal of Geography
Blackwell, 108 Cowley Road, Oxford OX4 1JF, UK; or PO Box 1320, Murray Hill Station, NY 10156, USA.

ARENA – A Marxist Journal of Criticism and Discussion
PO Box 18, North Carlton, Victoria 3054, Australia.

BERKELEY JOURNAL OF SOCIOLOGY
458A Barrows Hall, Dept. of Sociology, Berkeley, CA 94720, USA.

BORDERLINE
Dublin Resource Centre, 6 Crow Street, Dublin 2, Ireland.

BORDER LINES – Cultures, Contexts, Canadas
Bethune College, York University, 4700 Keele Street, Downsview, Ontario M3J 1P3, Canada.

CAHIERS GALILEE
c/o G. Valenduc, 5 rue de la Resistance, 1490 Court-St-Etienne, Belgium. Special issues on biotechnology, infotech.

CAPITAL & CLASS – Journal of the Conference of Socialist Economists
25 Horsell Road, London N5

CASOPIS ZA KRITIKO ZNANOSTI
Kersnikova 4, 61000 Ljubljana, Yugoslavia.

CATALYST – Socialist Journal of the Social Services
Box 1144, Cathedral Station, NY, NY 10025.

CIENCIA HOJE
Av. Venceslau Braz, 71 fundos casa 27. 22290 Rio de Janeiro-RJ, Brasil.

COUNTER-INFORMATION SERVICES (CIS)
9 Poland Street, London W1

CRIME AND SOCIAL JUSTICE – A Journal of Radical Criminology
PO Box 40601, San Francisco, CA 94140, USA.

CRITICAL SOCIAL POLICY
46 Elfort Road, London N5.

CRITIQUE – Journal of Soviet Studies and Socialist Theory
31 Cliveden Road, Glasgow G12.

CRITIQUE OF ANTHROPOLOGY
Luna, PO Box 6004, 1005 EA Amsterdam, Holland.

CULTURAL CRITIQUE
Telos Press, 431 E. 12th St, New York, NY 10009.

DEMOCRATIC PALESTINE
Box 12144, Damascus, Syria.

DESARROLLO – Tribuna para una Political Scientifico-Technologica
Apdo. 388, San Pedro 2050, Costa Rica.

DIALOGO SOCIAL
Ediciones CCS, Apartado 9A-192, Panama, R.P.

ECONOMIC & POLITICAL WEEKLY
Skylark, 284 Shahid Bhagatsingh Road, Bombay 400 038, India.

ETCETERA – Correspondencia de la Guerra Social
Apartado Correos 1.363, Barcelona, Spain.

GLOBAL ELECTRONICS
Pacific Studies Centre, 222B View Street, Mountain View, CA 94041, USA.

The GUARDIAN – Independent Radical Newsweekly
33 West 17th St. New York, NY 10011.

HEALTH/PAC (Policy Advisory Committee)
17 Murray St, New York, NY 10007.

HISTORY WORKSHOP – A Journal of Socialist and Feminist Historians
c/o Routledge & Kegan Paul, Broadway House, Newton Rd, Henley-on-Thames, Oxfordshire RG9 1EN.

INPUT – Initiative for the Peaceful Use of Technology
PO Box 248, Station B, Ottowa, Ontario KIP 6C4, Canada.

INSURGENT SOCIOLOGIST
Dept. of Sociology, Univ. of Oregon, Eugene, OR 97403, USA.

INTERNATIONAL JOURNAL OF HEALTH SERVICES
Baywood Publishing Company, 120 Marine St, Farmingdale, NY 11735, USA.

ISIS – Women's International Information and Communication Service
Via Santa Maria dell' Anima 30, Rome, Italy.

JERUSALEM INSTITUTE for the Study of Society
6 Bnai-Brith St, Jerusalem 95146, Israel.

The LEFT INDEX
511 Lincoln Street, Santa Cruz, CA 95060.

LITERATURE TEACHING POLITICS
c/o Andrew Belsey, Dept. of Philosophy, University College, Cardiff CF1 1XL.

MEDICINE IN SOCIETY – Quarterly Socialist Journal of Health Studies.
16 St. John Street, London EC1.

MIDNIGHT NOTES
Box 204, Jamaica Plain, MA 02130.

MODERN ZEITEN
Am Taubenfelde 30, 3000 Hanover 1, W. Germany.

MOTHER JONES
1663 Mission St, San Francisco, CA 94103, USA.

MONTHLY REVIEW – An Independent Socialist Magazine
62 West 14th St. New York, NY 10011, USA

MULTINATIONAL MONITOR
1346 Connecticut Ave. NW, Room 411, Washington, D.C. 20036.

NATURKAMPEN
c/o Politisk Revy, Vesterbrogade 31, 2 th, DK-1620 Kbh, Denmark.

NEW GERMAN CRITIQUE – An Interdisciplinary Journal of German Studies
Telos Press, 431 E. 12th St., NY, NY 10009.

OPEN ROAD – Anarcha-Feminist Edition
Box 6135, Station G, Vancouver, B.C., Canada.

OXFORD LITERARY REVIEW – A Post-Structuralist Journal
2 Marlborough Road, Oxford OX1 4LP, UK.

PANDORE – Problems of Science, Technology and Society
Denise de Pouvorville, 2 rue Conté, 75141 Paris, France.

PHILOSOPHY & SOCIAL ACTION
M–120 Greater Kailash-1, New Delhi 110 048, India.

PRACTICE – The Journal of Politics, Economics, Psychology, Sociology and Culture
7 East 20th St., 10th Floor, New York, NY 10003.

PRAXIS – A Journal of Radical Perspectives on the Arts.
Dickson Arts Centre, UCLA, Los Angeles, CA 90024.

PROCESSED WORLD – The Magazine with A Bad Attitude
41 Sutter Street, No. 1829, San Francisco, CA 94104.

PSYCH CRITIQUE
Ablex Publishing Co., 355 Chestnut St., Norwood, NJ, USA.

PSYCHOLOGY & SOCIAL THEORY
Triphammer Mall, Box 4387, Ithaca, NY 14852.

RACE & CLASS – A Journal for Black and Third World Liberation
Institute of Race Relations, 2–6 Leeke Street, Kings Cross Road, London WC1X 9HS.

RACE TODAY – Voice of the Black Community in Britain
165 Railton Road, London SE24.

RADICAL AMERICA
1 Summer St., Somerville, MA 02143, USA.

RADICAL BOOKSELLER
265 Seven Sisters Road, London N4.

RADICAL COMMUNITY MEDICINE
38 Weston Park, London N8 9TJ.

RADICAL HISTORY REVIEW – Mid-Atlantic Radical Historians' Organization (MARHO)
John Jay College, 445 West 59th St. New York, NY 10019, USA.

RADICAL PHILOSOPHY
c/o Ian Craib, Dept. Sociology, Univ. of Essex, Colchester CO4 3SQ, UK

RADICAL STATISTICS – Bulletin of BSSRS Radical Statistics Group
BSSRS, 25 Horsell Rd., London N5.

RED LETTERS – Communist Party Literature Journal
16 St. John Street, London EC1.

REVIEW OF AFRICAN POLITICAL ECONOMY
341 Glossop Road, Sheffield S10 2HP, UK.

REVIEW OF RADICAL POLITICAL ECONOMICS
URPE, 155 W. 23rd St., 12th Floor, New York, NY 10011, USA.

REVOLUON
Postbus 1328, 6501 Nijmegen, Holland.

SCHOOLING & CULTURE
ILEA Cockpot Arts Workshop. Gateforth Street, London NW8.

SCIENCE & SOCIETY
Room 4331 John Jay College, CUNY, 445 West 59th St. New York, NY 10019.

SCIENCE-FICTION STUDIES
Prof. Philmus, English Dept., Concordia University, 7141 Sherbrooke St. West. Montreal, Quebec, Canada H4B 1R6.

SCIENCE FOR PEOPLE – Magazine of BSSRS
25 Horsell Road, London N5.

SCIENCE FOR THE PEOPLE
879 Main Street, Cambridge, MA 02139, USA.

SE-SCIENZA ESPERIENZA
Via Nino Bixi 30, 20129 Milano, Italy.

SIGNS – Journal of Women in Culture and Society
University of Chicago Press, 5801 Ellis Avenue, Chicago, Illinois 60637, USA.

SOCIALISM AND EDUCATION – Journal of the Socialist Education Association
14 Branscombe St., London SE13 7AY.

SOCIALIST HEALTH REVIEW
19 June Blossom Society, 60A Pali Road, Bandra (West), Bombay 400 050, India.

SOCIALIST REVIEW
3202 Adeline, Berkeley, CA 94703.

SYGHRONA THEMATA
c/o Giorgos Goulakos, Valaoritou 12, Athens, 106–71 Greece.

TECHNOLOGY & CULTURE
University of Chicago Press, 5801 Ellis Avenue, Chicago, Illinois 60637, USA.

TELOS – A Quarterly Journal of Radical Thought
431 E. 12th St., NY, NY 10009.

TERMINAL 19/84
Centre d'Information et d'Initiative sur l'Informatisation
18 rue de Chatillon, 75014 Paris, France.

TESTI E CONTESTI – Quaderni di Scienze, Storia e Societa.
CLUP, Piazza Leonardo da Vinci 32, Milano, Italy.

UTUSAN KONSUMER
Consumers Association of Penang, 87 Cantonment Road, Penang 10250, Malaysia.

WECHSEL WIRKUNG – Technik/ Naturwissenschaft/Gesellschaft
Gneisenaustr. 2, 1000 Berlin 61, West Germany.

WETENSCHAP EN SAMENLEVING
VWW, Oude Gracht 80, 3511 AT Utrecht, Holland.

WIRE (Women's International Resource Exchange)
2700 Broadway, New York, NY 10025.

NOTES ON CONTRIBUTORS

Grazyna Baran studied physics at the University of Kent, taught science at several London secondary schools, and now teaches adult education at Morley College.

Ania Grobicki, having trained and worked as a chemical engineer in South Africa, is doing research at Imperial College in alternative energy sources. A member of the British Society for Social Responsibility in Science, she is interested in energy policy, women and science, and development issues.

Donna Haraway teaches feminist theory and history of science in the History of Consciousness Department at the University of California at Santa Cruz. She is currently writing about political imagination in feminist science fiction and finishing her book on contestations for what can count as nature in industrial societies, entitled *Primate Visions: History of the Craft of Story Telling in 20th Century Sciences of Monkeys and Apes*.

Ludmilla Jordanova teaches history at the University of Essex. She is editor of and contributor to *Languages of Nature: Critical Essays on Science and Literature* (Free Association Books, 1986). She is currently working on scientific and medical imagery.

Anne Karpf is a freelance journalist and critic. She is author of *Doctoring the Box: Health, Medicine and the Media* (Routledge & Kegan Paul, forthcoming).

Mary Kennedy lectures in women's studies and history in the Extra-Mural Studies Department, University of London. She is a founder member and secretary of the London History Workshop Centre, and co-author of *New Futures: Changing Women's Education* (Routledge & Kegan Paul, 1985).

Sonia Liff is a lecturer at Loughborough University. She has written a Ph.D thesis (at Manchester University) and numerous articles about gender, technology and work.

Pam Linn teaches in the Continuing Education Unit at Thames Polytechnic. She is a member of the Radical Science Collective.

Maureen McNeil is a lecturer at the Centre for Contemporary Cultural Studies at the University of Birmingham. She is also a member of the Radical Science Collective. Her research and teaching interests include gender and expertise, and science in culture. She is the author of *Under the Banner of Science: Erasmus Darwin and His Age* (Manchester University Press, 1987).

Alison Ravetz interrupted her study of archaeology to have a family, during which being a housewife interested her in housing. She has since published *Model Estate* and *Remaking Cities: Contradictions of the Recent Urban Environment*. She is now Co-ordinator of Shelter Studies on the Home Economics degree at Leeds Polytechnic.

Pam Smith did a combined hospital-community nursing course at the University of Manchester, then worked in Tanzania and Mozambique as a community nurse teacher. Recently she has done research into nurse training and patient care for Bloomsbury Health Authority, London.

Judith Williamson is a writer, teacher and film-maker. She is the author of *Decoding Advertisements* (Marion Boyars, 1978) and *Consuming Passions* (Marion Boyars, 1986). She teaches part-time at Middlesex Polytechnic, Maidstone College of Art, and abroad. Her film, 'A Sign is a Fine Investment', is distributed by the Arts Council.

Back Issues of RADICAL SCIENCE Series Still Available

RADICAL SCIENCE ESSAYS (nos 1–4, reprinted)
BOB YOUNG: Introduction / DAVID DICKSON: Technology and the Construction of Social Reality / JACK STAUDER: The 'Relevance' of Anthropology to Colonialism and Imperialism / MIKE HALES: Management Science and the 'Second Industrial Revolution' / SHEILA ERNST: The Politics of Abortion as 'Family Planning' / ALFRED SOHN-RETHEL: Science as Alienated Consciousness / SIMON PICKVANCE: 'Life' in a Biology Lab / CHARLIE CLUTTERBUCK: Death in the Plastics Industry / LUKE HODGKIN: Mathematics as Ideology and Politics / LES LEVIDOW: IQ as Ideological Reality / ALBERT EINSTEIN: Why Socialism?
Price: £7.95 pb, £25 hb

SCIENCE IS SOCIAL RELATIONS (no. 5)
BOB YOUNG: Science is Social Relations / PATRICK PARRINDER: Science and Social Consciousness in SF / DAVID TRIESMAN: The Institute of Psychiatry Sackings

THE LABOUR PROCESS (nos 6/7)
LES LEVIDOW: A Marxist Critique of the IQ Debate / MIKE BARNETT: Technology and the Labour Process / BOB YOUNG: Getting Started on Lysenkoism / RSJ SUBGROUP: Marxism, Feminism and Psychoanalysis / LES LEVIDOW: Grunwick as Technology and Class Struggle

SCIENCE AND HEGEMONY (no. 8)
DAVID DICKSON: Science and Political Hegemony in the 17th Century / WENDY HOLLWAY: Ideology and Medical Abortion / PHILIP BOYS: Detente, Genetics, and Social Theory

MEDICINE (no. 9)
KARL FIGLIO: Sinister Medicine? / GIANNA POMATA: Seveso – Safety in Numbers? / LES LEVIDOW: Three Mile Island / Critical Bibliography on Medicine

THIRD WORLD (no. 10)
DAVID DICKSON: Science and Technology, North and South: Multinational Management for Underdevelopment / RAPHAEL KAPLINSKY: Microelectronics and the Third World / LES LEVIDOW: Notes on Development / BRIAN MARTIN: The Goal of Self-Managed Science

SCIENCE, TECHNOLOGY AND THE SOCIALIST MOVEMENT (no. 11)
RSJ COLLECTIVE: Science, Technology, Medicine and the Socialist Movement / JONATHAN REE: The Anti-Althusser Bandwagon / PAM LINN: Designer or Drone? / MAUREEN MCNEIL: Braverman Revisited

MEDICALIZATION (no. 12)
Introduction: Unnatural Childbirth? / JANET JENNINGS: Who Controls Childbirth? / SHELLY DAY: Is Obstetric Technology Depressing? / EVAN STARK: What is Medicine?

SCIENTISM IN THE LEFT (no. 13)
STEVE SMITH: Taylorism Rules OK? Bolshevism, Taylorism and the Technical Intelligentsia / LES LEVIDOW: We Won't Be Fooled Again? Economic Planning and Left Strategies / DOUG KELLNER: Science and Method in Marx's *Capital* / JOE CROCKER: Sociobiology: The Capitalist Synthesis / TIM PUTNAM: Proletarian Science?

NO CLEAR REASON: NUCLEAR POWER POLITICS (no. 14)
Introduction: No Clear Reason / MIDNIGHT NOTES COLLECTIVE: 'Exterminism' or Class Struggle? / JAMES WOOD: Why Cruise and Pershing? / DAVE ROSENFELD: Don't Just Reduce Risk – Transform It! / LES LEVIDOW and BOB YOUNG: Exhibiting Nuclear Power: The Science Museum Cover-Up / MARTIN SPENCE: Exporting the 'Peaceful Atom' / DHIRENDRA SHARMA: India's Nuclear Estate / STEPHEN ROBINSON: Nuclear States of Terror
Price: £5 individual, £6 institutional

FREE ASSOCIATIONS: PSYCHOANALYSIS, GROUPS, POLITICS, CULTURE (no. 15)
Editorial / ROBERT M. YOUNG: No Easy Answers / RUSSELL JACOBY: Remembering 'Social Amnesia' / JANE TEMPERLEY: Our Own Worst Enemies: Unconscious Factors in Female Disadvantage / DAVID INGLEBY: The Ambivalence of Psychoanalysis / MARGOT WADDELL: The Long Weekend / BARRY RICHARDS: Civil Defence and Psychic Defence / MICHAEL RUSTIN: Psychoanalysis and Social Justice / KARL FIGLIO: Freud's Exegesis of the Soul / STEPHEN ROBINSON: The Art of the Possible / JOEL KOVEL: On Being a Marxist Psychoanalyst (and a Psychoanalytic Marxist) Price: £5.50 individual

MAKING WAVES: THE POLITICS OF COMMUNICATIONS (no. 16)
Editorial / URSULA HUWS: Terminal Isolation / ARMAND MATTELART: Infotech and the Third World / TOM ATHANASIOU: High-Tech Alternativism / RICHARD BARBROOK: Community Radio in Britain / DOUGLAS KELLNER: Public Access Television / DEE DEE HALLECK: Nicaraguan Video / MICHAEL CHANAN: The Reuters Factor / DAVID ALBURY: 'E.T.': Technology and Masculinity
Price: £5 individual, £6 institutional

ISSUES IN RADICAL SCIENCE (no. 17)
L.J. JORDANOVA: Fritz Lang's *Metropolis* / DAVE FEICKERT: Britain's Miners and New Technology / VINCENT MOSCO: Star Wars/Earth Wars / JONATHAN REE: Marxism from Above: Philosophy, Science and Prof. Kolakowski / BRUNO VITALE: Scientists as Military Hustlers / DOUG BOUCHER and ISADORE NABI: The New World Agriculture Group: A History / DON PARSON: One-Dimensional Planning Theory / DAVID DICKSON: Radical Science and the Modernist Dilemma / EDWARD YOXEN: Licensing Reproductive Technologies?
Price: £5 individual, £6 institutional

COMPULSIVE TECHNOLOGY: COMPUTERS AS CULTURE (no. 18)
RADICAL SCIENCE COLLECTIVE: Compulsive Technology / TOM ATHANASIOU: Artificial Intelligence: Cleverly Disguised Politics / KEVIN ROBINS and FRANK WEBSTER: Higher Education, High Tech, High Rhetoric / PAM LINN: Microcomputers in Education: Living and Dead Labour / GUY LACROIX: Infotech Newspeak / TONY SOLOMONIDES: Informing the Social Order / CHRISTOPHER KNEE: The Hidden Curriculum of the Computer / COLLETTIVO STRATEGIE: The 'Technetronic Society' According to Brzezinski / Critical Bibliography
Price: £5 individual, £6 institutional

GENDER AND EXPERTISE (no. 19)
MAUREEN MCNEIL: Being Reasonable Feminists / DONNA HARAWAY: Contested Bodies / GRAZYNA BARAN: Teaching Girls Science / MARY KENNEDY: Women in Adult Education / PAM LINN: Gender Stereotypes, Technology Stereotypes / ANNE KARPF: Feminist Approaches to Women and Technology / SONIA LIFF: Gender Relations in the Construction of Jobs / ALISON RAVETZ: Housework and Domestic Technologies / Critical Bibliography / plus reviews
Price: £8.95

SCIENCE AS POLITICS (no. 20)
NORMAN DIAMOND: The Copernican Revolution / JIM MOORE: Socializing Darwin / PETER TAYLOR: Dialectical Biology as Political Practice / T. JONES: Hazards for Export / LES LEVIDOW: Nuclear Politics in Yugoslavia / TIM ROWSE: Sociology Pulls Its Punches / ERWIN FLEISSNER: Salvador Luria / plus short reviews
Price: £6 individual, £8.50 institutional

Issues 5–13 Price: £4 individual, £5 institutional.
If ordering direct with payment in foreign currency, add equivalent of 60p to cover bank charges and use current exchange rates.
Radical Science, 26 Freegrove Road, London N7 9RQ

THE RADICAL SCIENCE series provides a forum for extended analyses of the ideology and practice of science, technology and medicine from a radical political perspective. Most contributions critically examine the role of scientism in society and culture.

We welcome suggestions for thematic numbers emphasizing particular topics around the critique of power exercised through expertise. We would like especially to develop a positive programme for the role of oppositional knowledge.

Radical Science Collective

Editorial Contributions

Ideally, articles should be less than 10,000 words and typed double-spaced. A number of copies would help: it is our policy that all articles should be read by as many members of the collective as possible. This usually takes some time so please bear with us – but remind us when your patience runs out.

Subscriptions

The subscription for three numbers per year is £18.00 post paid, libraries and institutions £25.00. Those who support us in our project are invited to add a donation to their subscription. Please add the equivalent of £0.60 to foreign cheques to cover bank charges involved. Subscriptions, donations, enquiries and articles should be sent to:

Free Association Books, 26 Freegrove Road, London N7 9RQ
Tel. (01) 609 5646.
FAB's catalogue is available on request.

Distribution

UK: Turnaround, 25 Horsell Road, London N5. Tel. (01) 609 7836.
USA: B. deBoer, 113 East Center Street, Nutley, NJ 07119. Tel. (201) 667 9300.
Carrier Pigeon, 40 Plympton St, Boston, MA 02118. Tel. (617) 542 5679.
CANADA: DEC, 427 Bloor St West, Toronto, Ontario M5S 1X7. Tel. (416) 964 6560
AUSTRALIA: Astam Books, 250 Abercrombie Street, Chippendale, NSW 2008.
Tel. Sydney 698 4080
SOUTH AFRICA: Ravan Press, PO Box 31134, Braamfontein 2017. Tel. 643 5552.

Copyright

ISSN 0305 0963.